CORPORATE CHARACTER

Corporate Character

Representing Imperial Power in British India, 1786–1901

EDDY KENT

UNIVERSITY OF TORONTO PRESS
Toronto Buffalo London

Toronto Buffalo London
www.utppublishing.com

ISBN 978-1-4426-4846-3 (cloth)

Library and Archives Canada Cataloguing in Publication

Kent, Eddy, 1978–, author
Corporate character : representing imperial power in British India, 1786–1901 / Eddy Kent.

Includes bibliographical references and index.
ISBN 978-1-4426-4846-3 (bound)

1. India – Politics and government – 1765–1947. 2. India – History – British occupation – 1765–1947. 3. East India Company – History. 4. Corporate culture – Great Britain – History. 5. Corporate culture – India – History. 6. India – Civilization – British influences. I. Title.

DS475.K45 2014 954.03'1 C2014-902344-8

This book has been published with the help of a grant from the Canadian Federation for the Humanities and Social Sciences, through the Awards to Scholarly Publications Program, using funds provided by the Social Sciences and Humanities Research Council of Canada.

University of Toronto Press acknowledges the financial assistance to its publishing program of the Canada Council for the Arts and the Ontario Arts Council, an agency of the Government of Ontario.

University of Toronto Press acknowledges the financial support of the Government of Canada through the Canada Book Fund for its publishing activities.

For Terri

Contents

Acknowledgments

The scholarly monograph is a misnomer. The only things I can fairly claim as mine alone are its intellectual poverties. All else has been produced in community – amid my mentors, colleagues, students, friends, and family members. With varying degrees of patience and encouragement, you have made this work possible.

My earliest academic debts are to Michael Bucknor, who inspired me to study imperial literature, and Ralph Crane, who got me started on the Raj. At the University of British Columbia, I benefited from the guidance of Nicholas Hudson, Jisha Menon, Ira Nadel, John Roosa, Janet Giltrow, Mandakranta Bose, Mark Vessey, and above all Jonathan Wisenthal, who through example taught me more about honourable conduct than I ever found in the pages of Burke or Macaulay. With dumb luck I stumbled into a wonderfully resourceful group of graduate students, including Alyssa Maclean, Greg Morgan, Mike Wells, Travis Mason, Sarah Banting, Colleen Derkatch, Kim Snowdon, Charles Barbour, Sean Saunders, Christine Stewart, Sharon Alker, Deanna Reder, Shurli Makmillan, Jennifer Schnepf, Emily Doucet, Jennifer Bowering Delisle, Steve Ney, Maia Joseph, Lisa Szabo-Jones, Katja Thieme, and Tunji Osinubi. Two deserve special mention: my good friends Tyson Stolte and Daniel O'Leary; both are models of serious, disinterested scholarship and sources of constant cheer. Without all of you, I may never have survived Vancouver's rainy seasons.

The book began to take shape during the wonderful year I spent as a postdoctoral fellow at Rutgers, where John Kucich offered an open door, critical eyes, and frank opinions. Beyond discussing the vicissitudes of imperial culture, he generously shared his accumulated wisdom on aspects of the profession. I didn't always listen but he was always right. My comrades in the online collective *The Floating Academy* have buoyed me up at important moments, as have more members of the Victorian studies community than I can mention individually. Sara Suleri and Tirthankar Bose made timely and valuable interventions to various drafts of the manuscript, as did the two anonymous readers appointed by the University of Toronto Press. Thanks also to my editor at the University of Toronto Press, Richard Ratzlaff, whose safe hands have made the journey from manuscript to book seem unnaturally easy.

In preparing this book, I incurred a special debt to the staff in the Asian and African Studies reading room at the British Library, who over the years have responded magnanimously to all my requests, great and small, pertaining to the India Office Records. By providing material support for this archive, making it freely available to the world, the British government goes some small way towards redressing the problematic, and often objectionable, circumstances attached to its assembly. For more direct material support, I have relied upon the Canadian public, whose long-standing, and hopefully continuing, commitment to publicly funded post-secondary research has made this book possible.

Finally, I must thank my family for keeping me on track. My parents, Ed and Eileen, never expected my life to take this path, but to me it makes their unwavering love and encouragement all the better. Debts to my brother David extend across our individual academic peregrinations; continents and oceans have interposed, but he remains my confidant. I am humbled by the kindness and hospitality of the Tomsky family in London, especially Marta, my second mother. Somehow, happily, during the research and writing of this book, I have acquired two lovely children. To Felix and Zara, I hope you'll understand why your dad kept such strange hours at various stages of your early lives. More than anyone else, you two know why I can only name and never fully thank Terri Tomsky – my best friend, my best critic, and my partner in all things.

Preface: The 8,000-Mile Screwdriver

Imperialism is a rummy business.

– Rudyard Kipling, 1900[1]

As Ernst Kantorowicz observed in his study of medieval political theology, a king has two bodies.[2] The first is a juridico-theological construct, an unlimited and perpetual sovereign; the second is the biological organism who occupies that office. Historically, this has had deep significance for the operation of imperial power, as human corporeality compelled emperors to seek networks of agents who would work on their behalf. Writing from prison in Mussolini's Italy, Antonio Gramsci provided the modern complement to Kantorowicz's observation. "The modern prince," Gramsci writes, "the myth-prince, cannot be a real person, a concrete individual. It can only be an organism, a complex element of society in which a collective will, which has already been recognized and has to some extent asserted itself into action, begins to take a concrete form" (129). Taken together, these ideas illuminate the basic fact that all empires are bound by the durability of agency relationships. Without the active consent and honest service of its agents, the imperium is jeopardized.

The possibility of corrupt or rogue agents is, of course, a threat shared by all forms of political organization. Yet for empires the problem is acute since geography substantially interposes between the emperor and his field agents. Simply put, empires are utterly dependent on their agents and yet they have no direct way to supervise or control them. To appreciate this fundamental problem, consider how it still affects the most technologically advanced of empires. Arguably no empire in history has entertained such fantasies of omnipotence as the United States, whose desire for projected power has led to such innovations as smart bombs, unmanned aerial vehicles, drones, and an array of surveillance satellites capable of producing high-resolution pictures of practically any spot on earth.

Yet even in this case, power cannot be projected perfectly. It must always pass through mediating layers. Nothing captures this better than the Abu Ghraib scandal of 2004, when photographs that depicted the torture and sexual abuse of Iraqi detainees by American soldiers were leaked to the public. The outcry, from Americans who believed that Iraq had been invaded to deliver freedom from tyranny, prompted a series of hurried apologies and condemnations from political and military officials alike. When the matter came to trial, the prosecution framed the crimes as the spontaneous and unauthorized acts of a few foot soldiers rather than as symptomatic of American detention policy.[3] The rogues were duly convicted and the system remained relatively unscathed. The only officer to be charged was acquitted and no public official resigned.

Without wanting to diminish the very important debates about torture and the human rights of prisoners that were prompted by the Abu Ghraib scandal, I want to consider the statement made by the then Secretary of Defence, Donald Rumsfeld, because of what it reveals about the internal mechanics of imperial power. In February 2005, Mr Rumsfeld was asked whether he felt responsible for the abuses. His response was characteristically defiant: "What was going on during the midnight shift in Abu Ghraib prison halfway across the world is something that someone in Washington DC clearly can't manage or deal with. And so I have no regrets" (King, par. 19). This represents a startling concession from a man elsewhere memorably described as trying to micromanage the war in Iraq with what Paul Bremer, the U.S. proconsul in Baghdad, described as "the 8,000-mile screwdriver" (82). In Rumsfeld's self-exculpation, the fantasy of imperial omnipotence founders upon the breakers of each agent's self-interest. Here, in the age of satellite communication networks and instant messaging, the most technologically advanced empire in the world admits itself incapable of either supervising or disciplining the actions of its representatives.

To apprehend the perennial challenge to the "rummy business" described in Rudyard Kipling's letter to the Duchess of Sutherland, we might consider how one of the British Empire's civil servants responded to questions similar to those asked of Secretary Rumsfeld. In 1852 John Stuart Mill appeared before a Parliamentary Select Committee, convened to review the system by which Britain governed its Indian territories. At the time, Mill was the most senior bureaucrat in the London headquarters of the Indian administration and he was called upon to rationalize what seemed for some to be its byzantine form of government. Two events from the previous decade coloured the interview: the first was Britain's defeat in the Anglo-Afghan wars of 1838–42; the second was General Charles Napier's unauthorized and violent annexation of Sind province in 1842–3, the act which led to the famous yet apocryphal one-word telegram "Peccavi." In both cases, the committee challenged Mill: would it not have been better were the central administration located in India rather than London? Mill countered partly by noting that India was a subcontinent, which meant that a local capitol would likely confront the same problem as London. He proceeded then to defend the perpetual *ex post facto* nature of the London correspondence:

> There are very few acts of the Government of India which it is possible for the authorities here to set aside when they are once done [in India] ... [We] have, however, a great power of making useful comments, which may serve as instructions for future cases of the same kind; and it seems to me the greatest good that the home authorities can do is to comment freely on the proceedings of the local authorities, to criticise them well, and lay down general principles for the guidance of Government on subsequent occasions. ("The East India Company Charter" 69–70)

Like Rumsfeld, then, Mill knew that there would always be a "midnight shift." The challenge for both empires, then, was to cultivate an indirect mode of managing the workers on the midnight shift, wherein the imperial agents would regulate themselves.

Gramsci calls such cultures of regulation, in which one group willingly and against its interest cedes superiority to another, hegemony. Uniting ideology from above with consent from below, hegemony explains how dominated classes participate in their subjection through their contact with institutions. In the colonial context, hegemony helps answer the riddle of how relatively small groups of colonizers could effectively manage the subjection of colonized peoples. The anticolonial activist and novelist Ngugi wa Thiong'o described life in colonial Kenya in just such terms:

> [T]he night of the sword and the bullet was followed by the morning of the chalk and the blackboard. The physical violence of the battlefield was followed by the psychological violence of the classroom. But where the former was visibly brutal, the latter was visibly gentle. (9)

Ngugi captures the subtlety of hegemonic articulations as he notes their visible gentility and he speaks for many in the anticolonial movement when he rejects the politics of armed resistance and instead puts the task of decolonizing the mind as the necessary first objective in any true liberation program.

The colonized mind, which is the universal goal of hegemony, guarantees political stability and this suggests that hegemony theory can usefully illuminate an empire's attempt to manage its otherwise independent agents. This book explores how the British Empire colonized the minds of the men it sent overseas to act in its name. A long way from London and invested with plenipotentiary powers, these agents had ample opportunity to enrich themselves through corruption or to embark upon heroic military campaigns. Instead, they nearly unanimously suspended their private pursuit of wealth or glory in order to serve an employer that offered meagre wages and little public recognition. The following chapters elaborate the visibly gentle ways that these otherwise free-thinking British subjects were incorporated within the empire's social organism.

CORPORATE CHARACTER

Introduction: Empire's Corporate Culture

In 1888, as part of his attempt to raise enough money to secure passage back to England, Rudyard Kipling published "The Man Who Would Be King" in A.H. Wheeler's Indian Railway Library series. The story, which tells the tale of two self-described "loafers" who set out across the Afghan border to carve out for themselves an independent kingdom, was immediately recognized as a commentary on the perennial challenges empires face when trying to regulate the behaviour of their agents. Because they disregard the standards of imperial conduct for personal enrichment, Daniel Dravot and Peachy Carnehan endure spectacularly gruesome fates: the first loses his head; the other is crucified and forced to trudge home carrying said head back across the desert to relay the tale of imperial folly with his dying breath. Rudyard Kipling's support of the British Empire is, of course, unambiguous, and "The Man Who Would Be King" is not a categorical critique of imperialism, but merely of imperialism done the wrong way. The secure "home" towards which Carnehan struggles in this story is British India, a model for Kipling and many others in the 1880s of imperialism done well. The story became a touchstone for subsequent authors and critics of colonial literature. Edmund Wilson, writing in the twilight of the British Raj in 1941, provided the characteristic criticism, calling it "surely a parable of what might happen to the English if they should forfeit their moral authority" (160). The thrill, in other words, for Kipling's colonial and metropolitan audience, derives from the contradiction between these rogues' actions and the expectations of virtuous service that prevailed in the late-Victorian period.

The mythos of "moral authority" underpinned many justifications for European imperialism in the nineteenth and twentieth centuries. However, unlike their continental rivals, British imperialists seemed reluctant to acknowledge the "rummy business" of empire. In 1883 the historian John Seeley delivered a series of lectures on the origins of imperial Britain. Reflecting on what he termed the "expansion of England," he famously pronounced that England had acquired its empire "in a fit of absence of mind" (8).[1] What Seeley meant was that, as far as he could tell, the historical record contained no evidence of any deliberate plan or conspiracy on England's part to extend its dominion into other parts of the globe. Moreover, Seeley contended, imperialism never really enjoyed the support of the English population or its political class. Instead, he explained, the empire grew unconsciously, sometimes by the unsanctioned selfishness of an enterprising few and other times through a series of accidents with unforeseen consequences. This did not, for Seeley, make the British Empire any less virtuous. It was, he pronounced, like "the full-grown giant developed out of the sturdy boy" (164), a natural if unintended by-product of England's national virtue rather than of any selfish design.

For Seeley, absent-mindedness distinguished the British Empire from both its antecedents and its contemporaries because it secured England's moral dignity. Though England might have an empire, its citizens, he maintained, were not imperialistic. In fact, he stresses that:

> It is essentially barbaric that one community should be treated as the property of another and the fruits of its industry confiscated ... [W]e may have acquired India by conquest, [but] we cannot and do no hold it for our own pecuniary advantage. We draw no tribute from it; it is not to us a profitable investment; we should be ashamed to acknowledge that in governing it we in any way sacrificed its interest to our own. (66)

Seeley's interpretation of imperial history had wide purchase in late-Victorian Britain even if some still contested the benevolence of Britain's Indian *imperium* on both ethical and factual grounds.[2] Partly this popularity was secured because Seeley complemented an already existing tradition of imperial apologias. Roughly, that tradition might be summed up thus: Providence had declared the English to be the trustees of good and liberal government; the English in turn accepted the imperial mantle reluctantly and even then only as trustees; once the colonies were prepared to govern themselves, the English would happily relinquish their burden.

In later chapters, I will engage texts from that tradition, including Edmund Burke's speeches during the impeachment of Warren Hastings,

John Stuart Mill's *Considerations on Representative Government*, and Thomas Macaulay's "Speech on the Government of India." For the moment, I am focusing on Seeley not because, as Cambridge's Regius Professor of History, his authority among his contemporaries was formidable. Public figures like Burke, Mill, and Macaulay were at least as influential in their day. What warrants attention, rather, is Seeley's clear statement of this empire's distinctive feature: sacrifice in the furtherance of the common wealth. Though all empires, to some extent, depend on myths of nobility and graciousness, few have returned as ardently and obsessively to ideas of duty and service as the British.[3] For Seeley, those ideas explained the wondrous durability of the British Empire. England, he reminds his audience, was but one of many small European nations that acquired empires in the early modern period. Whereas the French, Dutch, Spanish, and Portuguese empires had all declined, England's endured because it had transmuted the English nation's supposedly characteristic love of liberty and fair play into an imperial code of disinterestedness.

Though Seeley's ideas are structured by his cultural milieu and institutional affiliation, his empirical base is largely sound: for the majority of the nineteenth century, Britain maintained a very orderly empire. I should make clear what I mean here by "orderly." To speak of order is not, for one thing, to deny that abuses, injustices, and even atrocities took place. Nor is it, for another, to forget that racist, pseudoscientific, and what Edward Said called Orientalist discourses were deployed to dominate subject peoples. As scholars like Mike Davis have shown, the business of empire was underwritten by harrowing costs to economies, liberties, dignities, and lives (8–12). Elizabeth Kolsky's *Colonial Justice in British India* (2010) chronicles the quantity of abuse perpetrated by white Britons – overwhelmingly not part of the "official" classes, but rather planters, sailors, enlisted soldiers, and drifters – against Indians and concludes that such violence was part of ordinary colonial life rather than the stuff of exception. The orderliness I am thinking of concerns the internal coherence of imperialism in the nineteenth century. Kipling's audience, in other words, would have been unsurprised at the divine retribution visited upon Dravot and Carnehan because their rogue actions were so inconsistent with already established ideas and expectations of imperial conduct. *Corporate Character* engages the Victorian mythos of honourable and selfless service within the culture of colonialism. More specifically, the purpose of this book is to suggest why relatively few internal scandals took place over the historically long and geographically broad life of the British Empire. This should not be mistaken as a defence of empire of any sort, nor as an argument that somehow Britain's empire was better than any other. My intention, instead, is to explain how and why Britain's imperial agents so willingly served, when it was so obviously against any rational calculation of their self-interest.

Seeley's contemporary, W.E.H. Lecky identified that remarkable orderliness to be the true marvel of the British Empire. Delivering the inaugural lecture at the Imperial Institute in 1893, Lecky pronounced that "it is not an easy thing to secure honest and faithful administration in remote countries, far from the supervision and practical control of the central government" (27–8). The early modern age, he explained, had presented several European nations the opportunity to build empires. Like any large-scale operation, these nascent empires divested power to their agents and expected them to act in the national interest, to do their duty. England's global dominance at the end of the century, he concluded, was attributable to the consistently high levels of obedient and dutiful service it had obtained.

This book examines the culture of colonialism, by which I mean the ways that literature and other cultural productions contributed to establish expectations of high levels of service from colonial agents. Certainly, the image of stoic commitment to service at meagre pay and little recognition by men who might otherwise have indulged their desires in the opulent Oriental landscape is one of the more enduring in nineteenth-century imperial mythology. Rudyard Kipling's short story "On the City Wall" (1888) is an excellent example of this myth making. An allegory of power that engages two types of rebellious natives (the belligerent Sikh warrior and the Anglicized Muslim), the story opens with a few remarks on the difficulty of administering power:

> It is necessary to explain something about the Supreme Government which is above all and below all and behind all. Gentlemen come from England, spend a few weeks in India, walk round this great Sphinx of the Plains, and write books upon its ways and its works, denouncing or praising it as their own ignorance prompts. Consequently all the world knows how the Supreme Government conducts itself. But no one, not even the Supreme Government, knows everything about the administration of the Empire. Year by year England sends out fresh drafts for the first fighting-line, which is officially called the Indian Civil Service. These die, or kill themselves by overwork, or are worried to death, or broken in health and

> hope in order that the land may be protected from death and sickness, famine and war, and may eventually become capable of standing alone. It will never stand alone, but the idea is a pretty one, and men are willing to die for it, and yearly the work of pushing and coaxing and scolding and petting the country into good living goes forward. If an advance be made all credit is given to the native, while the Englishmen stand back and wipe their foreheads. If a failure occurs the Englishmen step forward and take the blame. (4: 305–6)[4]

Kipling here has identified the three distinct branches of the imperial governing apparatus: the ignorant political overseers, the nominally superintending central power, and the silently heroic individual field agents. A keen observer of imperial society, Kipling, like Lecky, insists that the colonial government is entirely contingent on the voluntary subscription by those agents to an idea.

In this book I will be calling such volunteerism the idea of the virtuous empire. Other scholars have noted the admixture of heroic masochism in Britain's imperial self-fashioning. Daniel Bivona's study of the imperial bureaucracy in the late-Victorian and early-Edwardian period proposes to explain how the "imperial bureaucrat comes to imagine his own mastery as a peculiar form of self-sacrifice – and especially, as an erotically charged, masochistically tinged, form of service to some higher power or higher ideal" (3), and John Kucich has argued that "elements of masochistic fantasy resonated powerfully" (2) within a great deal of colonial discourse. Angela Poon has called this compound of heroism and guilty suffering "the double nature" (75) of English colonial rule, especially in India. For Bivona, Kucich, and Poon, Rudyard Kipling is taken to be the high priest of this mythology – along the same lines, a generation earlier, Benita Parry called Kipling "the coarse figure who virtually invented the Anglo-Indian rhetoric of fortitude and self-sacrifice" (18) – but more broadly, their readings of the idea of the virtuous empire find its origins somewhere shortly after the Indian Rebellion of 1857, the event which prompted Britain to take sovereignty over the subcontinent away from its proxy agent, the East India Company. Stephen Patterson's recent history of the cult of imperial honour, for example, suggests that while the "discourse of honour and shame always existed to some degree in British India ... this system underwent radical changes with the establishment of the Raj in 1858" (13).

This book challenges the interpretation that takes the transfer from Company to Crown as a paradigm shift in the colonial culture of British

India, seeing it instead as one event on a longer historical continuum. Historians like C.A. Bayly have observed that, in terms of the day-to-day administration of the colonial territory, the 1858 Act for the Better Government of India was symbolic more than anything.[5] Charles Canning was both the last Company-employed governor-general and the first viceroy; Company civil servants remained in their offices, with the same roles and responsibilities but with new titles. By making these observations, I am not discounting the intense effect of the Rebellion on British consciousness, colonial or otherwise. Christopher Herbert is absolutely right to argue that the Rebellion was of "incomprehensible magnitude and historical importance" for Victorians (2) as is Maya Jasanoff's characterization of 1857–8 as "Britain's most desperate imperial scare" (10). However, Herbert adds, that significance is something of a "riddle" (19) since compared to, say, the Crimean war the Rebellion was rather small and rather well-contained. "Gauged purely in the light of its empirical scale and its practical consequences," Herbert writes, "the Mutiny might not seem an outstandingly momentous historical event" (1). Though he takes a position very much against Herbert's, ideologically, Guatam Chakravarty agrees in his study of cultural representations of the Indian Mutiny that the symbolic outstripped the pragmatic in terms of the Mutiny's significance for Anglo-Indian colonial relations (47–8).

This suggests a need to extend the historical horizon past the events of 1857–8, an extension which threatens critical assessments of Kipling's original genius. As a first step, we could turn to the opinions of Thomas Babington Macaulay, a man whose liberal politics arguably comprise Kipling's polar opposite.[6] Macaulay, like Kipling, recognized that the empire depended on the actions of employees over whom London had little if any control. His 1833 "Speech on the Government of India," reveals a man most impressed by the universal propriety of colonial field agents, men heroic to the point of self-sacrifice:

> I contemplate with reverence and delight the honourable poverty which is the evidence of rectitude firmly maintained amidst strong temptations. I rejoice to see my countrymen, after ruling millions of subjects, after commanding victorious armies, after dictating terms of peace at the gates of hostile capitals, after administering the revenues of great provinces, after judging the causes of wealthy Zemindars, after residing at the courts of tributary Kings, return to their native land with no more than a decent competence. (151)[7]

Here, fifty years before Kipling, is an exemplary piece of Kiplingesque rhetoric. Compare it, for example, to one of Kipling's first published short stories, "Only a Subaltern" (1888), which demolishes the idea that colonial servants could expect a glorious homecoming:

> Papa Wick had been a Commissioner in his day, holding authority over three millions of men in the Chota-Buldana Division, building great works for the good of the land, and doing his best to make two blades of grass grow where there was but one before. Of course, nobody knew anything about this in the little English village where he was just "old Mr. Wick" and had forgotten that he was a Companion of the Order of the Star of India. (3: 416–17)

In fact, "Only a Subaltern" carries the diminution of Papa Wick's heroic statesmanship to an extreme; both his career and anonymous retirement are pushed aside in order to emblazon the short and less honourable life of his son, Bobby, the titular subaltern.

Comparing Kipling and Macaulay supports the long-view approach to colonial culture advocated by Patrick Brantlinger. In *Rule of Darkness* (1988), Brantlinger cautioned that imperial ideology and its associated rhetoric were well developed before the fin-de-siècle era of Kipling and jingoism (6–8). *Corporate Character* follows Brantlinger and argues that we can understand the imperialism of an Anglo-Indian writer like Kipling only when we overcome our tendency to read him as radically original or to see his era as discrete.[8] The idea of the virtuous empire predates Kipling just as British imperialism predates its jingoistic expression in the last decades of the nineteenth century. In both cases, to assume otherwise risks misapprehending the imperialism of the 1880s and 1890s for imperialism as such – an error which can allow other forms of imperial discourse from other periods to escape without criticism.

Thinking about Macaulay not only helps situate Kipling within a larger tradition of imperial debates on duty and self-sacrifice but it also provides an opportunity to explain why I am approaching imperialism through the problematic of institutions and agency, rather than the more conventional lenses of race or nation. Repeatedly in his writings on India, in the essays on Robert Clive and Warren Hastings as well as in his parliamentary speeches, Macaulay maintained that the virtuous and self-denying behaviour of colonial administrators was a function of England's – and lately Britain's – national character. Yet, putting to one side the relative novelty of "Britishness" at this point in history, it is worth noting that in the 1830s the British Indian Empire was even newer, less than seventy years old, and even during that short tenure, the "character" of "British" agents had been inconsistent. We need only recall the notoriety of the "nabob," the vulgar and avaricious stock character of British stage drama in the 1760s and 1770s, whose ill-gotten foreign fortunes are often represented as a threat to the domestic body politic, to recognize that wherever Macaulay praises the virtue of the British Indian administrators his historical horizon is both limited and selective.[9] Chapter 1 will give its limit precisely: the 1788–95 impeachment of Warren Hastings. For Macaulay, like many other Victorian commentators, the trial was seen as the ritual break from the age of the corrupt nabobs, the robber-barons who plundered personal fortunes from Indian states while ostensibly serving their London controllers. For those earlier generations of agents, the men whose actions introduced the Sanskrit word "loot" into the English lexicon, British or English character was seemingly held in abeyance.

However, it would be wrong to dismiss Macaulay's invocation of national character entirely, since merely identifying a thing as artificial is not sufficient reason to dismiss its practical influence. A term like "British character" may or may not be essential or historically deep-rooted, but it was palpably felt across the diversity of the still-forming British nation.[10] In its operation, it contributes to the ineffable cultural temperament that Raymond Williams calls a structure of feeling. In *Marxism and Literature* (1977), Williams describes a method to apprehend "the sense of a generation or of a period" (131), a way to account for the social life of an ideology, the tension between institutional forms and private interpretations. A concept closely aligned to hegemony theory, a structure of feeling describes how ideology becomes common sense among a subjected people. Williams is careful to insist that structures of feeling are temporally and geographically rooted. In this, Williams illuminates Macaulay's appeal to character. In other words, I think Macaulay was right to argue that something peculiar was compelling overseas agents to behave as they did. He was only wrong to attach that behaviour to the cumulative effect of a particular (which we could call "English" or "British") historical progress. If British character is understood as a disposition cultivated slowly over a long period of time – and surely this is how Macaulay uses it – then, following Williams, we can clearly apprehend how inappropriate it is in the colonial context. Macaulay's error, if we can call it such, occurs when he extends the virtues of British character to the novelties of imperial power, alien geographies, and diverse new sets of cultural practices.

To be clear, I am not disagreeing with the historical fact that following the trial of Warren Hastings fewer colonial agents abused their power. Nor am I denying that there existed among those agents a belief in what could arguably be called (since it was certainly understood as) "British character." Rather, I am suggesting that the source of the British character in the colonial context, the ethic which regulated behaviour, is not as immemorial as Macaulay encourages us to infer. Sara Suleri makes a similar point in *The Rhetoric of English India* (1992), when she argues that the circumstances of empire outstripped the existing metaphorical registry of eighteenth-century English (64). To speak in ways that not only made that new experience sensible but also made it easier to control and regulate, imperial commentators, Suleri explains, had to craft a new language. Her conclusion suggests that we no longer attempt to understand imperialism as Seeley did, as a natural outgrowth of English culture, but instead attend to the specific institutions and cultural formations which coincided with the British Empire. For all the recent work on the cultures of imperialism in the late eighteenth and nineteenth centuries, little explains how the virtuous colonial administrator replaces the corrupt nabob in imperial self-fashioning.

One of my arguments in this book is that the "character" underpinning the idea of the virtuous empire was called into being by the Anglo-Irish politician Edmund Burke, the lead prosecutor in the impeachment of Warren Hastings. Burke is well known for demanding that Britain acknowledge its status as an imperial power and the attendant responsibilities attached to that power. To guide the morality of the nascent British Empire, Burke hearkened back to Rome, citing examples of virtue and corruption from classical literature and jurisprudence. However, as I will explain in chapter 1, the classical model did not quite fit the contemporary situation: the logistics of the British Empire differed markedly from the Roman; the advent of mercantilist capitalism and the emerging separation of private and public social spheres meant that classical ideas of virtue and corruption could provide, at best, only a point of departure. In other words, this book argues not that Burke established a moral code for the next century of imperialism but merely that he made the opening statement in what would become a century-long process of manufacturing imperial character.

In elaborating the social, economic, and political factors active in the manufacture of this imperial ethos, the task remains to identify and examine the series of administrative practices, organizations, and techniques developed specifically for that purpose. To do this, I will trace the relationships between different understandings of imperial agency by looking at the language and arguments of those who described it. Before I begin, though, the problem of imperial agency should be separated from the general issue of imperial morality – of whether it was or could be good that liberty-loving Britain subjected other nations and peoples under its authority. The sociologist Thomas Osborne has argued that the question of how "rulers justify their own rule for themselves ... actually has two sides" (289–90). Beside the moral justification of empire and its legitimation through ideology is the establishment of the ethical competence to rule. Working with a Foucauldian understanding of the ethical construction of authority, Osborne suggests that "there has to be some codification of the ethical type that bears particular competence to rule" (290).

Corporate Character complements Osborne's investigation into the ethics of imperial administration by focusing not on matters of sovereignty, but of agency. Imperial agency, as I am using it, refers to how power is administered and is therefore concerned not with the colonized subject but with the colonial administrator, the man Edmund Burke calls a "subject-in-power." My interest in this figure stems from my sense of his ambivalence, in both the etymological and psychological aspects. A colonial administrator is always suspended between power and service. As someone who wields plenipotentiary power in the colonial space but is concomitantly obliged to serve a distant master, his dilemma is summarized in another of Kipling's short stories, "A Sahibs' War" (1904). There, a Sikh trooper, by way of explaining why he is fighting in South Africa, offers the imperial equivalent of the paradox of Schrödinger's cat: "Ye cannot in one place rule and in another bear service. Either ye must everywhere rule or everywhere obey" (22: 90). But as another of Kipling's characters asserts, there is no quantum theory for human identity. Hurree Mookerjee, the Bengali agent of the British Secret Service in *Kim* (1901), clarifies the other difficulty of wielding imperial power when he tells his protégé, "One cannot be in two places at once. Thatt is axiomatic" (209). Mookerjee's axiom, offered to Kim as a consolation for the fact that neither of them can experience the full pleasure of their successful mission, reveals the simplicity of the Sikh's proverb: total, unrestricted power is an impossible fantasy in a modern imperial world. Yet colonial agents were expected to fulfil this fantasy when colonial logistics dictated that a solitary individual must *represent* and *embody* imperial authority. Knowing they would never be able to take full credit for any successes, it is easy to see how their actions were riven by deep psychological anxiety.

The ambivalence is harrowingly described in George Orwell's "Shooting an Elephant" (1936), an essay that reflects upon an episode from Orwell's time as a police officer in Burma. At its centre is the ethical dilemma prompted by his encounter with an angry elephant and an expectant group of colonial subjects. The narrator is conscious both of his official duty (to shoot the riotous elephant) and of the theatrical space (an audience waiting for him to perform), yet before he can enact imperial power, his private conscience intervenes:

> All this was perplexing and upsetting. For at that time I had already made up my mind that imperialism was an evil thing and the sooner I chucked up my job and got out of it the better. Theoretically – and secretly, of course – I was all for the Burmese and all against their oppressors, the British. As for the job I was doing, I hated it more bitterly than I can perhaps make clear ... But I could get nothing into perspective. I was young and ill-educated and I had to think out my problems in the utter silence that is imposed on every Englishman in the East ... With one part of my mind I thought of the British Raj as an unbreakable tyranny, as something clamped down, in *saecula saeculorum*, upon the will of prostrate people; with another part I thought that the greatest joy in the world would be to drive a bayonet into a Buddhist priest's guts. Feelings like these are the normal by-products of imperialism; ask any Anglo-Indian official, if you can catch him off duty. (3–4)

Orwell's indecision, his personal repulsion towards his official obligation to destroy a valuable asset (the elephant), has since become a favourite for both postcolonial and psychoanalytic theories of imperial discourse. For my purposes, it introduces the key themes of the agency crisis. Here we have a young man – an unfinished product – operating in a foreign territory thousands of miles away from both his home and his head office, a young man full of power yet without counsel, a young man with no recourse for his deliberation other than solitary introspection.

Orwell's reflection upon the awkward position he once occupied makes it clear that a colonial agent is never fully in possession of himself; rather he "becomes a sort of hollow, posing dummy" (8). Even though he intuitively knows what he should do – "As soon as I saw the elephant I knew with perfect certainty that I ought not to shoot him" – and admits that "I thought then and I think now that his attack of 'must' [i.e., rage or madness] was already passing off" he also realizes that, as a representative of imperial authority, there is no alternative *but* to kill the elephant (7). His struggle whether to obey his conscience or to play his role can hardly be described as decisive: though he eventually shoots the elephant, he does not immediately kill it. In case we missed the point that the elephant's condition as a rebellious beast of burden symbolizes the narrator's internally split subjectivity, Orwell commits a full fifth of the essay to the gory description of how he emptied his rifles into the elephant's head and heart. Yet even this disproportionate violence fails to resolve the problem; the narrator finally gives up and walks away, leaving the mangled animal to die from its wounds. The elephant's struggle, its wheezing presence, haunts the narrator because it is so like his own: suspended between life and death, struggling to maintain the illusion of agency when faced with its inevitable dissolution, the un-dead elephant symbolizes the impossible position occupied by the colonial official, the subject-in-power.

Agency and Institutions

It might be argued that the colonial context is only a particular form of a problem inherent in any complex social organism, or that the dilemmas faced by men like Orwell can best be understood via the way British culture sacralized tropes of duty following the famous Victorian loss of religious faith. But what distinguishes the imperial agency crisis is neither its extremity (an effectively unbridgeable distance) nor its scale (the amount of power vested in single agents) but rather its novelty. As I will show in the following chapters, the eighteenth-century debates about imperial morality were eclipsed in the nineteenth century by debates about the form and the style of the imperial administration. After the putative virtue of imperialism had been established, the threat of the deviant employee became *the* energizing principle behind nearly all discussions of reform or improvement. And because, according to historians like C.A. Bayly and P.J. Marshall, Britain basically improvised its approach to governance in India, this energizing principle had a great effect on colonial policy and colonial culture.[11]

This study uses the term "agency" in relation to its two popular understandings. On the one hand, I am interested in British citizens as agents, as contracted employees acting in the interest of another party.

This enters the territory of ethics, where it is very easy to imagine a plenitude of Orwellian conflicts of interest, where official obligation contradicts one's individual sense of what could or ought to be done. But since conscience is not always the thing preventing an order from being carried out, and since not all colonial officials were as "theoretically and secretly" moral as Eric Arthur Blair, my investigation will also account for other types of personal interests. For example, in most of the empire, and certainly in British India, there was always the risk that agents would abuse their unsupervised official positions for personal gratification. The early stages of Anglo-Indian history are replete with Kiplingesque men who would be kings; the most famous was Robert Clive, the clerk who in 1751 took charge of an army and won the battle that established Britain's territorial sovereignty in India. Yet Clive's is not simply a tale of Boy's Own heroism. Among his contemporaries, Clive's fame stemmed more from the immense personal fortune he extracted from those battles, via the private "pensions" he negotiated with the Indian princes whose thrones he had won. It is salutary to note that Clive's notorious pursuit of private profit set off a wave of speculative greed in London that nearly bankrupted his mercantile employers.[12] Indeed, in 1771 Ralph Griffiths, editor of the *Monthly Review*, warned those who hoped to reform Anglo-India through mere policy changes that such an approach "impl[ies] a degree of integrity in the officers of the East India Company, which will never be found among men who forsake their own country to amass wealth under an unkindly climate" (504).

Taking together the threats posed to those London-based principals by both moral objectors and selfish opportunists, I consider their various attempts to manage the response of their agents, to prepare employees to see official duties as coterminous with personal satisfaction. To do this, I need to clarify the other sense with which I use the word "agency": as an institution. There can hardly be any accounting of the way individual agency was managed in colonial India without addressing the institutional character of either the East India Company or the Indian civil service. For this aspect I intend partly to answer Mary Poovey's call for more specialized research into the influence of institutions on human subjectivity. Poovey argues that to complement the vast array of theories of representation, humanities scholars should now work to describe the active roles institutions "play in subject-formation, geopolitical relations, and imaginative productivity." Doing so, "we might be able to begin developing new theories about abstractions like nationalism or globalization" (431). Her call is timely since "imperialism" is certainly another of those abstractions which requires further explication. If we agree that imperialism has an ideology whose principles are meditated and reflected in various institutions (literary, religious, educational, economic, etc.), then we need to understand it as a social process, and thus open to both sociological and cultural scrutiny.

The Corporation

The British-Indian experience is an excellent place to examine how institutions fashion subjectivity because of the overwhelming influence of a single one: the English East India Company, a joint-stock corporation that for over three hundred years operated a monopolistic trade between Great Britain and all ports east of the Cape of Good Hope. Yet however interesting the internal sociology of this early modern corporation may be, it is the radical shift in purpose that makes it particularly fertile ground for study.[13] When in the 1760s the Company began to assume sovereignty in parts of India, the consensus among both its stockholders and its external critics was that this mercantile association was constitutionally and organizationally ill-suited to administer power or deliver justice to a subject people. At the same time, few could imagine a viable alternative for that overseas administration.[14] After all, the Company had been operating in India since the early seventeenth century. In that time, it had established political relations with local powers, maintained a militia, and, most important, knew more than any other British entity something about the local customs. Despite being in effect the best of a bad bunch, the corporate structure of the East India Company and its associated culture were hardly geared to administer an empire. When the Company accepted the *diwan* of Bengal, it inaugurated what criminologist Mark Brown has called "a unique experiment in private sector stateship" (78). The institution which for one hundred and fifty years had developed a specialized set of routines and practices to manage the commercial activity of their overseas employees found itself compelled to develop entirely new practices sensitive to its new responsibilities.

In its beginning the English East India Company was little more than a replica of the various Dutch companies which had been trading with the Spice Islands of the Indonesian archipelago since 1594. Late in 1599, a group of London merchants hastily assembled to decide whether they too could take advantage of the enormous return on capital being realized by the Dutch trading missions. One year later, Elizabeth I assigned these merchants a royal charter, which granted them a monopoly on condition that they work to increase "the honour of our nation, [and] the wealth of our people" through "the increase of our navigation, and advancement of trade in merchandize" ("Charter" 2). The inclusion of honour means that Elizabeth's charter reads curiously against recent explanations of how modern corporations operate, which generally agree that corporations are constitutionally compelled to maximize shareholder profits and to "externalize" the costs of doing business.[15] Even if we take into account the very recent scramble by modern multinationals to publicize their commitment to corporate social responsibility, the East India Company was bound to the national interest in a way more similar to the Bank of England than to, say, British Petroleum or Halliburton. As I have suggested, my focus is on what happened after this mercantile company assumed territorial hegemony in parts of India in the mid-eighteenth century. When previously well-regulated employees became, potentially, mercenary fortune-hunters, there were deleterious consequences not only for the Company's trading interest but also for the domestic British economy. One of the great fears in the 1760s was that the infusion of foreign capital would exert inflationary pressure on British goods. By the 1770s, both stockholders and a large portion of the British public agreed that the second condition of the Elizabethan charter was not being upheld and that if the national honour was to be salvaged then serious structural reform was necessary for the East India Company.

The way this institution refashioned itself supports Jurgen Habermas's theory of social systems. In critiquing the metaphor of a "body politic" Habermas observes that social systems, unlike actual organisms, can change their goals and alter constitutional elements. That flexibility gives the lie to the mythology that corporations are "bodies," no matter how often its employees speak of esprit de corps. Unlike individuals, corporations can assert themselves, and therefore possess agency, in what Habermas calls a "hypercomplex environment," masquerading as bodies in order to maintain themselves at a new kind of control (*Legitimation* 3). The East India Company's structural transformation has been well-studied by economic historians and sociologists interested in how the Company morphed from trader to sovereign.[16] However, since, as historian Huw Bowen argues, the East India Company "always represented ... a semi-formal expansion of the [British] State" (20), it is understandable that scholarly focus has tended to be on the macropolitical level. This study extends such scholarship by scrutinizing micropolitics at the level of the individual agent, the company man. My claim is to take the idea of a corporate culture seriously. To do that, I must first concede that the term "corporate culture" is anachronistic in the age of the East India Company; the nearest analogue is esprit de corps, the favoured phrase of Anglo-Indian writers seeking to explain in their memoirs, letters, and imaginative fiction the reason why such a thinly spread group of Britons could cohere across a subcontinent. To distinguish between corporate culture and an esprit de corps, though, I follow the arguments put forward by Karl Marx and Freidrich Engels in *The German Ideology*, that governing ideologies do not descend to humanity from the heavens (42–4). In other words, the spirit in the *esprit* cannot precede the material *corps*. Thus I favour the term "corporate culture" for its ability to signify the necessary cultural work and social interaction between individual humans to create the corporate body. In the mid-eighteenth century, with both an institution and its members undergoing significant interruption to an established practice of everyday life, being forced mutually to adapt to a new state of affairs, we are now well placed to test the theory that human subjectivity and morality are coproduced by agents and their institutional agencies.

Group Theory

This book argues that we must think about the social system bounded by the East India Company's agents as a group separate from the general British polity. But since groups and institutions take many forms, each with its own internal logic, I need to introduce a categorical distinction made by the nineteenth-century sociologist Ferdinand Tönnies. In *Gemeinschaft und Gesellschaft* (1887), Tönnies claimed that human associations could be characterized by two normative types. On the one hand there is an organic community (*Gemeinschaft*), bound together by ties of kinship, fellowship, custom, history, and communal ownership of primary goods (17, 36). On the other hand, there is a mechanical civil society (*Gesellschaft*), where free-standing individuals interact with each other through self-interest, contracts, and the external constraints of formally enacted laws (56–7).

This division provides a framework for understanding the administrative culture of the East India Company. Clearly, as a mercantile organization, the Company initially carried the aspect of *Gesellschaft*, an artificial society of unrelated individuals brought together by the pursuit of profit through trade and who undertook to be regulated by a set of rational, negotiated rules of conduct.[17] This worked well enough so long as the Company's interests were limited to the economic sphere. Yet when it became a political power, and when employees could enrich themselves economically through the corrupt exercise of their political power, London was at a loss. It is a measure of their desperation in the face of ongoing corruption that in 1765 the directors agreed to send none other than Robert Clive back to India to handle the problem.

In order to discipline their agents, the challenge for the East India Company was to create social capital and to associate its accrual with the successful discharge of administrative tasks. Yet for social capital to obtain value, the civil society of merchant-traders would have to become a community of administrators. Recalling John Stuart Mill's admission to Parliament that the Company could exercise no direct control over its agents once they had been sent to India and adding to this the fact that the agents themselves often worked in isolation from each other, I am arguing that the transformation can only take place at the level of culture. In short, to return to Tönnies's model, the East India Company militated against corruption by transforming their *Gesellschaft* into a *Gemeinschaft*, inaugurating one of the first deliberate attempts to fashion a corporate culture.

In describing that corporate culture, I want to link the culture of British imperialism to the structure of its administration through their shared concern with ethical dilemmas. My work is prompted by the fact that imperial necessity often asked colonial civil servants and readers to abandon personal scruples in favour of an ostensibly national interest. However, I argue that the object of imperial hegemony is not merely to convince people to suspend their moral code; it is equally important to ensure that agents or readers do not go too far, indulging in their new-found radical subjectivity by taking excess material, psychological, or affective pleasure from their imperial experience.

Because this is a study of how texts contributed to the management of individuals in the employ of a corporate body, I focus on those responsible for authoring and administering imperial policy: the clerks, officers, and merchants acting directly or indirectly as agents of the Crown. As a body, this small group certainly should not be confused as a metonym for British society nor can it even be thought to encompass the total number of British subjects living and working in India in the eighteenth and nineteenth centuries. For the most part, I have very little to say about the enlisted soldiers, missionaries, or private merchants who began to arrive in increasing numbers as the Company gradually ceded its monopoly on Indian trade and immigration.

To this end, one of my goals is to locate the dissonance between these company men and the larger pool (i.e., the white male British upper-middle class) from which they were drawn. It is commonly held that one of the great benefits of empire was its provision of a useful occupation for the second sons of Britain's landed families.[18] Work in the colonies sated the zeal of many who might otherwise have been motivated to social agitation by their arbitrary exclusion from the established domestic political economy. As Raymond Williams wrote in his reflection on George Orwell, "Only part of the [ruling] class was quite wholly in command: able to live on its property and investments, or to move directly into central metropolitan institutions. A much larger part had a harder and humbler function" (*Orwell* 14). An overwhelming mass of archival records testifies that the company men professed a different, or at least heavily inflected, creed of values when compared to their contemporary mainstream British middle-class ideology.

Recent work on this "second-sons" thesis has illuminated the importance of sexuality in the operation of imperial power. The historian Ronald Hyam has argued that "the driving force behind empire building" was "the export of surplus emotional or sexual energy," and that imperial expansion accelerated and intensified relationships between men (*Britain's Imperial Centruy* 135). For Hyam, this produced a cult of hypermasculinity whose deities included men like Henry Lawrence and Charles Napier and whose high priests spoke the language of James Fitzjames Stephen, who in *Liberty, Equality Fraternity* (1873), argued, "Strength in all its forms is life and manhood. To be less strong is to be less of a man" (221).[19] Christopher Lane's *The Ruling Passion* (1994) productively complicates Hyam's narrative of aggressive sublimation, whereby imperialism is a consequence of "rejecting or sublimating … physical desire for other men" (4), by suggesting instead a profound sexual ambivalence in the colonial theatre. Lane argues that "masculine identification" (13) often interrupted imperialist drives by fostering affective attachments within what he calls, following Helene Cixous, "The Empire of the Selfsame." This book is indebted to such work for highlighting the importance of homosocial bonds within imperial culture.

As I will demonstrate in my third chapter, the divergence between metropole and colony is palpable in the early literature of Anglo-India.

The crucial difference is the immense power enjoyed by these agents in territories that were not bound by the social conventions of their home country. In the employ of the East India Company, a colonial administrator wielded nearly despotic power over a massive foreign territory and population, and could reinvent both himself and that territory in the process; yet he was obliged contractually at a modest wage to follow the directives of a small court of proprietors located several months' correspondence away. That these proprietors often displayed ignorance of the conditions in any given agent's territory only exacerbated the situation. The resulting effect of anxious frustration became a recurrent theme in the writings of company men. However, despite the tension between corporate headquarters and its field agents, the company men somehow cohered enough to perpetuate British overseas hegemony for nearly two centuries.

Throughout this study I will refer to "aristocratic virtue" as the vehicle for that social stability. Briefly defined, aristocratic virtue denotes the psychosocial process whereby a British citizen (employee or reader) was reduced to the level of instrumentality precisely at the moment he believed himself entrusted as the agent of noble reform. The term in the Anglo-Indian context originates from the sentiment expressed by Governor-General Richard Wellesley in his memorandum to the Company directors on the matter of employee training. Wellesley's "Notes with Respect to the Foundation of a College at Fort William" (1800) argues that colonial agents would be easy to manage if they could be brought to think of themselves as "statesmen ... properly qualified to conduct the ordinary movements of the great machine of Government" (731). This hoped-for combination of liberally educated gentlemen capable of ruling but satisfied to serve soon became not only the object of corporate pedagogy but also an ideal in Anglo-Indian literature. We can find the supreme literary representation of aristocratic virtue near the conclusion of Kipling's *Kim* in the famous scene where the young hero collapses into aphasia because, for the first time in his life, this otherwise omnipotent teenager feels himself "a cog-wheel unconnected with any machinery" (234).

A new "good," aristocratic virtue facilitated the transformation of Anglo-India from a civil society to a community because it enabled both pleasure and social merit to be acquired through the *act* rather than the *result* of work. This change accords with Tönnies's distinction: in a community work is a vocation and something not separable from life, whereas in a civil society work is like a business organized for the attainment of some hypothetical happy end, such as a salary or a parade when one retires home to England (Tönnies 68). This explains why so little of Anglo-Indian corporate culture emphasizes the practical achievements of British imperialism – the bridges built, the hospitals founded, the famines averted – and instead celebrates the virtuous toil and self-sacrifice of the colonial servants in service to the idea of practical achievements.

Like all cultural topoi, aristocratic virtue became progressively more complex as it circulated. The rudimentary encouragement of a fraternal esprit de corps at Haileybury College anticipates the circles of proficient technocrats who populate Kipling's short stories. Likewise Wellesley's promise that noble sacrifice would lead to honourable distinction upon retirement is eventually critiqued by Anglo-Indian writers who maintain that work and achievements mean little to those outside the community of administrators. As such, aristocratic virtue belongs to an affective economy where the pleasures of imperialism are granted to colonial agents on the condition that they can only enjoy those pleasures secretly among themselves.

Corporate Culture

By emphasizing the continuity of aristocratic virtue across various iterations of British Indian imperialism in the long nineteenth century, *Corporate Character* analyses the influence of colonial texts both as desiring objects, directed towards some goal (real or imagined), and as practical contributions to the definition and structure of that goal. The material under consideration includes novels, short stories, poems, essays, memoirs, personal correspondence, and parliamentary speeches related to the East India Company and its bureaucratic after-image, the Indian Civil Service. What unites these texts is their interest in representing the agency crisis (or lack thereof) experienced by a colonial agent in power. Though it is true that, without exception, the subjects are men, the authors interested in them are drawn from both genders. From Frances Burney at the trial of Warren Hastings, through to Sara Jeannette Duncan and Edith Dell at the apex of the Raj, *Corporate Character* identifies a long tradition of women's writing fascinated with the ethical conflicts provoked by the circumstances of colonial rule.[20]

It is important to emphasize that this is a study of cultural representations. While I am interested in the relation between Anglo-Indian literature and the government of India, I do not mean to suggest, for example, that Anglo-Indian authors wrote in order to serve the disciplinary desires of the East India Company or the Indian government; in fact, many of the best Anglo-Indian writers did not strictly belong to the official class represented in their fiction. (Both Rudyard Kipling and Sara Jeannette Duncan, for example, were journalists and not administrators.) Neither do I intend to show a causal link between this literature and the ethical standards of its readers. What I am more concerned with is understanding the feelings, beliefs, and dispositions to act in certain ways that were prevalent in a society at a particular cultural moment, including not only those explicitly stated but also those that went without saying or were otherwise regarded as assumed and natural. And it is here that literature becomes a viable site of inquiry since literature, if Matthew Arnold has taught us anything, remains one of the deepest and abundant archives for the best of what has been thought and said by Anglo-Indians.

On the matter of historical accuracy, I want to invoke a letter written by Oscar Wilde to *The Times* in 1891, which responded to a complaint about his recent review of Kipling's *Plain Tales from the Hills*. In the review Wilde had praised Kipling as a master of vulgarity, a compliment which one reader took to be a pernicious slur on the character of Anglo-Indians. In his letter, Wilde begs not to be misunderstood, declaring "How far Mr. Kipling's stories really mirror Anglo-Indian society I have no idea at all, nor, indeed, am I much interested in any correspondence between art and nature" (105). The retort is classic Wilde: the voice of a world-weary artist who shrugs off reality to focus his energies on *l'art pour l'art*. But it is also a useful reminder that no piece of fiction, whatever its ideological claims or intentions, can ever represent the world as it was.

Such a distinction is important in the case of Anglo-Indian literature, since much of the early critical reception took Kipling's representations of colonial life at face value.[21] However, as Ambreen Hai has argued, even a writer as confident as Kipling readily acknowledged his inability to communicate what was "real" or "true" about the Indian empire to his English readers. Hai cites the way Kipling hedges the "truths" contained in the short stories of *Life's Handicap* (1891) with a facetious preface which "admits" these stories were not written by Kipling, but collected from a native informant. In the preface, Kipling alludes to a larger archive of salacious material, claiming that his putative informant's "tales were true, but not one in twenty could be printed in an English book, because the English do not think as natives do" (*Life's*

Handicap viii). For Hai, this is a technique of self-deprecation wherein Kipling "calls attention to missing stories, or parts of stories that are inaccessible because of his own limitations of class, gender or race, or that must necessarily be 'mangled' and censored in anticipation of the limitations of his British audience who could not understand the complexities of Anglo-Indian life" (608). Accordingly, this study is careful not to assume that textual or fictional life reflects real social life in any way; the speeches, memoranda, short stories, and novels under discussion here are not "representative" texts that tell us how things really were. Like all other characters in fiction, a company man cannot be said to point to a "real" Anglo-India; instead he comprises a mixture of the writer's social knowledge, social wishes, favoured literary conventions, and in some cases, autobiography. This fact holds whether he is the figure constructed by Edmund Burke in parliamentary speeches or the figure constructed by Rudyard Kipling in the *Civil and Military Gazette*. In reading my selections as social texts – that is, as reflective commentaries on social conditions intended to challenge, explore, and reframe the associated debates – the conclusions I draw are not meant to illuminate history but culture.

Yet there can be no doubt that "real" history informs this study of corporate culture and by bringing history and fiction into close relation, my work is in sympathy with what Pierre Bourdieu has called "constructivist structuralism." Like Bourdieu, I am confident that, in addition to symbolic systems such as language and myths, social worlds contain "objective structures independent of the consciousness and will of agents, which are capable of guiding and constraining their practices or their representations" ("Social Space" 14). These structures form what Bourdieu calls the "habitus" of a society, the totality of learned habits, bodily skills, styles, tastes, and other non-discursive knowledges that might be said to go-without-saying for a specific group (17–20). So, just as we are now inclined (thanks to Tom Nairn, Katie Trumpener, Linda Colley, and others) to agree that there was nothing "natural" in the notion of "Britishness," we should also realize that there was nothing natural about the *genus* Anglo-Indian.

To apprehend how the company man is structurally constructed, it is helpful to think about the Marxist understanding of a social class. Marx, of course, argued that human communities could be divided into a hierarchy of classes determined by the degree to which they have access to the economic means of production. However, the point that many overlook is that these classes are neither natural, nor fixed, nor even economically determined, but are *made* through political work.[22] This is Bourdieu's point when, in a vision indebted to Marx's comments upon humanity's relationship to history that open *The Eighteenth Brumaire*, he comes to consider how it is that human subjects (even those belonging to a non-dominant class) come to accept their position in society:

> No doubt agents do have an active apprehension of the world. No doubt they do construct their vision of the world. But this construction is carried out under structural constraints. (18)

In those cases when agents do perceive their social world as evident, Bourdieu continues, it is only because they have internalized the structures of that world. Bourdieu here closely approximates what Gramsci would call a hegemonic order: the vision of the social world which makes a given state of affairs seem natural and its moral code seem like "common sense" to everyone, not just the dominant class. Whether we use Gramsci's hegemony or Bourdieu's preferred "habitus," the point for both is that consent is not something produced through propaganda or imposed by symbolic systems but is, instead, something manufactured by exchange across networks of social structures and institutions. The corporate culture of colonial administrators in India – through the standard of aristocratic virtue established to purify mercantile imperialism, through the disciplinary apparatuses of the training colleges and the competition examination founded to train men who found that virtue through exile and sacrifice, and through the literary culture which continued to disseminate this orthodoxy long after the decline of Company power in India – exemplify a case of manufactured consent.

Chapter 1, "Corruption and the Corporation," examines how the idea of empire became virtuous in the first place by developing Edmund Burke's conception of Parliament as a public stage where state-level crises could be resolved symbolically. Siraj Ahmed has called Burke's speeches and writings on British India "the period's most elaborate vision of the degenerative influence of empire upon the civilized self" ("Theater" 29). My argument turns on the distinction between the public and the private spheres, in order to suggest that the impeachment of Warren Hastings is the first modern corporate corruption trial. The manager's corrupt character, Burke argued, threatened to undermine the institutional integrity of the East India Company and thereby compromised Britain's ability to justify its occupation of India. While later chapters will document Burke's influence on future generations of Anglo-Indian policy makers and cultural critics, this first examines how Burke cultivated the customary language, rituals, and values of eighteenth-century Britain to create new associations which made territorial imperialism palatable.

Chapter 2, "How the Civil Service Got Its Name: India as a Noble Profession," examines how the Company began to produce its social capital and pushes past the simple observation that the language of British imperial discourse in the nineteenth century demotes the aspect of commodity trade in favour of Burkean ideas of "duty" and "honour." Instead I examine two specific attempts by the East India Company to cultivate feelings of aristocratic virtue among its recruits. My starting point is that when it comes to analysing the ethics of a nineteenth-century British colonial administrator, describing either the empire or its hegemonic persuasiveness in terms of "duty" or "honour" is difficult because it is so clearly tautological: in India one "acts" ethically by "acting" British. The argument here is that imperial ethics were, indeed, informed by British identity, but that this British identity was brought into being by the practical demands of controlling one's distant agents. I examine texts written by Wellesley, Thomas Malthus, and Thomas Babington Macaulay in relation to the establishment of the East India Company's training college in Haileybury and of the later competition exam. By doing so, I demonstrate that the British identity which informed an agent's ethical choices was explicitly corporate in nature, not based on traditional or essential forms (whether British, English, Christian, European, etc.) but manufactured by a series of novel disciplinary apparatuses.

The next two chapters examine the literature of Anglo-India, and how it enabled social cohesion in the decline of those explicit training apparatuses. Chapter 3, "Representing Working Conditions in Company India," addresses the limited utility of the national-literature paradigm employed by scholarship in colonial and postcolonial studies. Examining the demography of Company India, and especially the major change caused by the implementation of the competition exam, as well as the conditions under which company men could write, I argue that these early exercises in self-representation show the dissonance Anglo-Indian writers felt between expectations of imperial virtue, metropolitan stereotypes of colonial life, and the realities of colonial service. Chapter 4, "Corporate Culture in Post-Company India," traces that dissonance into the years following the transfer of power from Company to Crown in 1858. Against the imperial myth-makers who maintained that transfer entailed a wholesale transformation of the imperial project, this chapter argues that the preponderance of work and professionalism confirms the enduring influence of the Company's ethos, long after the Crown assumed direct control. By focusing on the shared themes of social transparency and unheralded toil in the works of Henry Stewart Cunningham, Rudyard Kipling, and Sara Jeannette Duncan, this chapter illuminates both the growing hegemony of and the critical resistance to the corporate ideology.

The final chapter considers Kipling's novel *Kim* as the apotheosis of that corporate culture, both in its representation of unproblematically distributed power and in its description of the importance of social bonds among the thinly spread administrators. In *Kim*, the subjects of the previous chapters are worked out in fiction. In *Kim* the colonial bureaucracy is perfectly legitimate, an institution whose dominion over India has no end; in *Kim* the school of St Xavier in Lucknow presents a glimpse of the training methods of the junior class of company men; in *Kim* Creighton and Lurgan communicate the mores of professional behaviour; and in *Kim* the central drama culminates with the protagonist suffering an ethical crisis when Kim O'Hara breaks down at the successful conclusion of his secret mission. Recent interpretations of the novel have suggested that Kim's breakdown stems from his sense of conflicted identity and his inability to choose between loyalty to his Indian comrades and to his British compatriots. However, the ubiquity of terms such as British and Indian in these critiques reveals nationhood as the spectre which continues to haunt our reading of colonial texts. In this chapter, I argue that it is better to view Kim's collapse as precipitated by the unbearable pressure of being a company man, at once an individual moral being and also a representative, a physical manifestation, of a complex corporate body.

1 Corruption and the Corporation: The Impeachment of Warren Hastings

If we believe J.R. Seeley's declaration that Britain acquired its empire absent-mindedly, then one of the more intriguing moments of forgetfulness surrounds the point when a mercantile corporation became the authorized proxy for British power on the Indian subcontinent. The rise of the East India Company as a political and administrative entity stands out because it so clearly contradicted British attitudes to both commercial and foreign affairs, as they were popularly understood in the middle of the eighteenth century. From Bernard Mandeville's *Fable of the Bees* (1714) to Adam Smith's *Wealth of Nations* (1776), early modern British commercial discourse is characterized by its advocacy of industry, free trade, and the mutual benefits accrued by those parties who transact without ulterior interest. At the same time, it is worth recalling that Britain's two major wars of the period, namely the War of Jenkins's Ear and the Seven Years' War, marshalled domestic support in part by positioning Britain as the scourge of Spanish, Portuguese, and French tyranny. We do well to remember that James Thomson's patriotic ditty "Rule Britannia" (1740) simultaneously boasted not only that "Britons never will be slaves" (6) but also that their "cities shall with commerce shine" (26).

In this atmosphere – with liberty, commerce, and public opinion seemingly opposed to imperialism – it would seem difficult to reconcile the position occupied by the East India Company. By the 1770s not only had Britain's pre-eminent overseas trading company assumed territorial and judicial control of a foreign country, but it also stood accused of exercising that sovereignty in a despotic manner. Opponents to these developments ranged from Company stockholders who thought that the responsibilities of governance unnecessarily distracted their commercial agents, to moralists who expressed outrage that British subjects had manipulated the terms of the Company's Elizabethan charter and set themselves up in a private fiefdom.[1] Even Britons residing in India often complained that the present form of government was incompetent.[2] At home and in the wake of the American rebellion, some expressed concern that disgruntled Britons in India might imitate their American cousins.[3] In any case, there was an increasing consensus that what was bad for business was also damaging the national reputation.

These critics shared concerns about the relationship between the East India Company as a corporate body and its individual employees. The technological limits of eighteenth-century communication networks meant that the Company's agents lived and worked at an impossible remove from the supervision of its directors or stockholders. And since the Elizabethan charter granted that Company (and hence its agents) the power to raise armies, collect taxes, distribute justice, and negotiate political treaties, its agents had ample opportunity to enrich themselves. In *The Wealth of Nations*, Adam Smith summarized this difficulty:

> Nothing can be more completely foolish than to expect the clerks of a great Counting-House, at ten-thousand miles distance, and consequently almost out of sight, should, upon a simple order from their master, give up, at once, doing any business on their account, abandon forever all hopes of making a fortune, of which they have the means in their hands, and content themselves with the modest salaries which their master allows them. (2: 253)

Though he named none in particular, Smith could have pointed to any number of examples as proof that the contrary was taking place. By the 1770s, England was awash in recently returned agents, men who had made astronomical fortunes overseas in the service of the Company and whose *nouveaux* spending habits and questionable taste introduced into popular culture "the nabob," a figure to be pilloried alongside "the Cit," as a synonym for ill-gained riches.

The controversy over Britain's position in India culminated in 1787, when the "Scandal of Empire" – to use historian Nicholas Dirks's evocative phrase – resulted in the parliamentary impeachment of the East India Company's chief executive. The trial of Warren Hastings lasted over eight years and has since become a touchstone for studies of the British Empire, as well as an important development in the constitutional history of Great Britain.[4] Many, especially many of the pro-empire Victorian commentators like Macaulay, view the event as the site where the existence of the British Empire was contested, and where the governing principles of its future were debated between Hastings and his prosecutor, Edmund Burke.[5] This is certainly true, but the impeachment is additionally important since, before we can begin to examine the civilizing mission of nineteenth-century imperialism, we must reconcile how mercantile imperialism itself became civilized in the late eighteenth century.

Stephen A. Browne has called the impeachment "rhetorical action on a grand scale, an interplay of warring values, an epic contest between good and evil that sweeps into itself speaker, audience, and empire" (84). Historical accident put a man of Burke's political and moral temperament in charge of this rare and powerful political event, and while the consequence for the future British Empire has been frequently studied, the effects on the East India Company, a mercantile corporation seeking to manage the threat of the rogue agent, have yet to be properly reckoned. In what follows, I argue that the impeachment of Warren Hastings was a spectacular event whose significance is not the prosecution of one man's indiscretions, nor about which set of values won the war, but rather a ritual sanitization that allowed a commercial trading organization to access the kind of social capital previously held in monopoly by the state. In calling the impeachment a spectacle, I mean to build upon Michel Foucault's thoughts about the relation between the theatre and political authority. While Foucault was thinking of torture in France, his claim that "in the eighteenth century, judicial torture functioned in [a] strange economy, in which the ritual that produced truth went side by side with the ritual that imposed punishment" (42) suggests a new way to understand the function of the Hastings's impeachment.

Burke's Indian speeches are crucial to that transformation, not only for the effect they would have on the future shape of imperial government but also for their immediate contribution to the sedimentation of the idea of empire within the British polity. The historian P.J. Marshall observes that by the 1780s, "nearly every section of British political opinion was prepared to accept that serious crimes had been committed in India" (*Impeachment* viii). Despite this, few politicians were agitating for something to be done. In fact, we could almost say that the impeachment occurred accidentally, given that it originated with a man who by that time was a political afterthought. In 1786 Burke privately confessed himself startled when his motion to impeach Hastings succeeded. The year before, he had written to Philip Francis – Hastings's nemesis in Bengal and Burke's primary source of information – explaining that, in drawing up the motion, "my business is not to consider what will convict Mr. Hastings (a thing we all know to be impracticable) but what will acquit and justify myself to those few persons, and to those distant times, which may take a concern in these affairs and in the actors in them" (*Letters* 249). Burke's pessimistic forecast was accurate insofar as the trial, after eight years, ended in Hastings's acquittal.

My argument builds on Marshall's observation that, following the impeachment, the imperial question never attracted the same level of interest or scrutiny in Britain (*Impeachment* 189). To be sure, Marshall is not saying that debates on the necessity, viability, or sustainability of empire were suspended for the duration of the nineteenth and twentieth centuries; rather, his point is that when these debates took place, they asked questions of a different order. In other words, following the Hastings trial, British imperial debates no longer asked *should* but rather *(how) could* the empire be virtuous. Never again would the British public countenance the defence made by Warren Hastings, that morality is geographically relative, and since tyranny is the "natural" form of government in Oriental civilizations, so must Britons act the tyrant. If we read the impeachment less as a punitive exercise of parliamentary justice than as a normative event that made territorial imperialism comprehensible and palatable to the British public, then we come closer to seeing its political afterlife. Understood this way, the impeachment becomes a foundational "text" of the empire, situated somewhere between a Platonic dialogue on statecraft and a dramatic example of, in Burke's words, the British Parliament delivering "the Imperial justice which you owe to the people that call to you from all parts of a great and disjointed empire" ("Opening" 277).

Amid this spectacle, the previously separable and real figures of Warren Hastings and Edmund Burke transformed into antagonistic characters in a drama performed on the grandest stage in the kingdom, characters that in future would exist only in dialectical tension with one another. In this theatrical space, we begin to see limits drawn around a previously sprawling colonial subject, a discourse whose language would afterwards be bounded by the extremes of Hastings's pragmatism on the one hand and Burke's idealism on the other.[6] In some ways, this delimiting was unavoidable, since the degree, scale, and alien nature of territorial power was unprecedented in British history. It makes sense that a new language was required; the only thing left to do is to remark on the shape of that new language. In what terms henceforth would the British conceive of their ascendancy in India? A quick survey of later imperial debates reveals Orientalists vs. Anglicists, Globetrotters vs. Anglo-Indians, and Fieldings vs. Burtons. Yet while all these antagonisms engage the mode of imperial governance, none, not even E.M. Forster's 1924 liberal critique of imperialism, *A Passage to India*, can confront the possibility that empire is not an immediate necessity.

Raymond Williams, who had a great deal to say about power but rather little about empire, developed a theory that explains just such a process. In "Base and Superstructure" (1973), Williams argued that the functional antagonisms presented by a social order are not true expressions of class or group interests. Williams explains that while it may appear that a given social order tolerates a wide range of opinion or positions, the existence of a hegemony implies that each and every antagonism is incorporated. Such incorporated, or co-opted, antagonisms are "recognizable by the fact that whatever the degree of internal variation, they do not in practice go beyond the limits of the central effective and dominant definitions" (10). Here he follows Marx's precedent, by turning the Hegelian notion of historical progress on its head. Thus, for Williams, the synthesis or sublation in a hegemonic articulation is not the product of actual historical antagonisms but rather the thing that calls such antagonisms into being. What hegemony theory allows us to perceive is how the problem of imperial morality slipped out of the public sphere as an object of scrutiny and into ontological neutrality. Recognizing this, we can see how what became British imperial discourse assumes its hegemonic aspect only after an event like the impeachment, how the empire became a matter of common sense, a matter of fact.

In her study of imperial discourse, Sara Suleri rightly observes that the novelty of colonial power in Britain meant that Burke and his contemporaries lacked the proper linguistic register to discuss the issue coherently (49–53). But neither Suleri nor any other of the scholars of empire have addressed in sufficient detail the representation of the East India Company, either as the proxy agent of British power or as a corporate body which managed its employees in very specific ways. It is my belief that the insertion of a mercantile corporation into the offices of the imperial state opens a rich seam for colonial scholarship, not only because it demonstrates the interdependence of capitalism and imperialism but also because it reminds us that the historical artefact we call the British Empire was always unplanned, unregulated, and unstable.

What became the culture of imperialism had a great deal to do with the improvisational responses to dynamic situations by particular individuals.

In the impeachment we are furnished with a robust example of these contingencies: parliamentary impeachments are rare in themselves; an impeachment initiated by a private member in opposition was and remains unprecedented in British parliamentary history. Whatever his later fame, we must remember that up until the Hastings trial, Edmund Burke was never a particularly successful parliamentarian.[7] To be fair, this marginality enabled Burke to speak frequently on unpopular topics in tones that more calculating politicians might eschew. Among Burke's hobbyhorses, the case of India was perhaps ridden the most.[8] His interest in India was long-standing and although he frequently brought the plight of Company India to the attention of Parliament – most notably in support of Charles Fox's India Bill of 1783, whose failure toppled the Fox-North coalition and raised Pitt the Younger into his first ministry – his protests went largely unheeded because, according to historian Fredrick Whelan, few British politicians in the era of the American Revolution were prepared to expend political capital pursuing the questionable morality of men employed by a company operating under the licence of a sixteenth-century charter (Whelan 18–20).

As it happens, historians have yet to explain fully why the Hastings impeachment went as far as it did.[9] Burke was an opposition backbencher and it was popularly conceded that however unscrupulous Warren Hastings might have been he was no Clive. It was only the last-minute (and unexpected) support of Pitt that secured the parliamentary censure. But whatever the historical coincidences, Burke made the most of his opportunity and related the charges against Hastings in such a way as to guarantee their notoriety. The initial twenty-seven charges enumerated offences ranging from extortion to condoning torture. In his effort to halt the corruption of the nascent British Empire, Burke charged Hastings with High Crimes and Misdemeanours, "by each and all of which Practices the Welfare of the East India Company has materially suffered, the Happiness of the Native Inhabitants of India been deeply affected, their Confidence in English Faith and Lenity shaken and impaired, and the *Honour of the Crown* and the *Character of this Nation* wantonly and wickedly degraded ("Articles of Impeachment" 135, emphasis added).

In Burke's estimation, the disreputable conduct of an employee affected three parties: East India Company stockholders, Indian subjects, and British citizens. The intersection of these three previously separable interests reveals the importance of the corporation in the first coherent articulation of Britain's empire. By aggregating the interests of Company, the colonized, and the colonizer, Burke obliged the British public to confront serially the responsibility it bore to another nation. Were Hastings merely a rogue employee, he could have been disciplined internally; were he merely an aspiring despot, he might have been left to share the fate of Daniel Dravot in Rudyard Kipling's short story "The Man Who Would Be King" (1888); were he merely a domestic criminal, he could have been left to the municipal courts. But because Burke argued that Hastings belonged at once to all three categories simultaneously, he meant to establish that only one body, the British Parliament, could exercise jurisdiction. Accordingly, in his "Speech on the Opening of the Impeachment," Burke makes it clear that "it is by this tribunal that Statesmen who abuse their power are tried before Statesmen and by Statesmen, upon solid principles of State morality ... It is here that no subject in any part of the Empire can be refused justice" ("Opening" 272).

However, in applying "the oldest process known to the Constitution of this country ... [and] the individuating principle that makes England what England is," to the subject of the very new and very nebulous British Empire, Burke's prosecution had long-lasting and arguably unintended consequences (272). While he aimed to legitimize British authority in India by holding it to the same moral standard that justified British domestic power, he necessarily had to establish the moral standard for the organization acting on behalf of the British Crown. This meant arguing that the East India Company was a virtuous organization as such. Only once the Company's virtue had been established in principle could Burke contend that Hastings had violated the sanctity of the governor general's office by using publicly entrusted powers to further his private pecuniary interest. In other words, during the impeachment of Warren Hastings, a commercial organization accessed for the first time the institutional authority previously reserved for apparatuses of the state.

To purify the acts of Britons overseas, Edmund Burke necessarily confronted the impure amalgamation of merchant and sovereign famously criticized by Adam Smith. The problem, as Smith saw it, involved the separation of interests. Smith argues that "[a]s sovereigns, their interest is exactly the same with that of the country which they govern. As merchants their interest is directly opposite to that interest" (2: 480).

In other words, Company employees were obliged to maximize the price of goods exported from Britain (in order to enable the Company to purchase more Indian commodities); simultaneously, as sovereigns, they were obliged to maximize the price of Indian commodities (to create the surplus value which would enable the local economy's development). Yet as Smith continues his economic analysis of colonies in Book Four of *Wealth of Nations*, he realizes that the corporate structure of the East India Company presents an even greater problem. That is to say, even if the Janus-faced interests of the merchant-sovereign could be reconciled, the Company would still be forced to consider the fact that their employees, as servants of the Company, had no interest in the welfare of the people they governed:

> The country belongs to their masters [the stockholders], who cannot avoid having some regard for the interest of what belongs to them. But it does not belong to the servants. The real interest of their masters, if they were capable of understanding it, is the same with that of the country, and it is from ignorance chiefly, and the meanness of mercantile prejudice, that they ever oppress it. But the real interest of the servants is by no means the same with that of the country, and the most perfect information would not necessarily put an end to their oppressions. (2: 483)

In this, Smith's economic analysis draws upon the moral argument put forward by William Bolts in *Considerations of Indian Affairs* (1772).[10] Bolts, an expelled Company employee, explained that the "different interests of the Company as sovereigns of Bengal and at the same time monopolizers of all the trade and commerce of those countries, operate in direct opposition, and are mutually destructive of each other" (x).

Both Bolts and Smith in turn influenced Burke; nowhere is this clearer than in Burke's argument that the East India Company had become "that thing which was supposed by the Roman Law so unsuitable, the same power was a Trader, the same power was a Lord ... a State in disguise of a Merchant, a great public office in disguise of a Countinghouse" ("Opening" 283). From reading Bolts and Smith, Burke realized that the mission to eliminate corruption was twofold. On the one hand, the stockholders of the East India Company *qua* the political agent of the British public had to appreciate that India's political and economic interests were not opposed to but rather congruent with their own. At the same time, this enlightenment would be worthless if the actions of the Company's servants could not be regulated. So, on the other hand, the employees of the Company – a group of men who literally had no stock or share in the economic development of India or the spread of justice – would have to be subject to new forms of surveillance and discipline, forms that took into account the immense distance between London and India. The remainder of this chapter examines how Burke cultivated the customary language, rituals, and values of eighteenth-century mercantilism to create new associations which not only made territorial imperialism palatable for the domestic population, but also established a plan for managing the interests of employees.

The first part of this argument turns on the distinction between the public and the private spheres, by reading the impeachment of Warren Hastings as the first modern corporate corruption trial. I will focus on Burke's insistence that the corrupt character of a corporate executive threatened to undermine the institutional integrity of the East India Company and thereby compromised Britain's ability to justify its occupation of India. Of course, "corruption" will have a particular connotation to period scholars who, following J.G.A. Pocock's argument in *Virtue, Commerce, History*, understand it as an epithet for those monied interests which threatened to upset the natural stability maintained by Britain's landed gentry (115). Burke's own position in this debate is well known. An aristocratic Whig, Burke consistently rails in his Indian speeches and elsewhere against the potentially corruptive forces of new philosophies and technologies. Opposed to radical changes, he espouses instead a policy of cautious cultivation, the philosophical forerunner of what Matthew Arnold would two generations later call "Culture." Yet however prevalent the trope of corruption is in Burke's other writings, it deserves special attention in the context of a trial involving a commercial organization on the brink of moral and financial collapse.

To this end, the interpretive lenses of Pocockean virtue and Burkean cultivation might productively be refocused by drawing upon scholarship in the area of corruption theory. This subset of social theory is concerned with organizations in crisis and considers the role of individual agents in bringing about institutional decline. It builds from the generally accepted principle that a corrupt individual is one who has transgressed the putative division of interests and has utilized the powers of his or her public office in order to procure some private gain. Political scientist Joseph Nye provides the standard definition of corruption:

> behaviour which deviates from the normal duties of a public role because of private-regarding (family, close private clique), pecuniary or status

> gains; or violates rules against the exercise of certain types of private-regarding influence. This includes behaviour such as bribery (use of rewards to pervert the judgment of a person in a position of trust); nepotism (bestowal of patronage by reason of ascriptive relationship rather than merit) and misappropriation (illegal appropriation of public resources for private-regarding uses). (966)

As shorthand, we might say that actions are deemed corrupt when an element belonging to the private sphere makes itself visible in the public sphere. When these boundaries are transgressed, the restoration of public purity, the illusion upon which our notions of equitable democracy is founded, can only be effected through the public trial and punishment of offending individuals.

This interpretative model appears applicable to the Hastings impeachment since instead of attacking the Company, its modus vivendi, or even its board of directors, Burke focused overwhelmingly on its chief executive officer. While Burke reveals his distaste for mercantile imperialism, equally clear is his conviction that the available institutions of the British state were constitutionally incompatible with the responsibilities of administering a foreign empire and therefore liable to be corrupted. Of politicians, he declared:

> Ministers must wholly be removed from the management of the affairs of India, or they will have influence in its patronage ... It works both ways; it influences the delinquent, and it may corrupt the minister. ("Fox's India Bill" 443)

Burke's solution involved the substantial reform of the East India Company, a purge of malign forces that finds its modern echo in American President George W. Bush's "bad apples" defence, used to explain not only the abuses in the cells of Abu Ghraib, but also in the accounting departments of Enron and Tyco. In such ritualized processes, systemic critique is avoided through a process of scapegoating; Hastings the man became the vehicle for the purification of the East India Company's hegemony in India.

The afterlife of Burke's Indian speeches supports Paul Ricoeur's argument that ideology and rhetoric are inextricable.[11] That is to say, in order to appreciate why imperial ideology took this or that particular form in the nineteenth and twentieth centuries, we must begin with the rhetoric used by Burke in his excoriation of Warren Hastings. By pitching his accusations against Hastings in terms of peculation and tyranny, Burke simultaneously implanted an expectation that their antitheses – duty and self-sacrifice – should form the model for the future practice of company men in India. Likewise, by focusing his prosecution on the corrupt practices of an individual, Burke ritually cleansed the corporate entity. Amid those rhetorical flourishes of Oriental despotism, avarice, and grave threats to the national character were ideological movements of real substance as Burke established for the first time a set of moral preconditions for a just empire and a code of conduct for its future employees.

Credible Empires

We can better comprehend Burke's contribution to imperial discourse by way of a small detour through another of the so-called patriarchs of modern conservative thought, Benjamin Disraeli. In particular, I want to reflect on a scene early in Disraeli's novel *Tancred* (1847) where an idealistic son rejects the seat in Parliament offered by his father:

> You have proposed to me to-day … to enter public life. I do not shrink from its duties … But I cannot find that it is part of my duty to maintain the order of things, for I will not call it a system, which at present prevails in our country. It seems to me that it cannot last, as nothing can endure, or ought to endure, that is not founded on principle; and its principle I have not discovered. (38)

Britain, Tancred feels, has become a victim of its own successes; filthy lucre has obscured the "first principles" which made that material prosperity possible. So long as this remains the case, people supposedly working in the public interest by holding public office can only continue in "contributing to this quick corruption which surrounds us" (40). In this scene, Disraeli presents an archetype of conservative rhetoric: a great nation threatens to disintegrate because, tempted by a new philosophy or way of being, it has forgotten the ancient virtues which have made it great in the first instance; only through a redoubled effort to recover those lost virtues can the nation save itself and guarantee future prosperity. Tancred's lament might have been equally resonant in Burke's Britain, when waves of new wealth and exotic goods were pouring into the country from foreign territories and Britons grappled with the meaning of their newly acquired status as a colonial power.

Claiming "antiquity has lost all its effect and reverence on the minds of men," Burke called for a serious reformation of British imperial policy, warning, "Whatever does not stand with credit does not stand for long" ("Opening" 272).

Considering these jeremiads together, one could certainly locate the dissonance between Tancred's "principles" and Burke's "credit" as evidence of the powerful influence of the market economy in the eighteenth century. Pocock's argument shows how commercial terminology begins to function ideologically and serves to consolidate bourgeois interests by transcending its material connection with the marketplace and saturating British culture down to the level of language (108–16). To be sure, in the discourse of the eighteenth-century British public sphere, "credit" was as likely to refer to character or reputation as to fiscal solvency. On the other hand, it is difficult to imagine that Burke was unconscious of the metaphor's ambivalence when used in the specific context of the East India Company. Whatever resonance "credit" had within the moral vocabulary of his audience, its use could not fail to evoke images of the material, financial credibility of the Company as well. In this case we apprehend the translative character of metaphor, evidence that the bearing across involved in metaphoric meaning-making is not unidirectional. In his "Speech on the Opening of the Hastings Impeachment" Burke forces the metaphor of credit to refer simultaneously to its material and its moral index, to operate, that is to say, at once on its literal and sedimented levels. This catachresis signals a change in the way Britons conceived their emerging empire. By imposing the moral obligations of a just sovereign onto the vanguard corporation at the heart of Britain's imperial identity, Burke shattered one of the nation's self-fashioned images – that theirs was an empire of trade alone. By drawing attention to the multiple valences of credit or credibility in the speeches against Warren Hastings, I do not mean to imply that Burke's speeches in themselves altered the way empire was conceived in British public discourse. The historical record reveals manifold voices ranging across the political spectrum, aligned momentarily in their opposition to the powers exercised by the East India Company in India. The Company had acquired, through successive military campaigns, territorial control of several regions in India, using the plunder from one to finance the conquest of the next. Putting the crimes in foreign climes to one side, the Company's transactions in England appeared equally insalubrious as its precarious financial position had necessitated several government bailouts. Some commentators, reminded of the havoc caused by the burst South Seas Bubble, warned that the East India Company could fail at any moment. One anonymous pamphleteer wrote in 1768 that the collapse of the Company would affect "the whole publick credit of the kingdom, and almost renew the disasters of the South-Sea year" (*State of the East India Company's Affairs* 2). Another popular concern was the behaviour of Company employees who had been, since the time of Robert Clive, acquiring massive personal fortunes in India through morally questionable actions and returning to spend them in Britain, driving up the cost of property, rotten boroughs, and other commodities.

These robber-barons had been an object of public derision at least since Samuel Foote's popular drama *The Nabob* (1778), but because their money granted them access to public offices normally reserved for members of the aristocracy and their appointees they also engendered fears of a "Bengal interest" consolidating within the House of Commons and hijacking domestic politics. Lord Chatham, for one, remarked:

> The riches of Asia have been poured in upon us, and have brought with them not only Asiatic Luxury, but, I fear, Asiatic principles of government. Without connections, without any natural interest in the soil, the importers of foreign gold have forced their way into Parliament by such a torrent of private corruption as no hereditary fortune could resist. (qtd. in Lawson 120)

Aside from the matter of domestic stability, thornier existential questions were asked of the emerging empire by writers like the Tory sentimentalist Henry Mackenzie whose Man of Feeling momentarily descends from his pursuit of pure affect to pass judgment on more worldly matters:

> I cannot … rejoice at our conquests in India. You tell me of immense territories subject to the English: I cannot think of their possessions, without being led to enquire, by what right they possess them. They came as traders … and however great their profits were, they were then equitable [to Indians]. But what title have the subjects of another kingdom to establish an empire in India? to give laws to a country where the inhabitants received them on the terms of friendly commerce? (102)

William Wilberforce likened the injustices in India to the African slave trade (65). Others still, including Adam Smith, saw it as structurally unable to guarantee civil order in India, "necessarily composed of a council of merchants, a profession no doubt extremely respectable, but which in no country in the world carries along with it that sort of authority which naturally over-awes the people, and without force commands their willing obedience" (2: 480).

Compelled by its constitution to maximize trading profit, this mercantile organization was seen to be corroding both British and Indian societies and its radical potential was only increased by its uncertain tenure. The anxiety over the East India Company's destabilizing influence was no doubt accelerated by the contemporary debates about and the eventual loss of the American colonies as well as by the fact that "Britain" itself was conceptually nebulous in the eighteenth century. According to Linda Colley, victory in the Seven Years' War initiated a period of "collective agoraphobia" that unsettled traditional constructs of British national identities (101). When Burke told the audience at the Hastings impeachment that "whatever does not stand with credit does not stand for long," the imminent demise of the nascent British Empire – to say nothing of the shaky British nation – was a very real possibility.

Despite this robust chorus of critics, chroniclers of eighteenth-century Anglo-Indian relations often choose to represent Burke in terms not dissimilar to his legacy in other areas; that is to say, as a solitary figure who made an impassioned stance against the swirling revolutionary forces of his time. Among all the voices of his age, Burke's survives as the most important critique of the new imperialism. Among the panoply of available options, the choices he made, the affiliations he disclosed, and the rhetorical gestures he favoured became the principal attributes of a long and powerful tradition of imperial critique. By turning a legal impeachment into an allegorical battleground between imperial world views, Burke ensured that the events of 1788–95 would reverberate throughout subsequent imperial discourse. Whatever the British Empire would become – and this is not to say that Burke or Hastings somehow determined the future shape of imperial institutions – it would always trace its origins to the debates over the Hastings case, the first sustained public discussion on the moral consequences of Britain's imperial acquisitions.

Later I will explore some of the reasons behind and the consequences of this outcome but any analysis of Burke's textual afterlife must first build on an understanding of his Indian speeches that considers them as texts authored by one particular man and delivered at one particular historical moment. This analysis begins, then, in the cultural space situated somewhere between the constitutional *gravitas* of a parliamentary impeachment and the popular scandal of a British agent charged with acquiring, in the words of Elizabeth Ryves's mock heroic *The Hastiniad* (1785): "The mighty plunder dearly bought, / By deeds beyond the reach of thought" (1.13.51–2). In this space, the East India Company shed its mercantile skin and emerged as a legitimate apparatus of British authority.

Part of this metamorphosis can be attributed to the particular structure of feeling that informed Burke's avocations. While admitting the dangers of isolating a single strand of Burke's complex thought or of attributing to his writings an ideology which may never have entered his mind, it is possible nonetheless to identify a theme which illustrates his approach to the question of British rule in India. However unappetizing the prospect of a commercial organization exercising sovereignty in Britain's name may be, it was already a matter of fact that the East India Company had bound itself to the people of India when Robert Clive assumed the *diwani* of Bengal in 1765. According to Burke:

> When Great Britain assented to that grant virtually, and afterwards took advantage of it, Great Britain made a virtual act of union with that country, by which they bound themselves as securities for their subjects, to preserve all people in all rights, laws and liberties, which their natural original Sovereign was bound to enforce. (281–2)

During the "Speech on Opening" Burke presented a pragmatic plan for empire that might be classified as humanist in scope, contractual in articulation, and conservative in implementation. For example, no one who reads Burke's parliamentary speeches can deny his consistent call for a single, universal code of conduct that would give Britain's new-found Indian subjects access to the same rights enjoyed by their British counterparts. Neither can one overlook his conviction that British power in India was predicated on an obligation to increase the general well-being of its subjects. Finally, whatever gross acts of epistemic violence he may have committed in presuming to speak for the subaltern, Burke cannot be accused of treating the subject lightly. For fourteen years and the tenure of several parliamentary select committees, Burke took great pains to familiarize himself with Indian history and culture, a familiarity that distinguished him from his colleagues and that, moreover, informed his insistence on a cautious approach to Indian reform.

In the end, Burke did not suggest a wholesale withdrawal from India, nor did he propose the equally radical step that involved Parliament assuming direct control of India. Burke's speeches reveal a man who saw in the East India Company a potentially effective institution crippled by its inability to recognize the degree of responsibility it bore towards both Britain and India. Structurally, it remained "perhaps the best contrivance that has ever been thought of by the wit of men for the government of a remote, large, disjointed empire" (298). Made by humans, it had been neglected by humans and fallen into a corrupt state; only human action could bring about its rehabilitation. Reading Burke's Indian speeches as examples of curative reform illuminates how he cultivated the mercantile organization into a public institution.

Casting a glance over his political career, Burke declared that the efforts expended on the Hastings trial were "those on which I value myself the most; most for the importance; most for the labour; most for the judgement; most for the constancy and perseverance in the pursuit" ("Letter to a Noble Lord" 159). This valuation seems rather high given that the judgment went against Burke and Hastings was acquitted. To find the proper register for Burke's valuation of his efforts, we must extend the scope of inquiry beyond constitutional law and into a space where legal terminology and the rituals of jurisprudence intersect with discourses of morality, humanism, and natural law. Within the first few minutes of his speech, Burke established the solemnity of the occasion:

> My Lords, it cannot be conceived, God forbid that it should be conceived, that the business today is the business of the men. The question is, not solely whether the prisoner at the Bar shall be found innocent or guilty, but whether millions of mankind shall be miserable or happy. You do not decide the Case only; you fix the rule ... It is according to the Judgement that you shall pronounce on the past transactions of India ... that the whole rule, tenure, tendency, and character of our future government in India is to be finally decided. (270–1)

If Burke's case can be said to have failed for not securing a guilty verdict, it might just as easily be considered a success for cultivating a sense among the British public that the welfare of the Indian people was, for the time being, to be administered under trust by the British government. During the Hastings trial the question of whether Britain should govern India turned into one that asked what type of imperium Britain should exercise.

Setting the Stage

As part of his critique of the accusations made against Louis XVI, Burke insisted that the "punishment of real tyrants is a noble and awful act of justice" (*Reflections* 134). For the reader searching for a link between Burke's aesthetic and political theories, this statement neatly brings the romantic sentiment expressed in his *Philosophical Inquiry into the Sublime and the Beautiful* to bear on the subject of the French Revolution. Although many commentators engage Burke as an aesthetic or political philosopher, P.J. Marshall has argued that Burke scholars are reluctant to incorporate the most practical of Burke's works – his attempt to impeach Hastings – into their analysis ("Burke, Hastings, and the Higher Law" 31). Yet it is clear, as both Marshall and Fredrick Whelan have observed, that Burke himself knew the value of praxis.[12] Burke is nothing if not the harrower of abstract theoretical connections and his statement about punishing sublime tyrants, though made in the *Reflections on the Revolution in France*, could surely not have been made without regard for the other great Burkean project of 1790: the machinations of justice unfolding before the British Parliament in the form of the Hastings impeachment. Burke was not alone in appreciating the sublimity of these proceedings, for Hastings too, according to *The Morning Chronicle*'s report, opened his defence saying, "My Lords, I appear before this great and awful tribunal, equally impressed with a consciousness of my own integrity, and the strict and impartial justice of this great Court" (13 Feb 1788).

The invocation of the sublime is less a rhetorical gesture than it is a testament to the rare and awesome nature of this event. The novelist Frances Burney, who attended the impeachment as a spectator in the gallery, attests to the effectiveness of Burke's theatrics:

> I shuddered and drew involuntarily back when, as the doors flung open, I saw Mr Burke, as Head of the Committee, make his solemn entry. He held a scroll in his hand, and walked alone, his brow knit with corroding care and deep labouring thought … I trembled … and hardly could keep my place when I found Mr Hastings was being brought to the bar … What an awful moment this for such a man! – a man fallen from such height of power to a situation so humiliating – from the almost unlimited command of so large a part of the Eastern World to be cast at the feet of his enemies … Could even his Prosecutors at that moment look on – and not shudder at least, if they did not blush? (4: 56–9)

Burney's diary entry, punctuated by awful, involuntary shuddering and trembling reveals sentimentality as rationality's partner in the fashioning of imperial identities.

To Burke's prosecutorial team, such emotional responses were neither unexpected nor undesired. Instead, and suitably for a group that included Richard Sheridan, they explicitly sought not only to convict Hastings in the court of public opinion (although playing to the gallery was certainly one consideration) but also to create an atmosphere of solemnity. They understood that, as constitutional tools, impeachments function as a final check on power. But precisely because they lay claim to a higher authority than that of the monarch, impeachments are difficult to initiate and manage. While claiming to base its authority in such abstract notions as state morality, an impeachment can select only a limited number of citizens to operate as arbiters. Therefore, like the municipal court writ large, impeachments are as much about reification and spectacle as they are about dispensing justice.

In the case of the Hastings impeachment, *The Morning Chronicle* reports how steps were taken to ensure that the "grandeur and sublimity of the Court, when seated in judgement, could only be equalled by the immensity of the subject which engaged its attention; the fate of empires, kingdoms, and millions of their inhabitants, depending on the issue" (16 Feb 1788). To achieve this effect, Westminster Hall was specially renovated and its gallery expanded to accommodate 1,100 spectators, not including the special seating areas for the Lords and the Commons. The furniture was reupholstered in crimson and drapes of the same colour were hung throughout the hall. Sir Peter Burrell, the official in charge of the preparations, is reported in *The Morning Chronicle* to have "ordered the gallery on the west side to be continued or extended farther than he believed had been usual, in order to give more accommodation, as well as to add to the symmetry and beauty of the Court" (7 Feb 1788).

Such a renovation, the explicit fabrication of a putatively traditional space, is one of British history's more patent examples of what historian Eric Hobsbawm has called "the invention of tradition" ("Introduction" 2–3). In his examination of persistent yet often arbitrary and useless cultural signifiers in social spaces, Hobsbawm suggests that periods of significant upheaval often inspire groups to "invent" a tradition. For instance, the powdered wigs donned by judicial officers in modern courthouses are now undoubtedly part of the legal profession's tradition and certainly add solemnity to the dispensation of justice. Yet equally indisputable is the fact that such wigs only entered the British courts in the eighteenth century. According to Hobsbawm, the aristocratic pretension of the courtroom wig emerged in response to the increasing embourgoisement of the court itself via the increasing number of civil suits and contractual squabbles launched by middle-class traders and small-property holders. The impeachment of Warren Hastings, amid an era of very conflicting views on empire, should be seen as another invented tradition. Though Burke and his fellow prosecutors held that impeachments were customary procedures enshrined in the constitution, they also knew that they had precious few historical precedents. The previous impeachment, of Elijah Impey, took place seventy years earlier, just beyond the horizon of living memory. This granted the managers of the prosecution a good deal of flexibility in making their arrangements. Only once the stage had been set could the pageantry commence. Macaulay's famous essay would later describe the opening of the impeachment as the social event of the year ("Warren Hastings" 249–52). The *London Chronicle* published an account of the opening day in a format not dissimilar from conventional contemporary theatre notices:

> The Lords were then called over by the Clerk, and arranged by Sir Isaac Heard, Principal King at Arms, when upwards of two hundred proceeded in order to Westminster Hall. The Peers were preceded by
> The Lord Chancellor's attendants, two and two.
> The Clerks of the House of Lords.
> The Masters in Chancery, two and two.
> The Judges.
> Serjeants Adair and Hill.
> The Yeoman Usher of the Black Rod
> Two Heralds.
> The Lords Baron, two and two.
> The Lords Bishops, two and two.
> The Lords Viscounts, two and two.
> The Lords Marquesses, two and two.
> The Lords Dukes, two and two.
> The Mace Bearer.
> The Lord Chancellor with his train borne.
> (All in their Parliamentary Robes)
>
> The Lords Spiritual seated themselves on their Bench, which was on the side on which they entered; as they passed the throne, they bowed to it, as

> if the King was seated in it. The Temporal Lords crossed over the house, and each made a respectful bow to the seat of Majesty. (13 Feb 1788)

The presence of the "King-in-Majesty," emphasized by the obeisant lords, declares that the subject (i.e., the good government of India) fell under the jurisdiction of the British nation just as the absence of the king-in-body ensures that no attention is directed away from the central figure of this drama, the accused tyrant.

At least two things are achieved by this configuration. First, it would have harmonized with Burke's stated valuation of Parliament as a stage where the problems of the nation could be worked through symbolically. The customary authority embedded in rituals, he wrote in his *Reflections on the Revolution in France*, allows us to overcome the limitations imposed by our fallen state; they are the illusions "necessary to cover the defects of our naked, shivering nature, and to raise it to dignity" (128). Second, as figure 1 shows, the elliptical court takes Hastings and the Lord Chancellor as its foci. That it is the Lord Chancellor and not the king would have concentrated the spectators' attention on the accused. The prosecutors, divorced from the axial relationship between the King-in-Majesty and the accused, stand as dispassionate intermediaries, advocates of a public, rather than royal or private, interest.

Hastings's symbolic status is emphasized by the content of Burke's speech. Before elaborating the crimes, Burke proposed "to give your Lordships such an explanation of any thing in the laws, customs, opinions and manners of the people concerned," in order to "remove all doubt and ambiguity from the minds of your Lordships on these subjects" ("Opening" 269). Thus Hastings stood in court for several days, the subject of public scrutiny, as Burke explained the constitution of the East India Company, detailed the natures of Hindu and Islamic law, and summarized the history of Anglo-Indian relations. As the silenced subject at the centre of a novel spectacle, Hastings became the embodied symbol of British power in India. Having focused attention on this solitary figure, whom he depicted as a tyrannical example of an empire governed poorly, Burke could more easily attribute all criminal practices in India to his wicked personal character. This strategy required an ambivalent portrayal of Warren Hastings, one that hearkened back to the most famous impeachment in British history. To succeed, Burke appealed to the medieval legal construction that Ernst Kantorowicz has called the king's two bodies, a "man-made irreality" uniting the

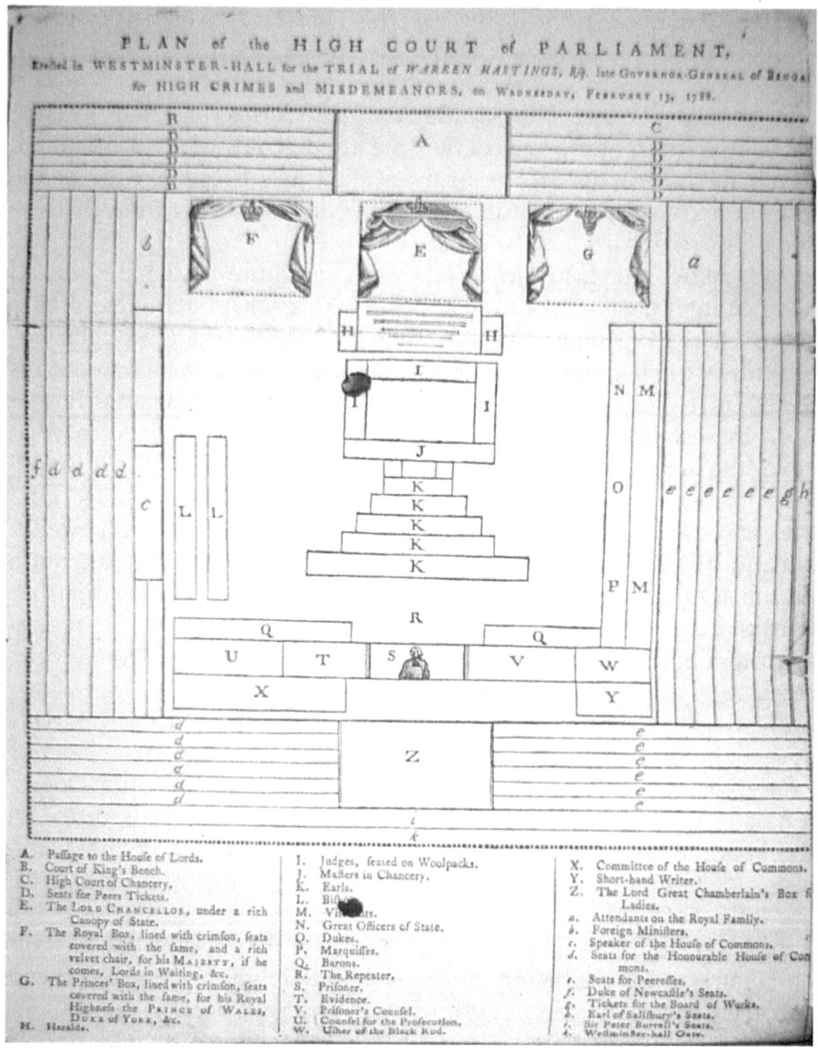

Figure 1: from Warren Hastings, *Memoirs Relative to the State of India* (1789) (Hastings is in Box S; his prosecutors are in Box U).

body politic to the body corporeal (5). Burke announced that here in Parliament was "one in whom all the frauds, all the peculations, all the violence, all the tyranny in India are *embodied, disciplined and arrayed*" ("Opening" 275, emphasis added). Like Charles I before him, Hastings stood accused of ignoring the responsibilities of his office; a man on trial for failing to meet the expectations society had invested in his metonymic status.

Corruption

Burke's case defined Hastings's criminality in terms of corruption. If accusing Hastings of tyranny allowed Burke to marshal support from a public still invested in the idea of Britain as the scourge of imperial tyrants, then convicting him of corruption would amount to a tacit admission by the public that empire *could* be virtuous. Before attending to the specifics of the Hastings impeachment, it is worth discussing the ambivalent position of the term "corruption" in eighteenth-century discourse. While we tend now to think of political corruption as the abuse of publicly entrusted powers in the interest of private gain, "corruption" has a history that predates this logic's assumptions of distinct public and private spheres. From the Latin *corrumpo* (to destroy, to spoil, to waste), corruption implies deviation from a normal state. Thus, we can casually observe that the mutability of political society means that political corruption is contingent on specific localities. Political theorist Mark Philp notes that the closest analogue in ancient Greece is the concept of *diaphtheirein*, which implies the destruction or severe restriction of a person's ability to perceive virtue or act virtuously (441). In the realm of jurisprudence, the Romans used *corrumpo* synonymously as a marker of diminished capacity. For example, the *Verrine Orations*, Cicero's famous prosecution of the proconsul Verres, begin with a rhetorical gesture which trades heavily in corruption in order to insinuate that the only virtuous outcome would be a conviction. Against Verres, Cicero imputes, "in spe corrumpendi iudicii perspicua sua consilia contatusque omnibus fecit" (1.2.5).[13] When Cicero speaks of corruption here, he refers only to the retardation of a public official's ability to behave virtuously in a particular situation. For instance, though part of the case against Verres involved his acceptance of bribes and gifts in exchange for political favours, Cicero nowhere calls Verres corrupt. For the Romans, whose culture knew of no division between public and private spheres, the act of accepting a bribe was irrelevant; only the perversion of justice signalled corruption.

H.V. Canter noted in 1914 that Burke took the *Verrine Orations* as a template for his prosecution of Hastings, and Burke certainly echoes Cicero when he states, "It is no derogation to us to suppose the possibility of being corrupted by that which by great Empires have been corrupted, and by which assemblies almost as great as your Lordships' have been known to be indirectly shaken" ("Opening" 277).[14] Siraj Ahmed follows this line when he argues that "for Burke, imperialism, like revolution, is antithetical to civil society" ("Theater" 29). Burke's imitation of Cicero adapted classical form to the present contingencies. In itself, this would be unremarkable since emulation of the Greeks and Romans had been popular practice in British culture (and especially in parliamentary orations) since the Augustan Age. However, it turns out that the mid- to late eighteenth century represents a pivotal period in the history of corruption as the emergence of separate public and private spheres turned the rhetoric of corruption away from diagnosis and towards proscription. The real source of Burke's agitation was not, as Ahmed suggests, that imperialism puts individuals into situations which "give the natural self that is civil society's primary threat the opportunity to pursue its ambitions without any form of restraint" ("Theater" 29). Rather, Hastings had violated the sanctity of his office, rupturing Britain's proud tradition of governing by rule of law:[15]

> [Warren Hastings] is staining not only the nature and character of office, but that which is the particular glory of the official and judicial character of this Country; and therefore in this house, which is eminently the guardian of the purity of all the offices of this Kingdom, he ought to be called eminently and peculiarly to account. There are many things undoubtedly in crimes which make them frightful and odious, but bribery, peculation, filthy hands, and a Chief Governor of a great empire receiving bribes from poor, miserable, indignant people; that is the thing that makes Government base, contemptible and odious, in the eyes of mankind. ("Opening" 376)

With filthy hands staining the purity of British offices, Hastings demonstrated "a pollution in the touch" (376).

In *Purity and Danger*, anthropologist Mary Douglas argues that our notions of filth are deeply contextual; a hair on the head does not evoke the same revulsion as a hair in one's sandwich. The modern understanding of political corruption follows a similar logic; a governmental advertising campaign to promote national unity is in itself benign. However, when an advertising agency with partisan allegiance is contracted to act as a middleman, and consequently siphons millions of dollars in bogus commissions from the campaign's budget, we have an instance of corruption. If we grant that political corruption depends on these contextual spatial relations, and if we seek to understand the Hastings impeachment as a corruption trial, then we must also consider the rules and expectations attached to the developing notion of the "public sphere" in eighteenth-century culture. Much of our modern understanding of the public sphere derives from the work of Hannah Arendt on what she called the rise of the social. For Arendt, society "is the form in which the fact of mutual dependence for the sake of life and nothing else assumes public significance" (*Human Condition* 46). Jurgen Habermas has taken up Arendt's idea in his work on modern cultures of communication, and associated the civil discourse of this mutual dependency with an emerging new class, the bourgeois professionals, who occupied "a commanding status in the new sphere of civil society" (*Structural* 23). Moreover, as Pocock has shown, the language of this sphere is inextricable from the new economic relations of commercial society. For Habermas, modern consciousness depends on a perceived faith in a manageable division between public (*oeconomos*) and private (*oikos*) spheres. To retain any political legitimacy, the public sphere has to appear as an impartial space where ideas can be exchanged and consensual decisions made. The visible influence of private interest threatens that perceived impartiality and therefore must be managed.

But risk management is not simply a matter of discipline and punish and the boundary between the sacred and the profane is one in constant if subtle flux. The Hastings impeachment shows how corruption trials can function productively in the consolidation of hegemony, depicting the transgressive in order to create new normalities. If political corruption is one term to describe the infestation of public office by private interest, then a corruption trial presupposes the existence of a public interest. Yet, as we have seen, in the build-up to the impeachment, though they may have been curious and though they may have been concerned, it was not at all clear that British people had any direct interest in the East India Company or in Indian affairs. Thus, for the student of empire, Burke's first great achievement was to turn Hastings's conduct into a matter of public concern. Unlike Verres, Hastings was charged not only with peculation and tyranny, but also with defeating the "excellent institution" that was the East India Company's Indian administration, and of perpetrating "the most shameful enormities that have ever disgraced a nation or can ever vex a people" (298–9). In Burke's view, Hastings's corrupt practices plagued both the Indian and the British nations and Burke chose to introduce the case to Parliament in terms of national prestige, warning that not only were other

European nations observing the outcome but that also "the credit and honour of the British nation will itself be decided by this decision" (271). In the opening lines of the speech, Burke makes it very clear that Hastings is on trial as a representative man, one whose plenipotentiary powers have placed the national character in jeopardy:

> We are to decide by the case of this gentleman whether the crimes of individuals are to be turned into public guilt and national ignominy, or whether the nation will convert these offences, which have thrown a transient shade on its glory, into a judgement that will reflect a permanent lustre on the honour, justice, and humanity of this Kingdom. (271)

For Cicero, corruption was a lamentable thing; for Burke, it threatened civic order. Within the "Speech on Opening" Burke's description of corruption contains a metastasis not found in Cicero's orations. When Burke declares that Hastings's crimes are rooted in "a heart blackened to the very blackest, a heart dyed deep in blackness, a heart corrupted, vitiated, and gangrened to the very core," the litany of diseased images suggests that the classical understanding of corruption-as-impairment has now been alloyed to the notion of corruption-as-contagion (277, 275). The distinction is important given Burke's Whiggish faith in the organic nature of civic institutions. His synthetic view of institutional development is expressed in the *Reflections*:

> By a slow but well-sustained progress, the effect of each step is watched; the good or ill success of the first gives light to us in the second; and so, from light to light, we are conducted safely through the whole series ... One advantage is as little as possible sacrificed to another. We compensate, we reconcile, we balance. (217)

In this dialectical tension between past and present, the progressive future can only be assured through the vigilant policy of cultivated reform detailed in his "Letter to a Noble Lord": "Reform is not a change in the substance or in the primary modification of the object, but a direct application of a remedy to the grievance complained of" (155). A failure to attend to such grievances gives rise to institutional decay and, earlier in his career, Burke railed against "corrupt influence which is itself the perennial spring of all prodigality and of all disorder" ("American Taxation" 410). In that "Speech on American Taxation," Burke warned that corruption spreads naturally through systems and that the "only method which has ever been found effectual to preserve any man against the corruption of nature and example is an habit of life and communication of councils with the most virtuous and public-spirited men of the age you live in" (423).

Taken together in the context of the Hastings trial, these positions shed light on Burke's prosecutorial strategy. Institutions such as the East India Company may be founded on principles "so great, so excellent, so perfect that … human wisdom has never exceeded [them]," but their present virtue is contingent upon those who occupy their offices (296). Throughout his opening speech he emphasizes the corporeality of the corporation, stating that the merchants and employees of the East India Company constitute a "public body ... responsible, their body as a corporate body, themselves as individuals … to the high justice of this kingdom" (281). A sense of collective identity and collective responsibility is enhanced because no Briton "can go there [to India] that does not go in its service … [and so] the *Esprit de corps* is strong in it – the spirit of the body by which they consider themselves as having a common interest" (285–6). The conditions of the British in India therefore gave rise to a society unique in human history, a community where one's profession became the condition of membership. As a consequence,

> the English Nation in India is nothing but a seminary for the succession of Officers. They are a Nation of placemen. They are a Republic, a Commonwealth without a people. They are a State made up wholly of magistrates. The consequence of which is that there is no people to control, to watch, to balance against the power of office. (285–6)

Presented with the potential for a Platonic utopia, Burke wonders, in quintessential Whiggish style, *quis custodiet custodies* when the affiliative bonds of society were overdetermined by the organizational structure of the administration. Because employment in the Company was the precondition for communal relations and because that community had until now lacked the proper checks against power, Company employees were susceptible to corrupt influences. In Warren Hastings, Burke suggests:

> We have not chosen to bring before you a poor, puny, trembling delinquent, misled perhaps by the example of those who ought to have kept him in awe … No, my Lords, we have brought before your Lordships the first man in rank, authority and station; we have brought before you the head, the chief, the captain general in iniquity ... if you strike at him you will not have need of a great many more examples. (275–6)

Burke accused the governor general not only of personal avarice and tyranny, but of setting the example for his subordinates to imitate. Hastings, the vicious man, was perverting the esprit de corps into a confederacy of equally implicated criminals.

> The consequence is that he who has taken but one penny of unlawful emolument (and all have taken many pennies of unlawful emolument), that he dare not complain of the most abandoned extortion and cruel oppression; and he who has taken a penny to do a good act is obliged to be silent when he sees whole nations desolated about him ... The great criminal has the laws in his hand ... He has such a hold of corruption that he has linked it, got it bound above, below, and on all sides about him, by one common participation and connivance. And accordingly he has had no complaint from the Service against him ... because, as nobody is free from small offences, the great offender can always crush the small one. (290)

The crime was particularly egregious since the office of governor general demanded precisely the opposite; as one who enjoyed a "great superintending trust," Hastings was "responsible for the acts and conduct" of his subordinates (380).

The approach Burke took in the Hastings impeachment registers the lesson he learned from his unsuccessful defence of Fox's India Bill. Then Burke appealed to the humanity of his fellow parliamentarians, urging them to act to alleviate the suffering of a people to whom they owed no specific political allegiance. His famous apocalyptic vision of Company rule depicts the pillaging of India by untutored and ungoverned swarms of greedy youths:

> The natives scarcely know what it is to see the grey head of an Englishman. Young men (boys almost) govern there, without society, and without sympathy with the natives. They have no more social habits with the people, than if they still resided in England; nor indeed any species of intercourse but that which is necessary to making a sudden fortune, with a view to a remote settlement. Animated with all the avarice of age, and all the impetuosity of youth, they roll in one after another; wave after wave; and there is nothing before the eyes of the natives but an endless, hopeless prospect of new flights of birds of prey and passage, with appetites continually renewing for a food that is continually wasting. ("Fox's India Bill" 402)

Having seen Fox's India Bill defeated, an incident which led to the collapse of the North coalition and Burke's brief reprieve from the opposition benches, Burke turned away from the individual act and focused instead on the system of governance in order to encourage parliamentarians to see the problem in terms of an institution corrupted by an individual who had co-opted a public body to serve his private interest. Having "subverted," and "defeated this excellent institution," by overriding its constitution in favour of a private "system of corruption" ("Opening" 290), Hastings was therefore not only overseeing the criminal despoilment of India but also diminishing the authority of other British institutions. In the "Speech on Opening," Burke makes it very clear that all public institutions are potentially vulnerable to decay, that the corruption of the East India Company was not a unique case, somehow endemic to Indian geography or morality. The corruption, Burke reminded his audience, was a contagion that could spread back to the metropolis as well: "For though at the first view bribery and peculation do not seem to be so horrid a matter, but may seem to be only transferring a little money out of one pocket into another, I shall show that by such a system of bribery, the Country is undone" (373). The decline of the East India Company is "only the beginning of a great, notorious, system of corruption" (385). Without a direct and swift corrective from Parliament the plague would spread to England "with most grievous and terrible consequences" (386).

The Ideal Company Man

The East India Company, now properly understood as the arm of the British government responsible for governing its Indian empire, could begin to be spoken of in terms of a state and Hastings in terms of a tyrant. Burke's recommendation, condensed in his declaration that "you strike at the whole corps if you strike at the head," is that virtue could be restored by a simple matter of regime change (276). Having established the idea of the East India Company as a virtuous institution, Burke turned his attention to its future officers. Consistent with his faith that a corporation, once properly entrusted with sacred rights and responsibilities by a sovereign power, functions as an immortal institution, Burke arrived at two standards by which a Company official could be measured: the standards of God and the standards of man. Because the empire had come into being "by the providence of God," Burke insisted its offices should be measured by divine standards, not least of which would be the ability to dispense "Imperial justice" (277). However, he admitted that its officers could only be held to the standard of men:

> The Commons are too liberal not to allow for the difficulties of a great and arduous public situation. They know too well that domineering necessities will frequently occur in all great affairs. They know that the exigencies of a great occasion, in its precipitate career, do not give time to have recourse to fixed principles, but that they oblige men frequently to decide in a manner that calmer reason would certainly have rejected. We know that, as we are to be served by men, the persons who serve us must be tried as men, and that there is a very large allowance indeed for human infirmity and human error. (274–5)

Burke's allowance does not absolve a company man but rather exposes his ambivalent position, his split allegiance between those who govern him and those whom he governs. Burke reconciles the paradox of the subject-sovereign by uniting the two allegiances under the principles of natural law, a universal order which he refers to as the "Law of Nations" (367).[16]

Rather than name Burke an international jurist *avant la lettre*, it suffices to note that he perceived the company man as obliged

> to pursue the good of the [Indian] people as much as possible in the spirit of the Laws of this Country [i.e., Britain], which intend in all respects their conservation, their happiness, and their prosperity ... We call for that spirit of equity, that spirit of justice, that spirit of safety, that spirit of protection, that spirit of lenity, which ought to characterise every British subject in power. (345–6)

In that final noun phrase, "British subject in power," Burke clarifies the imperial hierarchy, but his vision turns on the word "ought." Throughout his speeches Burke relies on "ought," strengthening his rhetorical appeals by luridly juxtaposing the colonial present and the principled imperial future. Yet "ought" invokes a higher order or legislation and is a word particularly well embedded in the language and thought of Judaeo-Christian societies. In describing what ought to be, Burke evokes his contemporary David Hume, who observed that the journey from "is" to "ought" cannot be made without passing through human nature (*Human Nature* 469–70). Burke believed in a common human nature created by God as the supreme norm but he also knew that human nature realizes itself only partially in history through conventional forms, customs, and traditions, which constitute what he called the second nature of a particular people. Thus, although Burke's principled demand would later mutate into the moral imperative energizing the so-called "civilizing mission" of late nineteenth-century imperialism, Burke himself nowhere ascribes a monopoly of virtue to the British nation.[17] Faults Indian society may have, but he stated that it would be haphazard for Company employees to tinker with the natural institutions of a people "who formed their Laws and Institutions prior to our insect origins of yesterday" ("Opening" 304). Therefore, "if we must govern such a Country, we must govern them upon their own principles and maxims and not upon ours, that we must not think to force them to our narrow ideas, but extend ours to take in theirs; because to say that that people shall change their maxims, lives, and opinions, is what cannot be" (302).

In the final analysis, Burke can be called an imperialist only insofar as he believes that the possession and judicious application of Britain's cultivated principles legitimate its presence in India; to lapse into cultural relativism is to surrender the right to rule. In this sense Burke's excoriation of Hastings resembles David Hume's critique of Thomas Hobbes's moral philosophy. Hobbes put forward the case that humans are essentially amoral and what morality they do possess is determined by a combination of self-interest and social specificity (31–3). Hume rejected this explanation, arguing that a priori there are "particular *original* principles of human nature," shared by all humans that remain unalterable over time and space (*Human Nature* 590, emphasis in original).[18] In the impeachment, Hastings took the part of Hobbes, arguing that the laws and customs of India obliged him to utilize autocratic power at times. Burke rejected this "geographical morality" out of hand, insisting that "the laws of morality are the same every where, and that there is no action which would pass for an action of extortion, of peculation, of bribery and of oppression in England, that is not an act of extortion, of peculation, of bribery and of oppression in Europe, Asia, Africa, and all the world over" ("Opening" 346).

In Burke's assessment, company men cannot remain just rulers if they "unbaptize themselves of all that they learned in Europe and commence a new order and system of things" (346). The baptismal metaphor evokes not only those traditions of ritual cleansing which Burke is attempting to replicate through the impeachment spectacle but also the irrevocable commitment made by an initiate to a particular religious confession. The image is both apt for and recurring in Burke's discussion of Company officials. To emphasize how the Company's organizational structure could reduce the agency of its employees, Burke trumped baptism – which a casuist might argue is a commitment made on behalf of rather than by an individual – with confirmation:

> For the Servants of the company are obliged, when they enter into the Service, to enter into it not only with the general duty which attaches upon all servants, but they enter into a specific covenant with their Masters to perform all the duties described in that Covenant under heavy penalties. They are bound by them ... [and] they are bound to renew these covenants by something (I speak without offence) which may be said to resemble confirmation in the Church. (289–90)

These sacramental motifs illuminate Burke's vision for the future governance of India by suggesting that a company man's character should already be formed, founded in solid unalterable British principles, before he undertakes an Indian appointment.

Such expressions disclose Burke's debt to Aristotelian ethics as he speculatively answers his own question: "What should a British Governor in such a situation do, or forbear to do?" ("Opening" 345). Normally, ethics derive from a familiarity with custom; one's understanding of a community's laws or traditions fosters a sense of obligation that influences choice. The two major streams of post-Enlightenment moral philosophy measure ethics in these terms. Both utilitarian and deontological ethics theorize duty and obligation in terms of discrete actions in relation to an abstract set of ideal or divine rules, be it the greatest good, rationalism, or the Word of God. Such theories presume that the agent exists in and understands the norms of a community. But the conditions of imperial rule placed British men in positively un-British surroundings; in India, company men could have no recourse to the familiar. Therefore, argues Burke, ethical choices must be contingent on a preconfigured and essentially unalterable set of humanistic principles, that is to say, the character of the covenanted company man.

While literature scholars most often read Burke as a romantic, in the context of empire it is equally important to recognize his affiliations with the neoclassicism of the early century. His imitation of Cicero's *Verrine Orations* in the Hastings impeachment only partly discloses this affinity. More significant for the future of company men are the invocations of an Aristotelian humanism in those parts of his speeches where he discusses the ideal imperial administrator. When Burke invokes character, he invokes a type of Aristotelian virtue ethics. In *The Nicomachean Ethics* Aristotle suggests that the measure of an action will not be found in examining the act in isolation but by examining the actor: "Actions, then, are called just and temperate when they are such as the just and temperate person would do" (28). So virtue is as the virtuous person does. In Aristotelian terms, the virtuous person becomes the model for other community members when they themselves must deliberate over a course of action; in Burkean terms, "I do then declare, and wish it may stand recorded for posterity that there never was a *bad man* that had the ability for *good service*. It is not in the nature of such men" ("Opening" 403, emphasis in original).

Deprived of the advantages deriving from customary familiarity, the British could best serve India by being British. A British governor "ought to govern upon British principles, not by British forms." Such a virtuous service would bring "order, peace, happiness and security to the Natives," but it would also benefit the home countries:

> It would have been glorious to us too, that in an enlightened state of the world, possessing a religion, an improved part of the religion of the World – I mean the reformed religion – that we had done honor to Europe, to our Cause, to our religion, done honor to all the circumstances of which we boast and pride ourselves. ("Opening" 315)

Thus far, "it has happened otherwise; it is now for us to think how we are to repair it" (315).

With the corrupt influence purged and the example set for future governors of India, one final obstacle needed to be removed to preserve British India from future tyranny. No matter how virtuous the reformed company men might be, "the emoluments that belong to them are so weak, so inadequate to the dignity of the character that it is impossible (I may say of that service absolutely impossible) for the subordinate parts of it to exist, to hope to exist, as Englishmen who look at their home as their ultimate resource, to exist in a state of incorruption" (286–7). Inadequate pay alienates an agent from his principal, leading to a divergence of interests. To understand such situations, economist Jacob van Klaveren puts forward a market-oriented interpretation of corruption where

> a civil servant regards his public office as a business, the income of which he will, in the extreme case, seek to maximize ... The size of his income then does not depend on an ethical evaluation of his usefulness for the

> common good but precisely upon the market situation and his talents for finding the point of maximal gain on the public's demand curve. (39)

The unwelcome prospect of the merchant-administrator is precisely what animates Burke's Indian speeches. However, van Klaveren's neo-liberal nightmare scenario is, as he says, "an extreme case," and any measurement of political corruption in such exclusively economic terms can only take place in a world view that subordinates the political to the economic. Antonio Gramsci and, later, Pierre Bourdieu and John Guillory have demonstrated that ideology does not merely reflect a given state of affairs but can also function to create new social and cultural capital as well. Burke pointed towards such alternative forms of capital when he reminded the Lords that "often the greatest situations are attended with little emoluments because glory, family reputation, the love, the tears of joy, the honest applause, of their Country, pay those great and mighty labours which in great situations are sometimes required from the Commonwealth" (287). Such a statement corrects any extreme interpretations of Pocock's thesis in *Virtue, Commerce, and History* that commerce, exchange, and neo-Harringtonian thought redefined the principles of classical republicanism in the eighteenth century. As Burke reminds us here, the Whig commercial regime may have redefined but it did not replace republican virtues. Whatever influence market forces had in articulating the public sphere, they could not affix a determinate value to acts of public service. Those perennial socioethical benefits outlined by Burke would continue to be accrued by public officials, mitigating their temptation to treat their offices as private businesses.

By declaring the welfare of India to be a part of the British public good, Burke intended to establish conditions that would prevent the further exploitation of its Indian subjects and halt the decay of British institutions. This strategy calcified an imperial relationship and so the British Empire, a concept reviled only a generation before, became a matter of fact. In prosecuting Hastings and in highlighting the structural deficiencies in the present constitution of the East India Company, Burke passes over the ignoble details of British conquest, arguing that history cannot be undone. All governments, he submits, have their origin "in some matters that had as good be covered by obscurity." The impeachment of Warren Hastings was, then, one of those "secret veil[s] to be drawn over the beginnings of all governments," an illusory ceremony declaring the end of corrupt mercantile imperialism and enunciating a new and purified formation, an empire based on virtue, duty, and service ("Opening" 316–17).

2 How the Civil Service Got Its Name: India as a Noble Profession

A calling is not produced naturally, nor by high or low wages but by a long and arduous process of education.

– Max Weber

Whether to create the just empire of Burke's vision or to sustain the interests of the court of directors, it was clear that servants of the East India Company needed to be inoculated against the temptations in India which might inspire them to act irregularly. This was because the administrative system established by the Company put those employees in charge of large, populous, and prosperous districts, and simultaneously demanded that they govern in extreme isolation from either the London or Calcutta headquarters. In *Vanity Fair* (1848), William Makepeace Thackeray (himself Calcutta-born) gives a likely picture of district life in Napoleonic times:

> Boggley wollah is situated in a fine, lonely, marshy, jungly district famous for snipe shooting and where not unfrequently you may unflush a tiger. Ramgunge, where there is a magistrate, is only forty miles off, and there is a cavalry station about thirty miles father – so Joseph wrote home to his parents, when he took possession of his collectorship. He had lived for about eight years of his life quite alone at this charming place, scarcely seeing a Christian face except twice a year, when the detachment arrived to carry off the revenues which he had collected to Calcutta. (20–1)

The collector, Jos Sedley, is a literary descendent of the nabob, the stock character of eighteenth-century drama whose wealth derived from a corrupt exploitation of these same situations.[1] Thackeray's anti-hero, Becky Sharp, instantly makes that connection in her conversations with his sister Amelia, asking, "Isn't he very rich? They say all Indian Nabobs are enormously rich" (17). Jos Sedley's actual salary is never made clear in the novel. At one point, his father cites it at four thousand rupees a month (approximately £4800 annually), though since this is given in the context of Sedley Sr trying to raise money to support a new business venture, some inflation must be accounted for. This is hardly the "enormity" that the British public, including Becky Sharp, had come to associate with the nabob.[2] Even so, it is a substantial salary, which enables Jos a comfortable lifestyle while on furlough in London. Throughout the novel, Thackeray plays with the stereotype of the nabob to establish Sedley's character. He is introduced as "a very stout puffy man, in buckskins and hessian boots with several immense neckcoths that rose almost to his nose" (18). Though not a youth, he behaves "like a gay young bachelor" (21) and pursues all the latest fashions; a decade later, his obsession with appearance persists, with the narrator measuring him "as vain of his person as a woman" (573). Despite these airs, Jos Sedley "scarcely knew a single soul in the metropolis: and were it not for his doctor, and the society of his blue-pill, and his liver complaint, he must have died of loneliness" (21). His efforts to appear gallant are offset by his famous act of cowardice, abandoning the women and children during the Battle of Waterloo. Likewise, upon the news of his father's bankruptcy, Jos "acted as a man of his disposition would" (174) and establishes an annuity to support his parents; however, the annuity is a meagre £120 (in a world where George Osborne complains that £1,000 annually could not sustain him). Eventually William Dobbin browbeats Jos into doing his duty by his family. He dies overseas, friendless and penniless, having squandered his fortune on high living and financial speculation.

Yet despite these personal flaws in character, his occupation is an honourable one, a source of both social capital and money. The narrator describes the collectorship as "an honourable and lucrative post, as everybody knows" (20) and Dobbin confirms as much when he views Jos Sedley's "position and dignity, as collector of Boggley wollah" as assets that might "compensate" for the Sedley family's loss of station following Sedley Sr's bankruptcy (223). Sedley Sr likewise tries repeatedly to capitalize upon his son's honour, using that reputation as collateral against prospective loans. In fact, though Thackeray's description of the conditions in Boggley wollah make it abundantly clear that Jos Sedley could have enriched himself at the expense of the public purse, though Thackeray's contemporary audience knew that Company agents had become nabobs in the eighteenth-century precisely by these means, and though Thackeray's narrator positively delights in skewering Jos Sedley's avarice, selfishness, cowardice, and vanity, the novel makes no suggestion whatsoever that Jos Sedley takes advantage of his official status. In a way, his personal insalubrity ironically testifies to Burke's victory over corruption. By the late 1840s the popular opinion of empire, if the immensely popular Thackeray is any guide, is no longer troubled by rogue agents. Sedley's professional incorruptibility registers the first phase of the virtuous empire's hegemonic aspect: if a scoundrel like Jos can be thought beyond graft then, post-Hastings, corruption can hardly be a matter of concern in the imperial mentality of Thackeray's Britain. By 1859, the poltical economist Harriet Martineau was defying anyone "who take[s] an interest in the India of our own day," to argue "whether the history of any nation presents a picture of a more virtuous devotion to public duty" (55).

Yet suggesting that the threat of corruption disappeared from public scrutiny does not mean that it did not exist. No one should adduce that Burke's rhetoric, however brilliant, eliminated the possibility of peculation. Whatever reforms he called for, the basic agency relationship that caused problems for the East India Company in the eighteenth century remained intact throughout the nineteenth. Imperial agents still exercised plenipotentiary powers and continued to do so at an unbridgeable distance from the imperial centre. Recall that only four years before *Vanity Fair*, Sir Charles Napier disobeyed orders and launched the illegal invasion of the Sindh province, so scandalous as to birth a Victorian urban legend, Napier's one-word message to London: *Peccavi* ["I have sinned"].[3]

Napier's is not an isolated case, for these are also the years in which Thomas Babington Macaulay wrote his rehabilitative essays on Robert Clive and Warren Hastings. Macaulay's Whig historiography recast Clive and Hastings as likeable villains, men who were not without flaws, to be sure, but whose flaws could generally be overlooked in deference to their contributions in securing the first pieces of what was now Britain's progressive and noble empire. To Macaulay's picture of Clive and Hastings, one could easily apply the gentle self-admonition cast by Napier over his disobedience: "We have no right to seize Sind, yet we shall do so, and a very advantageous, useful, and humane piece of rascality it will be" (qtd. in Sorley 183). This transition, from the rapacious tyrants depicted in Burke's rhetoric to the noble rascals of the 1840s, forms the subject of this chapter, where I will examine how it was that India became a noble profession.

Emile Durkheim, who never applied his sociology to imperialism, imagined a hypothetical society uncannily familiar to Anglo-India in his theory of civic morals. "Imagine a population scattered over a vast area," he writes, "without the different elements of being able to communicate easily; each man would live for himself alone and public opinion would develop only in rare cases entailing a laborious calling together of these scattered sections" (8). In such a case, when individuals are deprived of the traditional immediate and frequent solidarity with other members of the group, Durkheim argues that collective consciousness can only be produced within stable and organized corporate structures, like those offered by the liberal professions which grant their members an ethical code through which they imaginatively and positively identify with each other. The great puzzle of modernity, he continues, is how this structure might emerge in the economic sphere, where "the ideas current on what the relations should be of the employee with his chief of the workman with the manager, of the rival manufacturers with each other and with the public ... are so slight that they might as well not be" (9–10).

Charles Napier diagnosed this absence of ethics as the condition of Company India, a "shopocracy" which cared little for the welfare of the people under its charge (22). In the twentieth century, economists have theorized the implications of this amoral capitalist logic, stating that individuals in a free market can always choose between competing offers for their services.[4] Eric Noreen explains that at "the heart of agency theory ... is the assumption that people act unreservedly in their own narrowly-defined self-interest with, if necessary, guile and deceit" (359). Taking the contract as the basic unit of relation, agency theorists study what happens with the introduction of new variables into systems. They speak of the gap between the most lucrative choice and the next best option, a "reservation utility" (Gintis and Ishikawa 196). In the case of the East India Company, when merchant-agents began to assume the function of political and judicial administrators, the opportunities for agents to augment their personal wealth increased. Economic agency theory proposes that, to maintain loyalty, the principal – the East India Company – had to respond by increasing either its incentives or its monitoring. Factually, we know that salaries did not increase significantly; practically, monitoring could not be increased since India lacked efficient communication and transportation networks.

By reading the East India Company as an organization unable to regulate the actions of men in the field and finding their authority confined to the rhetoric of praise and blame, I will show how the Company initiated a process whereby the isolated agents would govern themselves. In this sense, Edmund Burke's most significant contribution to the stability of the British Empire in India was his insistence that if the Company could be seen as an honourable institution then its employees could be obliged through the pursuit of impecunious emoluments. That is to say, I want to suggest that men like Jos Sedley did not consider corruption because, following Burke's advice, the Company rewrote the conditions of employment, introducing as compensation forms of social capital, expressed in terms of honour, duty, and national service. By the time of *Vanity Fair*, Thackeray's reflection on England during the Napoleonic wars from the perspective of the 1840s, the title of collector – even in a backwater like the district of Boggley wollah – has added nobility to its mercantilism; according to Thackeray's narrator it is "an honourable and a lucrative post, as everybody knows" (28). What made the collectorship of Boggley wollah an honourable post was the belief emerging as early as the 1840s that Britons, through their employment in the East India Company, were doing good and selfless work for the mutual benefit of Britain and India.

Histories of Company India have credited this transformation to the steady infiltration of middle-class ideologies of evangelicalism, utilitarianism and, eventually, liberalism.[5] Granting that any discussion of nineteenth-century English liberalism must acknowledge Richard Bellamy's caveat that it remains a "notoriously elusive notion" (1),[6] Thomas Metcalfe has argued that, in India, "liberalism, as a programme for reform, developed a coherence it rarely possessed at home" (29). As Eric Stokes has shown, India provided a laboratory for the experimental social engineering of the English utilitarians.[7] If the liberal spirit of early nineteenth-century England presumed that all humans are intrinsically equal and that human happiness could be improved by judiciously applying rational thought to administrative problems, then India provided the opportunity to test new models of governance. The historical record bears this out insofar as social reforms as diverse as universal state-sponsored education and competitive entry into the civil service were tested in India before making their way back to Britain.

However, what this proposition fails to account for is why men of Jos Sedley's character voluntarily relinquished the opportunity to profit personally in exchange for some noble idea of human advancement. To be clear, I am not dismissing the influence of either evangelicalism or utilitarianism on the shape of the administrator's character as much as I am suggesting that neither generated it. The profligacy of the eighteenth-century nabobs demonstrates that the "English character" contained no essential or traditional internal prohibitions against vice. It is equally haphazard to presume a spontaneous and universal level of volunteerism. Instead, if one considers Company employees as individual agents it becomes clear that obedience was encouraged through the creation of a corporate identity which rose not out of a response to new social ideologies of evangelicalism or utilitarianism but out of a crisis of control. According to Durkheim, "ethics will be the more developed and the more advanced in their operation, the greater the stability and the better the organisation of the professional groups themselves" (8).

We are now in a position to consider the East India Company as an agency and its employees as members of a professional service. A letter from the court of directors to the Board of Control in 1803 shows that the Company was well aware that systematic efforts would have to be made in order to "impress a permanent character upon the British disposition and habits in India" ("Representation" 403). The letter expresses scepticism that Wellesley's college at Fort William could deliver those results on a sustained basis, but it endorses the principle of collegiate education, asserting that India's government could only proceed by combining "the voluntary exertions of some and the stimulated exertions of others" (404).[8] In tracing the way this discipline of "stimulation" evolved in the first half of the nineteenth century, we encounter a familiar narrative of state evolution in a slightly altered corporate form. From explicit and cloddy ideological apparatuses such as the colleges at Fort William and Haileybury to the more subtle hegemonic articulation of the competition exam, the history of the East India Company's training regime reveals progressively more sophisticated and diffused technologies of control emerging in response to an ever more complicated imperial relationship.

In examining those systems established to co-opt the interests of Company employees and subordinate them within the corporate order, I draw on Antonio Gramsci's illumination in *Prison Notebooks* that a rise to power in a modern state can only be made and sustained by the consent of the governed. In the case of the East India Company, its employees consented to relinquish the chance to become nabobs in the style of Robert Clive or the avaricious protagonists of Kipling's short story "The Man Who Would Be King." Instead, they chose a life of relative anonymity full of bureaucratic toil in an unfamiliar country, a condition they themselves often describe as exile. As one twentieth-century Anglo-Indian civil servant remembers it, British citizens willingly joined a collective of "homeless vagrant governing-machines" (Beames 103). As I have argued in the previous chapter, the path to that submission was blazed by Edmund Burke, who facilitated the transformation of a mercantile operation with shaky credit into an honourable enterprise. The public spectacle of the impeachment powerfully symbolized Britain's intention to govern India justly. It asserted a public interest, which Burke felt would act as a check against corruption. Indeed, he argued in his *Reflections* that the "degree of estimation in which any profession is held becomes the standard of the estimation in which the professors hold themselves" (93).

What remains to be answered is how this newly acquired honour was translated into feelings of duty, loyalty, and public integrity and then imposed upon Company employees. To do this, we must go beyond the observation that the language of British imperial discourse in the nineteenth century bulges with a figural repertoire which demotes the aspect of commodity trade and geopolitical manoeuvrings in favour of "duty," and "honour." These words are little more than cliché since nearly every commentator appeals to them. When analysing the ethics of the imperial administrator, to describe either the empire or its hegemonic persuasiveness in such terms is difficult because it is so clearly tautological: one "acts" ethically by "acting" British. To puncture this loop, I want to suggest that imperial ethics were, indeed, informed by British identity, but that this "British" identity was brought into being by the practical demands of controlling one's distant agents. In other words, the Britishness that formed the basis for ethical action was an explicitly corporate identity, not grounded on traditional or essential forms (whether British, English, European, Christian, etc.) but manufactured by a series of novel processes and disseminated among would-be colonial civil servants. This chapter considers two of these disciplinary apparatuses, the training college and the competition examination, built by the Company to socialize recruits into its corporate culture.

To understand the intention behind the design of these institutions, we can look at the contributions of three men prominent in their development. Richard Wellesley, Thomas Robert Malthus, and Thomas Babington Macaulay are all successors of Edmund Burke in their belief that the control crisis could only be resolved by preparing employees to accept the idea of the virtuous empire before they undertook their official positions. All recognized that because the Company recruited such a small number annually, it would be possible for the entire body of future administrators to be selected, educated, and trained with great scrutiny. Of the three, Malthus expresses the view most concisely: "In India there is only one line of employment, and that is the Company's service" (*Statements* 38). None of these men, despite their connections to the Company, are themselves members of the administrative class that would be subject to their proposed apparatuses. Yet their writings remain important not only because they address the control crisis but also because their recommendations had a direct impact on the early training of a great majority of Anglo-Indians.

My concern is not to evaluate their writings aesthetically but, through a comparative analysis, to use them to illuminate how the idea of the virtuous empire became a corporate ethos in the first half of the nineteenth century. It needs no sophisticated argument to show that all modern political projects, especially of the imperial variety, appeal to virtue when defending their actions. Yet it remains the particular characteristic of the British Empire that it so often measured its virtue through its ability to spread stable political institutions throughout the world. The apotheosis of the empire, claimed liberals like Macaulay and John Stuart Mill, would be the moment of its dissolution. Britain proposed to give the world good government. Its representative agents were thus charged not with bringing the *pax* or the *prosperitas* Britannica but with securing the place of institutions, including the rule of law and private property rights, which would then, presumably, produce peace and prosperity of their own accord. This necessitated a new type of functionary: the imperial agent as bureaucrat.

A certain amount of engineering was necessary to create this figure and Wellesley, Malthus, and Macaulay influenced this process. Each engages the problem of the disobedient servant and each proposes a systematic solution. The concerns they express – over an individual's relation to society, the absence of privacy, the scale and degree of work allotted to each official, the saturation of a public morality, and the eradication of individual agency – would come to dominate Anglo-Indian fiction and memoirs in the closing years of the century. That cultural legacy will be taken up in later chapters. For now, the narrative of the virtuous empire begins with formal training colleges established in England and in India, which taught its students not, as in the other great public schools or in the universities, to be public citizens but rather instruments of a regulated system. It culminates with the introduction of the competition exam, Macaulay's great plan to open the Indian service to any citizen of the empire who could prove himself a liberal gentleman.

"For their Guidance, Improvement, and Restraint"

In detailing the case against Warren Hastings, Edmund Burke lamented the deficient education of the Company's disgraced governor general:

> He quitted Westminster School almost a boy. We have every reason to regret that he did not finish his education in that seminary which has given so many lights to the Church and ornaments to the State. Greatly we lament that he did not go to one of the Universities ... instead of studying in the School of Cossim Ally Cawn. If he had lived with us, he would have quoted the example of Cicero in his Government, he would have quoted several of the sacred and holy prophets, and made them his example. ("Speech on Opening" 367)

This critique was used to support Burke's claim that only fully formed British characters could govern India justly. The problem of how to train Company employees remained unresolved until an Old Etonian, Richard Wellesley, became governor general. Unsurprisingly, considering his younger brother's views on the virtues of the Eton playing fields, Wellesley felt that the foundations of character were best laid in formal educational institutions. Insofar as the only qualification for an Indian career in the early nineteenth century was a patronage appointment from a director, Wellesley argued that the East India Company was risking a repetition of the Hastings affair and jeopardizing the stability of its commercial interest in India.

On 10 July 1800, Wellesley's despatch to the London directors contained his "Notes with Respect to the Foundation of a College at Fort William" (hereafter "Notes"), which proposed a solution. The despatch is remarkable for two reasons. First, because it simultaneously introduced the idea of a college to the directors as it announced the Fort William College as a *fait accompli*, "Notes" documents an audacious act of insubordination. In it, Wellesley reveals what has been learned since the Hastings scandal. Knowing that the document would become part of the public record and could, like Hastings's self-incriminating diaries, be subject to parliamentary scrutiny, Wellesley aligns his proposition with the general public interest. "If the good Government of this empire be the primary duty of its sovereign," he writes, "it must ever be a leading branch of that duty to facilitate to the public officers and ministers the means of qualifying themselves for their respective functions" (730). In contrast, he complains that the current cohort of Company recruits "are unequal to their prescribed duties" and consequently "the principles of public integrity are endangered, and the successful administration of the whole Government exposed to hazard" (725).

Wellesley proposes to "facilitate" the means of qualification through the establishment of a comprehensive training college, where private individuals would learn the characteristics and sentiments of statesmen. Anticipating dissent for such an expansive and expensive reform, he characterizes any putative opponents as motivated by less than noble interests, arguing that "objections of a private nature might be stated against this plan; but those which are founded on public considerations appear to be absolutely insurmountable" (733–4). Fusing Hastings and Burke, Wellesley explains the "reasons which induced [him] to found the College without any previous reference to England," as a combination of his local expertise and his awareness of the superintending responsibility the East India Company bears to its Indian subjects (740). His exploitation of the Company's structural weakness – the distance between the principal and the agent in the field – established the speaker's unique authority to judge what is appropriate, and Wellesley's rhetoric provided a template for future generations of civil servants seeking to defend their actions through their memoirs.

Second, "Notes" is the first imperial text to suggest the need for a systematic production of a corporate identity and is also the first to confront the implications of introducing social capital as a form of compensation. According to Burke, graft could be reduced if employees could be made to see their stations as equivalent to those of statesmen. Following on, Wellesley insists that "the views of the servants of the Company should terminate in the prospect of returning to England, there to enjoy the emoluments arising from a due course of active and honourable service in India" (734). But the governor general realizes that one cannot produce statesmen without a state:

> Duty, policy, and honour require that [India] should not be administered as a temporary and precarious acquisition … [It] must be considered as a sacred trust, and a permanent possession. (731)

The "sacred trust" discloses Wellesley's Burkean inheritance, but the concept of India as a permanent possession is altogether novel. Here,

Wellesley is one of the first British statesmen to speak in the vocabulary of our modern notion of imperialism, a prepositional sleight of hand which makes it possible to speak not of the British in India but of British India.[9]

Beyond its novelty, the idea that historian Francis Hutchins calls "the illusion of permanence" is also demonstrably necessary once one begins to trade in social capital, a commodity which demands stable social institutions as a condition of its production. For a heuristic we can turn to the liberal professions, whose rise only slightly predates that of the Company's civil service.[10] Two prominent Victorian essays show how well Victorian intellectuals themselves understood the function of social capital. In "The Roots of Honour" (1860), John Ruskin argued that a profession is honourable inasmuch as it requires its members to sacrifice on occasion for the welfare of the state or of their charges (145–6). Similarly, John Stuart Mill's *Utilitarianism* identifies this willingness to sacrifice as evidence of the superiority of the anticipated pleasure (12–14). More recent social historians, including Penelope Corfield, have theorized this further, observing that professionals differentiate themselves from merchants and labourers by deriving their social status from more than mere money. According to Corfield, since "a proportion of individual remuneration was paid in the form of unquantifiable social respect," professionals depended on "public endorsement" within a stable political entity (177). Thus each of the three liberal professions – clergy, lawyers, and doctors – derived social capital through the performance of some "public" service.

This concept of service led to the fetishization and even a reification of abstractions, such as the rule of law, around which a professional ethos developed.[11] A comprehensive code of professional ethics enabled individual members of the profession to pursue their practice efficiently without frequent or direct monitoring from a centralized body, thereby preserving the "liberal" character that enabled a gentleman to acquire income through work without compromising his honour. In India, Wellesley saw that "the stability of our own interests" (719) could be assured if Company employees began to conceive of their employment as constituting a "public service" (740) and "Notes" enunciates the imperial ideology of virtuous sacrifice. The organizing principle of its professional ethics would not be, for instance, the salvation of heathen souls or the codification of Indian laws. These elements, associated as they are with evangelicalism and utilitarianism, were seen by Wellesley as effects of good government. Rather, the ethos for the company employee would be the spread of good government, "the *extension* of this beneficial system" (719, emphasis added). Thus the civilian employees of the East India Company were to be transformed into a body of men "properly qualified to conduct the ordinary movements of the great machine of Government" (731). The company man steps down from the heroic pedestal of nabobs who won Britain an empire and were motivated by "glory, wealth and power" (730). Instead, like a vicar, barrister, or doctor, he becomes a repository of "useful knowledge, cultivated talents, and well ordered and disciplined morals" (732); in other words a professional in Britain's first comprehensive civil service.

Of course for the Company directors, it was not at all apparent that such costly organizational changes were necessary. Relatively speaking, Company operations during Wellesley's tenure were running smoothly and, thanks to the land reforms of his predecessor, Charles Cornwallis, their administration of Bengal was now being funded on a solid tax-base. Wellesley pre-empted this objection by declaring this very prosperity to be the spur for reform: "The British possessions in India now constitute one of the most extensive and populous empires in the world ... in which property, life, civil order, and religious liberty are more secure, and the people enjoy a larger portion of the benefits of good government, than any country in this quarter of the globe" (718–19). Now that the Company possessions had assumed an imperial character, it was incumbent on the Company to act rather as a government than a mercantile corporation. But since the Company lacked established political institutions, "the general happiness and prosperity of the country must essentially depend on the conduct of the commercial servants" in its employ (721). In this, Wellesley saw a problem, for while the East India Company had always been a quasi-public institution by virtue of its royal charter, its employees were contracted to serve the private interests of a mercantile corporation. As such, they operate, "without rule or system to direct their duties; without any prescribed object of useful pursuit connected with future reward, emolument, or distinction; without any guide to regulate, or authority to control their conduct, or to form, improve, or preserve their morals" (728). This condition was not a problem until the Company acquired sovereignty over Indian territory. Until then, the agency relationship was purely material and it was sufficient to furnish one's agent with a "commercial education" (721). However, the assumption of political and judicial powers entailed responsibilities exceeding the limits of commercial education and as a result, "some succeed, in the ordinary progress of the service, to employments in which their incapacity or misconduct becomes conspicuous to the natives, disgraceful to themselves and to the British name, and injurious to the State" (727). To remove these threats to Company and imperial interests, Wellesley presented the directors with a plan to regulate their employees through a process of what today we would call professionalization. He acknowledged that while "extraordinary efforts of individual diligence" (729) had won Britain an Indian empire, "the Company's investment [can never] be conducted with the greatest possible advantage and honour to themselves, or with adequate justice to their subjects, *unless their commercial agents shall possess the qualities of statesmen*" (721, emphasis added). Looking back on Wellesley's proposition from our position in an age where universities host centres and departments design programs for this express purpose, it is difficult to recognize how innovative this proposal was. Wellesley is adamant that a mere liberal education of the sort deemed sufficient to prepare a gentleman for public life in Britain was insufficient for the demands of the profession. To "those branches of literature and science which form the basis of the education of persons destined to similar occupations in Europe," an Indian civil servant required "an intimate acquaintance with the history, languages, customs and manners of the people of India, with the Mahommedan and Hindoo codes of law and religion, and with the political and commercial interests of Great Britain in Asia" (722). To be clear, in 1800 no country anywhere in the world offered professional training in statesmanship. Given that his task is to persuade the directors to accept an expensive addition to their mercantile operations, Wellesley makes no effort to prove its uniqueness, deeming it "unnecessary to enter into any examination of the facts to prove, that no system of education, study, or discipline, now exists, either in Europe or in India founded on [these] principles" (723).

Content that he has established necessity, Wellesley begins to enumerate the means by which to guarantee "a sufficient supply of men qualified to fill the high offices of the State with credit to themselves and with advantage to the public" (723). One of the easier ways to impress upon employees the gravity of their situations, Wellesley suggests, is to evacuate the nominal remnants of the commercial character of the administration. He asks the court of directors to recognize that "the denominations of writer, factor, and merchant ... are now utterly inapplicable to the nature and extent of the duties discharged" (719):

> The Civil servants of the English East India Company, therefore, can no longer be considered as the agents of a commercial concern. They are, in fact, the ministers and officers of a powerful sovereign; they must now be viewed in that capacity. (722)

By openly declaring the responsibilities of employees to be matters of public concern, Wellesley argued that the East India Company would be able to police the behaviour of its agents more effectively. Made conscious of obligations not only to their employer but also to a "high public trust," those who would otherwise be mired in "despondency and sloth" would be energized and those tempted to corruption chastened (725).

But though titular reform might make employees more conscious of their behaviour and to a certain extent create a culture of self-regulation, it hardly equipped them with the skills necessary to undertake "the complicated and extensive relations of those sacred trusts and exalted stations" (722). Wellesley argued that only a systematic form of education could "establish a just conformity between their personal consideration, and the dignity and importance of their public stations" (722). Because of the unique demands of these stations, the education of civil servants "must therefore be of a mixed nature, its foundation must be judiciously laid in England and the superstructure systematically completed in India" (733). Like Burke, Wellesley hopes that properly trained civil servants will "be enabled to discriminate the characteristic differences of the several codes of law administered within the British Empire in India, and practically to combine the spirit of each in the dispensation of justice" (723).

However, when Wellesley speaks of foundations and superstructure he is using a spatial metaphor, an architectural topography that would influence the development of imperial ideology. Like every metaphor its purpose is to make something visible. The effect in this case is to make the foundation the most important, that which is necessary in the last instance. Taking the foundation as that part of one's education which took place in Britain, British character thus becomes the sine qua non of the Indian civil servant, a declaration which signals a move away from the previous policy of cultural appreciation, sympathy, and mutual understanding exemplified by the Orientalist project, led by William Jones, Charles Hamilton, and Nathaniel Halhed. Wellesley proposes to build on the English foundation by establishing a specialist college at Fort William in the Bengal Presidency where all Company recruits would be required to spend three years building their Indian superstructure. Wellesley's metaphor shows further how the superstructure is related to the foundation as he argues that the principal function of the college would not be, for example, to teach Indian languages or history but rather "to fix and establish sound and correct principles of religion and government in their minds at an early period of life" (737). Through the college, "the Government of India … will be enabled … to bring the general character of the servants of the Company to such a standard of perfection as the public interest require[s]" (740).

Standards were desirable since imperial policy, Wellesley admitted, had thus far been improvised. British agents like Clive found themselves in unfamiliar situations and made spontaneous decisions. Wellesley's chief insight, from the perspective of the British Empire, is to have realized that this improvisational aspect could never be removed. This is, on reflection, a profoundly anti-Orientalist sentiment, one which perhaps explains why a figure as influential as Wellesley is so rarely considered in postcolonial studies of Anglo-India.[12] I say anti-Orientalist because it amounts to an admission that knowledge of Indian culture and society either is impossible to calculate and commodify in academic collegiate discourse or, if it were, is of little practical use to its future administrators. Wellesley's insistence that all political situations are necessarily contingent entailed his recommendation that one cannot create procedures for every possible contingency in a country whose diverse customs were alien to its administrators. Wellesley instead sought to limit the range of that improvisation by establishing a standardized ethic. Arguing that behaviour is a product of habit and exercise he therefore urges that

> early habits should be so formed, as to establish in their minds such solid foundations of industry, prudence, integrity, and religion, as should effectually guard them against those temptations and corruptions with which the nature of this climate, and the particular depravity of the people of India, will surround and assail them in every station … The early discipline of the service should … form a natural barrier against habitual indolence, dissipation, and licentious indulgence. (723)

Wellesley's rhetoric of safeguards and barriers would come to feed the self-fashioned identity of the Victorian colonial administrator, who distinguished himself from his Roman, Spanish, Portuguese, or Mughal predecessors by enforcing strict embargos against social or sexual assimilation with their colonial subjects.[13]

For his part, Wellesley suggests that the moral character of employees would be greatly improved if, rather than spending their first years in India as clerks in close association with native writers, they associated freely in a collegiate atmosphere where they could lay "the foundations of private character and public reputation" (739):

> It cannot be supposed that many will be so insensible to their own honour and interests, and so destitute of every liberal feeling and sentiment, as not to prefer the proposed course of studies in the College to the menial labour imposed upon them of transcribing papers in an office where, in the nature of their duty, they are levelled with the native and Portuguese clerks, although infinitely inferior in its execution. (739)

Described in this fashion, the college promises to educate an elite, to appeal to the liberal (read: aristocratic) sentiment of recruits by offering them the opportunity to separate themselves from menial labour. The immediate effect of Wellesley's policy is apparent in the prize-winning essay from the first cohort of the college's graduates. In his disputation "On the Advantages to be Expected from an Academical Institution in India," W.B. Martin defends,

> the necessity, then of an enlightened and unremitting attention to those subjects of study, which are calculated to impress a virtuous and manly bias on our thoughts, to mould our character to a consistence with the principles of honor and liberality, and to render us valuable and ornamental members of society … But the importance of our character in India is such, our intercourse with society, and our influence on its general spirit and habits are so extensive, as to display the necessity of a more enlarged knowledge, and plainly demonstrate the propriety of adopting every method of instruction, which tends to open the mind, and sow the seeds of manly thought and dignified conduct. (6)

Martin's essay demonstrates the extent to which Wellesley's objectives have been internalized by the student. It does not matter so much whether any consonance exists between these statements and the student's personal opinions. Instead, it demonstrates the successful transference of imperial obligation. Martin, the institutionally sanctioned (because prize-winning) voice of the new generation of civil servants, speaks in overtly aristocratic tones. As "ornamental members" of Indian society, the chief purpose of the company men in India is to provide "dignified" models of "character" and "conduct" which could then be emulated by their Indian subjects. Running an empire, in other words, had become a matter of playing British. The deep irony, as we shall see, was that "acting" British affected the administrators as much as those they administered.

Imperious Necessity and Habits of Industrious Exertion

The court of directors, while upset by Wellesley's impudence, approved his plan in principle and agreed to fund a training college. Perhaps the most appealing aspect of the college was the opportunity to establish an esprit de corps among its initiates. The directors decided, however, that the purpose would be most efficiently achieved if the college were in England, closer to East India House and therefore easier to supervise. In 1806 East India College, commonly called Haileybury after the town where it was built, admitted its first cohort.

Haileybury was not without its detractors. Perhaps this was inevitable given the sheer novelty of a privately funded training institution purposely built to prepare young men for the task of statecraft in overseas territories. From its establishment until the early 1820s many newspapers, notably *The Times*, regularly ran pieces relating scenes of anarchy, riot, and general irregularity.[14] In 1812 Lord Grenville gave a speech in the House of Lords calling for its closure. In 1817 a group of Company stockholders, who were aggrieved at the expense of maintaining the college, united with local squires, who were aggrieved by the unwelcome influx of hundreds of rowdy boys into their sleepy corner of England, for the same purpose. These commotions were such that they animated Thomas Robert Malthus, Haileybury's Professor of History and Political Economy, to write a tract in reply. Published first as *A Letter to the Rt. Hon. Lord Grenville* (1813), the argument was slightly modified and reissued in 1817 as *Statements Respecting the East-India College with an Appeal to Facts*.

Little scholarly attention has been paid to Malthus's time at East India College, a strange fact given that Malthus is the first in a series of British political economists, from the Mills to John Maynard Keynes, whose speculative thought remains indebted to the patronage of the Company. As Keynes reminds us, Malthus's chair in political economy at Haileybury was the first of its kind to be established in England, predating Oxford and Cambridge by nearly twenty years (108). Nor do I think it an accident that a company charged with managing the affairs of an overseas colony should be so progressive in this field. But this is not a study in political economy or economic history; I am more interested in Malthus as an employee and the unique position this afforded him to comment on the East India College. As he asserts to Lord Grenville, "My situation, as one of the professors in the East India College, has given me the best opportunities of observing its effects on the young men who have been educated there" (*Letter* 1–2). In Malthus's pamphlets, we receive a clear picture of the structure, intent, and function of this institution, how it disciplined middle-class British boys into company men. Through Malthus's defence we see that the East India College was deliberately built to fashion industrious and obedient agents. In other words, it facilitated the transition from eighteenth-century nabob to nineteenth-century sahib.

Malthus's arguments need to be read as both a reflection of and a contribution to the structure of feeling that determined British attitudes to its empire. His arguments are based on the foundation of aristocratic virtue laid by figures like Burke and Wellesley. Consider, for example, how an emphasis on individual interest inflects his parse of Adam Smith's famous objection against Company rule in India: "One of the great objections urged by Adam Smith against the government of an exclusive Company is, that their interests, as a sovereign, are generally considered as subordinate to their interests as individuals, or as a body of merchants" (*Statements* 31). However, there is an important discrepancy between Malthus's parse and Smith's actual words. Though Malthus intimates otherwise, Smith never in *The Wealth of Nations* referred to the interests of individuals in his analysis of the East India Company. The threat of the rogue agent acting in private interest is instead part of the legacy of the Hastings corruption trial. As Malthus continues, it is that threat of individual agency which the structure of the East India College sought to nullify.

In order to lend moral authority to his argument, Malthus employs the same strategy used by both Burke during the Hastings impeachment and Wellesley in "Notes," namely, accusing one's opponents of private interest. In the preface to the *Statements*, Malthus pledges his name and character:

> [Those who] continue their attacks upon the college in the public prints, should adopt the same candid and manly mode of proceeding. If they do not, the inference will be pretty strong, that they cannot reveal their names without discovering to the public some probable motives for their attacks, different from a desire to promote the welfare and good government of India. (vii)

Rather than capitulate to those motivated by "feelings of temporary disappointment and irritation" (1), Malthus argues that "the great object ... must be kept in view by the legislature and the public" (2). His appeal indicates how deeply the idea of empire had sedimented in the British consciousness within a generation of the Hastings impeachment. To place in the British public sphere the interests of either India or the private company acting as its governor, Malthus need not make Burkean appeals to grandiloquent ideas of national honour or the Law of Nations. Instead, Malthus simply picks up where Wellesley left off, claiming empire as a fact which, in turn, obliged Britain to render certain services to India.

While the structure of his argument implies a progression from the general need for a college to the specific case of the college at Haileybury, all is predicated on imperial fact; justification is made on the basis of that which is, in Malthus's wonderfully euphemistic phrase, "imperiously necessary" (*Letter* 19). Imperious necessity means that stockholders of the Company must bear the expense of preparing a class of properly trained administrators; and imperious necessity means that a patch of English domesticity and tranquillity must be sacrificed to the service of the empire. Having dismissed his opponents summarily, Malthus turns to describe what type of administrator was "imperiously necessary" and what type of institution was most able to produce him.

Although the great public schools and the two Universities were thought to provide excellent preparation for a young man intending to enter public life in the early nineteenth century, Malthus notes that Haileybury is the first educational establishment exclusively dedicated to the training of civil servants and he cheerfully discloses that Haileybury is in the business of manufacturing character:

> [In] the judgement of the most competent and distinguished authorities, the students at East-India college are *formed in their morals, prepared in their character, and qualified in their education,* for the most important stations they are likely to fill, and that the Hertford college, instead of being the disgrace of England, has been rendering, and is rendering, most essential service to India. (*Statements* 84, emphasis in original)

If we focus only on Malthus's emphasized words, we discover nothing outside the usual claim of any schoolmaster. However, the subsequent phrase, "for the most important stations they are likely to fill," reminds us that this college exists for a very particular reason: the students at Haileybury were not being trained to spread Britannia's fame but to manage its acquisitions as quietly and effectively as possible.

Malthus defends this purpose by making the Wellesleyan appeal that the nature of the British Empire has changed. First he refers to the past as a period of expansion and acquisition when it was enough to rely on "military and political power." Here,

> circumstances rarely fail to generate the qualifications necessary. All ages and countries have produced warriors and statesmen. A few great and illustrious individuals ... might be sufficient so as to animate the whole body of their countrymen. But it is a very different thing when the question is no longer about the acquisition and the maintenance of an empire, but the administration of justice and of a good internal government to sixty millions of subjects. (19–20)

In Malthus's estimation, what was acquired by accident could only be maintained through a "system of discipline" (25). Burke and Wellesley made similar appeals for the reform of the body of imperial agents, but Malthus's writing reveals a great deal more sophistication. Whereas Burke called for British character and Wellesley called for liberal gentlemen, Malthus takes a more pragmatic approach. By 1813 the concern for the Company and even for enlightened thinkers like Malthus is not to produce a cohort of Clives or even Wellesleys but to establish an infrastructure capable of consolidating power.

The difference in what was needed can be measured by the subtitles of Philip Mason's two-volume history of British India, *The Men Who Ruled India* (1954). India had been won by "The Founders"; it was to be administered by "The Guardians." But whereas Mason argues that the change in attitude coincided with the Indian Mutiny of 1857 and the Crown's assumption of power in 1858, Malthus's writings show that this cultural adjustment was well underway in the early years of the nineteenth century. It would be equally remiss to presume that Malthus was a visionary in this regard. On the contrary, the religious instruction at East India College regularly imparted the same message in their end-of-term sermons. Symbolically the last opportunity to impress moral teaching on company men like Jos Sedley who would in Thackeray's words, "scarcely [see] a Christian face except twice a year, when the detachment arrived to carry off the revenues he had collected," these sermons often focused on the biblical Joseph who, like the graduates, was sent from his kindred to be a ruler in a foreign land. For instance, in 1827 Reverend Henry Walter advised the students, "You are summoned to be the instruments of a government, which must seek for strength by deserving the approbation of its subjects; and which, therefore expects its officers to save the weak from oppression ... In the hour of temptation, like Joseph, view with abhorrence, any proposal to violate a trust which has been generously and fully reposed" (9–10).[15]

Malthus concedes that great men will continue to emerge but, now that the purpose of empire has changed, such men will be comparatively without power:

> They cannot act without instruments. These instruments must necessarily be a considerable body of civil servants, not only possessing the means of easy communication with the natives, but of improved understandings, of acquired knowledge, and of habits of steady application and industry. (*Statements* 20)

Because of this change, Malthus continues, "it is abundantly evident that an improved education for the civil service of the Company [is] not an imaginary and theoretical, but a real and practical want – a want which, in some way or other require[s] unquestionably to be supplied" (23). The instrumental metaphor alludes to an idealized agency relationship, where the human subject is stripped of his individual will and made a tool in the service of his principal's interest. As evidence of the progress already being made in pursuit of this ideal, Malthus refers to a despatch sent in 1810 from Governor General Minto to the court of directors which praised the college students "for regular attendance; for obedience to the statutes and discipline of the college; for orderly and decorous demeanour; for moderation in expense, and consequently in the amount of their debt; and, in a word, for those decencies of conduct which denote men well born and characters well trained" (qtd. in *Statements* 53).

Minto makes no mention of intelligence, ingenuity, adaptability, creativity, eloquence, or any other trait one might expect of men who are nominally trained to hold the offices of statesmen. I would argue that he makes no mention because statesmanship was not the true object of the collegiate education but rather the veil thrown over the eyes of Company recruits and the British public in general. One might sum the Haileybury project up as the process by which a British citizen was reduced to the level of instrumentality even as he believed he was elevated to the aristocracy. Malthus, at least, confirms that "the feelings of the sovereign conspicuously predominated" at East India College (*Statements* 31).[16] Yet Haileybury was in the business of producing instruments, not sovereigns. The "feelings" then must be understood as structured, set in place and cultivated for an ulterior motive. The reason for this structure is clear: an employee who conceives himself a sovereign will affiliate more positively with the pleasures derived from immaterial civic virtues as compensation for his work. The success of this structure of feeling is measured not only in the reduction of corruption but also in the universal faith expressed by Anglo-Indian writers and memoirists in the anticipated pleasures derivable from one's retirement to the proverbial gabled villa in Surrey.

Malthus goes so far as to suggest that the collegiate mode of education itself contributes to the formation of this character. He submits that "the strict discipline and constant superintendence of a school would be but a bad preparation for the entire independence, and complete freedom from all restraint, which would await them on their arrival in Calcutta" (27). The task of administering an empire requires an institution

> where a more liberal system of discipline might be introduced; and where, instead of being kept to their studies solely by the fear of immediate observation and punishment, they might learn to be influenced by the higher motives of the love of distinction and the fear of disgrace, and to depend for success upon their own diligence and self-controul; upon the power of regulating their own time and attention; and on habits of systematic and persevering application, when out of the presence of their teachers. Nothing but an institution approaching in some degree to a college, and possessing some degree of college liberty, could either generate such habits, or properly develop the characters of the young persons educated in it. (28)

The phrase "college liberty" neatly captures the type of discipline the Company attempted to develop in response to the logistical contingencies of their agency relationships. "College liberty" is, after all, liberty within a system, an illusory freedom that masquerades as true liberation only insofar as a member has internalized the fundamental rules, the hegemony, of the ideological apparatus.

The work underway at the East India College as described by Malthus is very close to what social theorist Herbert Marcuse calls "repressive desublimation." In *One-Dimensional Man* (1964) Marcuse proposed the term to describe the process by which instinct is directed away from its natural expression and appears, instead, in some other form of (socially acceptable) expression (75–8). Unlike sublimation, which offers a surrogate object, desublimation offers the desired object itself. Desublimation explains how a social system manages and sanctions the release and pursuit of primal instincts with the aim of maintaining a higher discipline over its membership. This apparent liberty, while operating under a higher level of authority, Marcuse called "unfreedom" (1). Take the example of the argument that the East India Company addressed the immobility of Britain's restrictive class society by offering men the chance to be kings, to wield absolute power over a human population: this opportunity is one of "unfreedom," where the human individual can only pursue the primal drive (agency; power over others) when he has tacitly agreed to do so under the rubric of the overarching social order (serving as Company employee; behaving in an orderly fashion).

In the case of Malthus's idealized Haileybury, the horizon of "college liberty" becomes apparent if we contrast it with actual freedom. While Haileybury's critics are complaining that its students are too free – from academic regulations, from surveillance, from punishment – Malthus counters that it is precisely this freedom which shall guarantee their obedience. It is a conservative force masquerading as liberation. As one Haileybury alum, W.S. Seton-Karr, recalled,

> It was there [at Haileybury] that we first became cognizant of the fact that we were members of the Civil Service ... It was there that we first became firmly impressed with a conviction that, as members of such a body, there were certain traditions to be kept up and handed over to our successors, a political faith to be cherished, and a code of public and private honour to be rigidly maintained. (qtd. in Monier-Williams 94)

For Malthus, one of the clearest indications of institutional strength was the way it cultivated the higher motives of the love of distinction and the fear of disgrace, an awareness that one's actions are being assessed by a silent group of auditors. Malthus explains, for example, how the professors published examination results along two indices, the first being the bands of first-, second-, or third- class results familiar in the Oxbridge system and the second being a relative ladder ranking each individual in relation to his peers. Haileybury was unique among contemporary English educational institutions in that not only were the students being measured against some abstract standard but they were also being measured, constantly, against each other. Moreover, Malthus boasts, "These means of exciting emulation and industry have been attended with great success ... a more than usual proportion seem to be animated by a strong desire, accompanied by corresponding efforts, to make progress in the various studies proposed to them" (*Statements* 49). By the time the students had graduated, they were quite used to the idea that constant surveillance was taking place even as they lived and worked in the remotest outposts of the empire.

The *idea* of publicity would become a defining feature of nineteenth-century Anglo-Indian society. Helen Mackenzie, for one, recalls of her six years in India: "One learns to know people in India most thoroughly. Everybody lives, as it were, in a glass case – one knows the income, style of living, debts, and position, of every one else" (118). The noticeboard of the quadrangle would be succeeded by the *Gazette* and its lists of promotions, salaries, and achievements of every member of every Anglo-Indian civil and military administrator which was, if we recall, tantamount to the entirety of "respectable" Anglo-Indian society.

It would be insufficient to argue, however, that simply by a stricter or more detailed publication of student grades, the East India College transformed the superego of company recruits. Fortunately, Malthus himself considers publicity but one component of the disciplinary process. Another, equally important, innovation of the Haileybury system was its remarkably diverse curriculum, wherein a student would study simultaneously classical literature and languages, two "Oriental" languages (Persian and Sanskrit), the elements of mathematics, natural philosophy, the laws of England, general history, and political economy. For many of the college's critics, this breadth invariably prevented the acquisition of any tangible skills. To Malthus, these critics are missing the point since the purpose of the curriculum is not to teach anything of use but "to encourage most effectually habits of industry and application" (47). The barrage of courses and assignments has, he argues, "been useful to them in rendering a methodical arrangement of their hours of study" (47), thereby preparing them for the diverse tasks associated with their impending administrative posts. H. Morse Stephens, a Victorian chronicler of the East India College, drew a similar conclusion by observing that, "the chief advantage of such a college as Haileybury lay not so much in the actual instruction afforded, as in the association together of young men intended for a career in common, in which they specially needed the traditions of a noble service, while labouring side by side for the promotion of the welfare of the peoples of the East" (346).

In such a configuration, we can see how imagination is subordinated to methodology, and how independent thought is swamped by the pressure to complete the work at hand. Similarly, an anxiety runs through Anglo-Indian literature, especially but not exclusively in Kipling's fiction, over the fact that much work needs to be completed before the British can begin to spare the time necessary for metaphysical considerations.[17] Recall that Lord Minto's approbation was based on orderly and obedient graduates rather than incisive or talented ones. Malthus goes further, baldly stating,

> All the offices in India may not require talents; but all must require a certain degree of industry, good conduct, and inclination to the service. And beyond all question, [that is] one of the most important uses that the college can answer. (*Statements* 80)

The best defence of the college that Malthus can find is that it answers Burke's imperative, delivered on the opening of the Hastings impeachment, "My Lords, to obtain empire has been a common thing – to govern it well more rare" ("Opening" 314). The establishment of a college which combined universal publicity with a rigorous curriculum and college liberty tempered the characters of prospective company men. No longer, Malthus argued, could an Indian appointment be an opportunity for second sons "whose conduct and attainments do not promise a very fortunate career at home" (34). It was now the training ground for the servants of Britain's just empire.

Competition and Naked Ambition

Macaulay shared with Malthus a concern that the separate interests of the East India Company, its Indian subjects, and the British Crown would be best served if company men could be turned into well-regulated instruments of administrative machinery. But unlike Malthus, he was not confident that a college could create a *Gemeinschaft* in and of itself. For Macaulay, it was equally important to attend to the natural disposition of the recruits before they ever entered a collegiate environment. In particular he saw the existing system of patronage, where recruits entered the civil service on the basis of a personal recommendation by one of the Company directors, as a terribly inappropriate way to select men who would be asked to work as disinterested administrators. In response, he suggested that entry to the Company's service be opened on the basis of intellectual competition. His plan for a competitive examination, first made in his 1833 "Speech on the Government of India," would quickly become one of the rallying calls for Victorian liberalism. Since the reform of the Indian civil service served as the foundation for the abolition of patronage on the domestic front, Macaulay's campaign has been generally understood as an attack on one of the last vestiges of feudal arbitrariness, and the inauguration of meritocracy into the public service.

To get a quick thumbnail of the status quo in the era of patronage, we could do worse than turn to the Barnacle family in Charles Dickens' *Little Dorrit* (1855–7). According to the narrator, the Barnacles have infiltrated not only the Circumlocution Office but, through viral nepotism, had "dispersed themselves all over the public offices ... Either the nation was under a load of obligation to the Barnacles, or the Barnacles were under a load of obligation to the nation" (107). Now over and against those who thought it proper to leave appointments to the discretion of gentlemen, mandarins, or the Barnacles of the world, men like Mill, Macaulay, and Charles Trevelyan championed open competition.[18] To be clear though, the advocates of both patronage and competition shared the belief that the best man was needed for the job. Where they differed was in how to determine who that best man is. Generally speaking, liberal reformers agreed with the ideal for public service outlined in John Stuart Mill's *Considerations on Representative Government* (1861) as the state of affairs "in which the interest of the functionary is entirely coincident with his duty" (194–5). If we combine this with the old liberal canard that Britain held its empire reluctantly and only for as long as it would benefit its colonized peoples, then we quickly apprehend what the reformers really wanted: a group of disinterested men with a worldly appreciation of and a willingness to represent Indian interests.

Between 1833 and 1853, Macaulay committed a great deal of his intellectual energy to achieving this goal, but today his contribution to imperial pedagogy is more often characterized by his "Minute on Indian Education," which has become the standard-bearer for the canon of colonial discourse. Its suggestion that England endeavour to create a class of colonial administrators Indian in blood and English in character is now understood by postcolonial critics as one of the most egregious excesses of the Eurocentric cultural chauvinism which dominated the imperial age. By introducing the "Minute" at this point, my intention is not to offer a defence of Macaulay's Anglicist policy or to deny that it "enabl[ed] the humanistic ideals of enlightenment to coexist with and indeed even support education for social and political control" (Viswanathan 5). Rather, I want to draw attention to its contemporaneousness with his plans to reform the colonial civil service in total.

In both cases, the problem Macaulay confronted was no different from the one that faced Wellesley or Malthus: how best to create instruments for the machine of government. In each, the flaws in Macaulay's argument were manifold and based on a combination of inexperience and specious logic. Even Mill, always broadly sympathetic to Macaulay's politics, disagreed with the "Minute on Indian Education," calling it impractical and, in a letter to the Company's directors, "chimerical."[19] However, dismissing the "Minute" on the grounds of essentialism, racism, or hypocrisy is to mistake its rhetoric with its purpose, which is to create a new class of people. In Macaulay's day, the Company was expanding, continually drafting native clerks into its service. At Governor General Bentinck's request, and functioning in his capacity as Legal Member of Council in India, Macaulay was charged with advising the best means for the education of these future employees. Macaulay was concerned with English as the vernacular of administrative power, and with Englishness as its character.

The concept of Englishness as a transmissible code is behind the best postcolonial critiques, but those same critiques miss some of the point when they limit their analyses to the colonized subject.[20] If we contextualize the "Minute," we realize that Macaulay also intended to use the idea of Englishness to regulate the behaviour of English men. My contention here is that Macaulay was less a chauvinist than one who held all men equally to a standard that was as unnatural to an Englishman as to an Indian. This view is not possible if we limit ourselves to his "Minute," but if we engage his writings and speeches on the matter of domestic reform, we approach a fuller picture of his liberal intentions. Before he ever turned to the subject of Indian education, Macaulay sought to reform the method of selecting and training Company civil servants. In his "Speech on the Government of India," delivered amid the debate over the renewal of the Company's charter, Macaulay opposed the system of patronage through which writers were appointed to attend East India College on the grounds that imperial duty "entitled" India to "the best talents which England can spare" (155). To ensure that condition was met, he advocated the establishment of an open competition for these positions, through the process of a set examination. The principle of competition, he asserted, rather than the content of the exam, would be the best way to secure such candidates.

> Whatever be the languages, whatever be the sciences, which it is, in any age or country, the fashion to teach, the persons who become the greatest proficients ... will generally be the flower of the youth, *the most acute, the most industrious, the most ambitious of honourable distinctions* ... If, instead of learning Greek, we learned the Cherokee, the man who understood the Cherokee best, who made the most correct and melodious Cherokee verses, who comprehended most accurately the effect of the Cherokee particles, would generally be a superior man to him who was destitute of these accomplishments. (156)

On the one hand, Macaulay's speech is a simple defence of the value of a liberal education to a young man preparing for public life. On the other hand, he reveals that the measure of that value is not made in the content of such subjects, but in their rigour. Those inclined towards success in competition, that is to say, those who combine natural talent with ambition and industry, would become the best servants of the public good.

It would be twenty years before the competition examination was introduced, but in its founding document, Macaulay indicates that the basic elements of his philosophy have not altered. Macaulay's *The Indian Civil Service: A Report* (1855) contains the practical framework which later scholars including Terry Eagleton and D.J. Palmer would link to the establishment of English literature as a discipline in British schools and universities.[21] As a piece of Liberal political philosophy, its advocacy of meritocracy over arbitrary promotion makes it a worthy companion text to the tracts of the Administrative Reform Association and Mill's *Considerations on Representative Government*. However, whatever work this document did towards the institutionalization of certain academic subjects or to the broad reform of the domestic civil service, the *Report* also articulates a psychological profile of what Macaulay thought was the ideal employee. A civil service appointment should not be "a matter of favour, but a matter of right" and he who obtains the appointment should "owe it solely to his own abilities and industry" (*Report* 18). As in the 1833 "Speech," the 1855 report insists that the subjects examined are not as important as the principle of competition:

> Skill in Greek and Latin versification has, indeed, no direct tendency to form a judge, a financier, or a diplomatist. But the youth who does best

what all the ablest and most ambitious youths about him are trying to do well will generally prove a superior man. (*Report* 13)

Quite opposed to Malthus and the Haileybury philosophy, Macaulay urges that the best civil servants will be those committed to distinction rather than those capable of managing multiple subjects simultaneously. "Nothing can be further," he insists, "from our wish to hold our premiums for knowledge of wide surface and of small depth" (12). A candidate's commitment will also be tested in exams designed to belie "the delusive show of knowledge which is the effect of the process popularly called 'cramming'" (14). Throughout, the exam should be so designed as to indicate those candidates who possess the "qualities which are securities against vice – industry, self-denial, a taste for pleasures not sensual, a laudable desire of honourable distinction, a still more laudable desire to obtain the approbation of friends and relations" (21). Because the exam offered papers in many subjects and because deep knowledge of a subject was demanded, Macaulay wrote, "It seems to us probable that of the 6,875 marks, which are the *maximum*, no candidate will ever obtain half" (11). As one of the examination's critics noted in 1875, the limits of the papers were "almost co-extensive with human knowledge itself" (Griffin 529).

As we have already seen, these are the perennial qualities demanded by Company reformers from Burke to Wellesley and Malthus. Yet each figure has offered different proposals and the characteristic features of Macaulay's plan highlight his more sophisticated grasp of managing individual agents. Both the college and Macaulay's competition system disciplined on the basis of publicity. But whereas the collegiate construction of an esprit de corps regulated through an economy of shame underwritten by a fear of the public exposure of one's inadequacy, the competition exam *presumed* inadequacy and promoted the discovery of virtue through struggle. In this way, Macaulay's competition exam was designed to overcome not only the gap between London and India but also the gaps among the thinly spread Indian officials themselves. "Competitioners," or competition wallahs as they became known in India, were to be made conscious of their incomplete ability long before they reached positions of responsibility in India. Already, they would be prepared to fail in the equally onerous task of administering an empire.

The best civil servant, Macaulay seems to be arguing here, is the idealist: the man who holds the idea of the virtuous empire and its notional civil servant in the highest esteem; the man who realizes how far he is from incarnating that notion; and the man who is most driven to reduce that gap. If this is the case then the competition examination should be understood as the inaugural point for a system of self-generating subjectivity. This is quite unlike the collegiate system, whose disciplinary capacity was circumscribed by acts of remembrance after graduation. Whether or not civil servants would retain the feelings cultivated within the quadrangle once they had assumed positions of power – whether they would, in other words, remain attached to the idea of the virtuous empire – could not entirely be assured. Macaulay reasons that "the servant of the Company is often stationed, during a large part of his life, at a great distance from libraries and from European society, and will therefore find it peculiarly difficult to supply by study in his mature years the deficiencies of his early training" (*Report* 3–4). Alternatively, Macaulay's plan is self-generating, requiring neither library nor society, because it internalized the inadequacy, placing alienation at the centre of the individual agents' subjectivity.

Were it possible to implement successfully, Macaulay's plan would eliminate the need for elaborate surveillance and disciplinary networks. Like the collegiate system, the competition exam was designed to produce a particular psychosocial effect, but whereas Haileybury aimed for positive attachment through esprit du corps and a career-long nostalgia for collegiate fellowship, the competition exam operated negatively on its subjects. The competition exam takes the idea of the virtuous empire, that ethos which putatively transformed self-interested British subjects into dutiful colonial agents, as an impossible ideal. Macaulay's intention was to create an eligibility test that made the gap between the ideal and its aspirants palpable: even the best candidates would never "pass" his exam. The ideal company man, then, is a concept which the exam configures as *originally lost*, lost at the moment of its enunciation, named as something which will never come into being. And here lies the difference between the Haileybury graduates and Macaulay's candidates (who would soon become known, aptly, as "competitioners"). Properly trained, the competitioners represent a collective for whom process – doing the job – has replaced finite goals. For them, identity is not based on their shared ambition to recover or rebuild the lost idea of the virtuous empire, even if this is the declared, stated goal. Instead, their identity is based on loss itself. Recalling once more Macaulay's impossible expectations, I would argue that self-worth is a product of the pursuit, not the attainment, of a goal. In fact, achievement only indicates that one has not desired enough. That is to say, the most masochistic would be the best administrators; those most conscious of their inability to succeed in full would be most likely not to fail in total.

In imperial discourse the notional English civil servant is as universally acknowledged as his material incarnation is non-existent. The most ostensibly admirable characters in imperial fiction are those who exhibit masochistic commitments, rendered noble, of course, through the lexicon of duty and sacrifice. John Lang's novel *Wetherbys: Father and Son* (1853) is representative here. Consider the scene where young Wetherby describes his pensioned father:

> In India he was a tremendous talker, and usually spoke in a loud sonorous voice; but in England he was silent, reserved, and seemingly timid. If they could have got him upon ... any of the various questions on which he was accustomed to write and converse, he would have astounded his hearers with the mass of facts which he had in his memory, and the vigour with which he gave utterance to his thoughts: but his sympathies were now but rarely or never aroused, and he must have felt that he was regarded, if not as a stupid person, anything but a very clever fellow. (24)

The degree to which Anglo-Indian writers knew their hope would be thwarted is evident in the literature from the beginning. However, whereas young Wetherby writes in tones of bitter disappointment, later Anglo-Indian characters will take pleasure from knowing their toils should but inevitably would not be recognized. This shift has less to do with the collegiate training model than with the type of character cultivated by the competition examination. The publication of a document like Macaulay's *Report on the Civil Service* represents a point in the evolution of imperial discourse which realized that ethics were most efficiently (financially or pedagogically) instilled not through explicit ideological apparatuses like the East India College but instead through the construction of impossible goals.

3 Representing Working Conditions in Company India

The history of Anglo-Indian literature prior to the arrival of Rudyard Kipling usually receives scant critical attention. Partly this is a matter of quantity since, as Allen J. Greenberger wrote in an early review of Anglo-Indian literature, "It was only after the great success of Kipling that novels and stories set in the sub-continent were published in large number" (1). More often, however, the judgment is levelled based on quality. As Udayon Misra determined in his study of Raj fiction, most nineteenth-century Anglo-Indian literature is "not of sufficient literary merit or intellectual worth to engage our attention" (2). When scholars do turn their eyes to Anglo-Indian fiction, they more often do so reading for historical or sociological significance. The purpose of this chapter is not to overturn a century of criticism and reveal the previously undiscovered features of these texts that would qualify them as literary. Following the great achievements over the last forty years by scholars working on women's and working-class writing, our understanding of taste, literary quality, and canon formation has transformed substantially. The audience, the marketplace, and the socio-political context have replaced arbitrary and universal standards as the indices of literary worth. The argument of this chapter is that the early literature of Anglo-India does have literary merit, if we recognize the community of writers and readers, the corporate culture, out of which such literature emerged.

In 1887 Rudyard Kipling wrote an ironic send-off to his Anglo-Indian readers in the *Civil and Military Gazette* that proposed to explain Anglo-Indian society to itself. Kipling was nearing the end of his tenure at the *Gazette*, which for the last two years, under the editorship of Kay Robinson, had been publishing the short fiction that made Kipling an

Anglo-Indian celebrity. His observations in "Anglo-Indian Society" (1887) seem immediately to undercut both his own literary competence, and the literary tastes of readers who had by then become fans of Kipling's oeuvre:

> There is no society in India, as we understand the word. There are no books, no pictures, no conversations worth listening to for recreation's sake. Every man is in some service or other, has a hard day's work to do, and has very little inclination to talk or to do anything but sleep at the end of it. (186)

The hinge in that potentially bleak assessment of Anglo-Indian society is the equivocal phrase "as we understand the word." The reference is to established conventions of metropolitan social life, the Indian imitations of which Kipling regularly skewered as hopelessly pretentious in his short fiction. Like Edmund Burke a century before, Kipling is arguing against the possibility of imposing or planting English culture upon foreign territory. Unlike Burke, Kipling is talking about the colonizers rather than the colonized.

This chapter looks at the emergence of an Anglo-Indian society distinct from its metropolitan analogue. To appreciate, in the first instance, the size of that gap, consider the impish prefaces that Kipling prepared for the first English edition of *Departmental Ditties* (1890). The first would be addressed "To my Anglo-Indian Public":

> Dear Folk,
>
> [My metropolitan readers] still believe that all white men in India sleep for three or four hours in the middle of the day and spend most of their waking moments in "kicking the poor dear native downstairs." They are quite certain that the Indian administrator is much too near to affairs to be able to form impartial judgments, and every gentleman and every other lady … knows exactly how India ought to be governed … You however can read between the lines I have written and know exactly how far the ditties tell truth, and by how much they err in describing the frivolous, gilded, idle, irresponsible life. ("Unpublished Prefaces" 25)

The second was intended for that same metropolitan reader:

> This is a book on Anglo-Indian subjects. An Anglo-Indian subject is a person who was once an Englishman, but who through the effects of climate,

> overfeeding, and underwork becomes something quite different. His duties are to live luxuriously on the money wrung from the teeming millions of India, who are all very highly educated, peaceful, and open minded folk, more than capable of administering a government of their own. The Anglo-Indian is vastly inferior to the Englishman in physique, endurance and mental power. ("Unpublished Prefaces" 25–6)

Though he left these prefaces unpublished – explaining to William Thacker, "No use telling the public you think 'em a damned ass" (qtd. in Kemp and Lewis 169) – he did feel it necessary to attach some prefatory verse to the English edition of the collection, addressed to his Anglo-Indian readers, which concludes thus:

> I have written the tale of our life
> For a sheltered people's mirth,
> In jesting guise – but ye are wise,
> And ye know what the jest is worth. ("Prelude" 9–12)

Kipling's contempt for the metropolitan reader who does not understand the truth of the colonial situation is an extreme but also characteristic feature of Anglo-Indian literature in the nineteenth century, which often speaks to two audiences simultaneously.

Such prefaces, published and unpublished, show that by the fin de siècle the distance between Anglo-Indian and mainstream British culture is almost insuperable. My interest in this chapter is to retrace the history of this separation in the poetry and prose of Anglo-Indian writers. Many scholars, literary critics, and historians, have trodden this path before me in order to establish to what extent – if at all – Anglo-Indian literature was national.[1] That question, I believe, has been answered definitively in the negative. Given that the morphology provided by "the nation" is inadequate, this chapter proposes to read nineteenth-century Anglo-Indian literature as that of a professional, or corporate, society. My decision is guided by the overwhelming influence of work on the social lives of Anglo-Indians. As A. Claude Browne, editor of the Calcutta-based newspaper *The Empress*, explained to a London audience in the early twentieth century, "One's occupation, not one's birth, breeding, education, or even financial standing, determines one's place in the Indian scheme of things" (23). Following Browne's advice, this chapter takes work, rather than nation, race, or class, as the animating force of Anglo-Indian literature.

In the context of domestic Victorian fiction, Carolyn Lesjak has argued persuasively that the literary history of the novel must be read in coordination with developments in capitalism. Lesjak reveals an ideological attempt to separate the domains of labour and pleasure, emphasizing pleasure, leisureliness, spare time, and introspection as the proper topics of literary representation. Lesjak insists that, "pleasure figures as a space or site free from the vagaries of production" (16). In the context of Anglo-India, such a division – of labour from art – is simply not possible. To articulate the characteristic features of Anglo-Indian society, we must observe Kipling's warning: "Nothing seems to impress the Anglo-Indians except their work" ("Anglo-Indian Society" 191). If Anglo-Indian literature is the union of art and labour, it is significant as one of the few archives of nineteenth-century Anglophone writing that remains relatively immune from the commodifying vicissitudes of capitalism – whose ideology seeks to alienate the worker from the work.

Kipling's contemporary, William Morris, called such a culture socialist. In his lecture "The Socialist Ideal: Art" (1891), William Morris distinguishes between the socialist and the capitalist view of art:

> To the Socialist a house, a knife, a cup, a steam engine, or what not, anything, I repeat, that is made by man and has form, must either be a work of art or destructive to art. The Commercialist, on the other hand, divides "manufactured articles" into those which are prepensely works of art, and are offered for sale in the market as such, and those which have no pretence and could have no pretence to artistic qualities. (33)

Without wanting to suggest that Anglo-Indians, least of all Kipling, were socialists, this chapter builds on such a socialistic view that art "is the expression of pleasure in the labour of production" (33). It is this union of work-pleasure in the spare-time writing of company men, which supplies the basis of the literary merit, the differently understood society, of Anglo-Indian literature.

Corporate Culture

Helping the domestic reader-as-citizen to think of empire as a potentially virtuous enterprise is one thing; far more difficult is encouraging a reader to make great personal sacrifices on its behalf, and in particular to eschew opportunities for personal enrichment. George Orwell cannily remarked that "civilized men do not readily move away from the centres of civilization" ("Rudyard Kipling" 83) and so, in addition to the powerful tradition of what we might call domestic imperial discourse, there exists a genre of colonial literature concerned neither with life in Britain in the age of empire nor with explaining the colonial Other to fellow Britons. In the Indian context, this genre was more concerned with articulating a distinct Anglo-Indian and, this chapter argues, corporate culture. To support the claim that there was an Anglo-Indian literature distinct from a metropolitan centre, I must first establish the degree to which such literature was capable of self-reflection and self-fashioning. This is not as easy as it perhaps sounds since, as Edmund Burke said during the Hastings impeachment, "The Company in India does not exist as a national colony ... The English in India are nothing but a seminary for the succession of officers. They are a nation of placemen; they are a republic; they are a commonwealth without a people" (285–6). P.J. Marshall confirms that Burke's estimation held true for at least the next forty years, when the Company in 1833 lost its monopoly on immigration.[2] Marshall adds that as late as 1901, according to the census, less than one-quarter of respondents listing their background as "European" were born in India ("The Whites of British India" 26).

With the East India Company – and later the Crown – recruiting its soldiers and administrators in Britain, and with the vast majority of these employees retiring back to Britain (the 1901 census reveals that only 5 per cent of the European population was over fifty years old), British India was never a settler colony like Australia, Canada, or New Zealand. William Browne Hockley, a retired Company man, prefaced his fictional sketches *The English in India* (1828) arguing against those who held fast to the stereotypes of the nabob:

> I have endeavoured to portray the English in India as they really exist – such as my own experience found them. Educated, for the greater part, in England, and forming in the East a society almost exclusively British, it is evident that they cannot exhibit differences of feeling, and scarcely of habit, so marked as some imagine. (v)

Yet if Anglo-India never conformed to the evolutionary models of nationalism in the settler colonies, Kipling's writing at the fin de siècle suggest how wrong it is to collapse Anglo-India with metropolitan culture.

If neither national nor even protonational, Company India was always unusually literary. In 1784 William Jones, Henry Thomas Colebrooke, and Nathaniel Halhed founded the Asiatic Society in Calcutta to enhance the study of Oriental research, the practice that would become known as Orientalism. As the seat of government, Calcutta had a lively print culture, and the college at Fort William from 1800 onwards produced a steady stream of educated, literary men whose amateur poetry frequently appeared in journals such as *The Calcutta Journal, The Asiatic Miscellany*, and *The Asiatic Journal*. Nigel Leask describes such poets as "eager to show off their imitations of the latest metropolitan models" (53). Leask admits, however, that the amateur quality of this poetry, written by civil servants in their leisure time, makes it challenging to sustain any claims of "geo-political self-consciousness" (55). The poetry by early nineteenth-century Company men, whether the romantic orientalism of John Leyden or the anti-romantic burlesques of Charles D'Oyly, could not be described as the basis for a national literature. Instead, Leask argues, they chronicle the "the idiosyncrasies and ennui of colonial life" (53) rather than revealing "any positive sense of identity or unity of purpose" (82).

It is not until the 1840s – when, as Mary Ellis Gibson argues, poetry ceased to be the dominant genre of belletristic writing (8) – that the sense of community begins to appear. One of the first Anglo-Indian poets to do so is James Henry Burke, whose *Days in the East* (1842) speaks of

> the mysterious mission which has sent
> The sons of Britain to a distant land, –
> The dispensation which nor battlement
> Nor armed phalanx ever can withstand;
> Nor by the mortal breath of ardour fanned,
> Or fenced by dictates of erratic zeal;
> But, heaven-directed, breaks upon the strand,
> A nation's thousand miseries to heal, –
> The true intent of all in glory to reveal. (2.36.316–24)

By the late 1840s and early 1850s, as in Britain, the novel replaced poetry as the predominant mode of literary expression. However, given the conditions under which Anglo-Indian poetry was produced – by writers writing in their limited spare time – the change in genre entailed a change in writer as well. Company India offered little space to sustain "professional" writers, as those emerging in London in the 1830s and 1840s. Like poetry, the early fiction of Anglo-India was still predominantly written by company men, but now often by company men at the end of their official careers. The major Company novelists – William Browne Hockley, John Lang, and William Delafield Arnold – each sketched the conditions of Anglo-Indian life from the perspective of retirement. This change altered their approach to representing Anglo-Indian life; alloyed with the generic capacity of the novel to represent entire social worlds, Anglo-Indian writers began exercises of critical self-reflection (a tendency borne out in the other major prose genres of Anglo-Indian writing: travelogues and memoirs). The remainder of this chapter is devoted to analysing two such novels, William Delafield Arnold's *Oakfield; Or Fellowship in the East* (1853) and George Otto Trevelyan's *The Competition Wallah* (1864). Neither Arnold nor Trevelyan is writing explicitly for an Anglo-Indian audience, but theirs are the first major literary representations of official Anglo-Indian life, its potential virtues, and the hazards that interpose between the ideals and the practicalities of imperial service.

William Delafield Arnold's *Oakfield; or Fellowship in the East*

William Delafield Arnold's *Oakfield* is based on the novelist's experience in the Company's military and civilian services, but was written in Britain and published for a British readership. Like an autobiography or a history, therefore, it is primarily a mediating text, purposing to explain a foreign object to a domestic audience.[3] However *Oakfield* is important because its "foreign object" is Anglo-Indian society, rather than Indian society. Indeed *Oakfield* is the first sustained novelistic representation of Anglo-Indian life. Moreover, since Arnold's purpose was to critique the unscrupulous behaviour of Anglo-Indians who were putatively serving Britain's national and moral interest, it is an excellent point of departure for a discussion of the distinguishing characteristics of Anglo-Indian corporate culture.

Set during the years surrounding the First Afghan War (1839–42), there is strong evidence that neither Arnold nor the novel's eponymous protagonist liked their Indian experiences very well.[4] Both saw a want of moral strength in the average Anglo-Indian, a fault that, in their minds, was compounded by an esprit de corps, which encouraged every individual to behave according to the standard of the lowest common denominator. The fate of Oakfield's first regimental friend, a young cadet named Arthur Vernon, demonstrates the corrupting effects of that corporate spirit. Vernon, an essentially good adolescent, lacks the courage to insist that his regimental colleagues behave properly and so instead he tolerates, before ultimately participating in, their debauchery. The demise of this cherubic character represents, in Arnold's mind at least, the greatest tragedy of Anglo-Indian society, namely that esprit de corps snuffed out all moral sparks, preventing the emergence of true Christian gentlemen and leaving the administrative classes of Company India as little more than a confederacy of rogues.

In short, Arnold in 1853 saw the same faults with Anglo-Indian society as were perceived by Edmund Burke in 1786.[5] For both men, the employees of the East India Company were failing to uphold the honour of their station and were discrediting not only the good name of Britain but also, in Arnold's view, of Christianity as well. Because it argues that very little has changed since the days of Hastings, *Oakfield* can be read as a serious indictment of the collegiate training system. Of course, such a reading could not be pursued without qualification; one would have to note that Edward Oakfield sees far more debauchery among military regiments than among the covenanted civil service; once he secures his transfer from the military to the civilian branch, he begins to enjoy his Indian experiences more, and finds less obnoxious behaviour among his colleagues. Despite these qualifications I think that the general critique still holds for, outside the Company of a small circle of kindred spirits, Oakfield never finds personal satisfaction in Anglo-Indian society. From the beginning, the novel's epigraph alludes to the pleasure Oakfield finds in solitary introspection. Taken from Mycerinus, it tells the reader, "He within / Took measure of his soul, and knew its strength, / And by that silent knowledge, day by day / Was calmed, ennobled, comforted, sustained." Even the "success" of his civilian career exists in proportion to the isolation granted by his solitary employment as a district collector in the tradition of *Vanity Fair*'s Jos Sedley.

There are only two significant deviations between the life of the author and his protagonist and these are the moments of dramatic conflict around which the plot is organized: Oakfield's court martial and his battlefield heroism during the Second Afghan War of 1848. Since these scenes, which combine elements of fantasy, melodrama, and moral exposition, are little more than set pieces deployed to "prove" the truth and the merit of Oakfield's position, they are of little interest other than to illuminate the continuing relevance of romantic conventions in the mid-century Victorian novel. The world view expressed by Oakfield, on the other hand, is very significant since it emanates from a member of one of the most influential families in the period. William was, even more than his brothers, morally akin to Dr Arnold and by his own admission it was out of deference to the Arnold fame that he published the first edition of *Oakfield* pseudonymously. It is only in the preface to the second edition, responding to accusations that anonymity is the refuge of cowards, that "Punjabee" reveals his true identity. There Arnold explains that he chose the disguise "because I did not wish that a name, for the sake of which I have so frequently met with kindness, should in any degree be compromised by any performance of mine" (x). In 1944 E.M. Forster praised the novel not because he thought William Arnold "an artist," but because, for him, *Oakfield* exemplifies the "Arnold integrity" (411). Until the 1970s, Forster's was the only appeal to extend Arnold's readership beyond area specialists.[6] For Forster the value of this novel is its scrutiny of how what I have been calling the virtuous empire holds up under a stern application of the Arnold family values.

When literary scholars began to focus more on imperialism, *Oakfield* received renewed attention as a novel of empire.[7] After all, this novel is basically a critique of British India by a young man who feels that Britons are not completing what he views as their duty towards the natives. With India providing the exotic setting and Indians providing the silent subjects for Arnold's disquisitions on Britain's imperial duty, it is almost as if *Oakfield* was written especially to provide grist for the mill of postcolonial critique. Certainly it would be easy to apply Gayatri Spivak's argument that even the best-intentioned critiques of empire from within inevitably perpetuate the epistemic violence of colonial discourse by continuing to represent the colonized as a silent mass unable to speak for themselves.[8] However, one could counter, Oakfield himself seems unwilling to participate in ignorant Orientalism, asking "What does, what can a subaltern in a native infantry regiment see or know of the people?" (1: 244). This is not to say that Oakfield does not subscribe to the Burkean conditions for a virtuous empire; on the contrary, Oakfield shows himself to have been, prior to his departure for India, convinced of the imperium. Privately, he wonders, "Was not every European in India engaged in the grand work of civilising Asia?" (1: 16); publicly he writes home, "The obvious work of every European in India seems to me to be to justify his position in a country not his own, by helping to civilise it" (1: 42). To his friends he confides, "I came out to this country with vague general notions of a great work of civilisation and reform, calling for labourers and so on; but I find this notion fade entirely away before the stupid realities of daily life" (1: 171).

Given Oakfield's confidence that the empire could be made virtuous, if only the colonial soldiers and administrators would behave as

Christian gentlemen, it is better to read the novel as a critique of imperial manners and psychology, in sympathy with Joseph Conrad's *Heart of Darkness*. Granting that the ways in which Oakfield corrects the behaviour of scoundrels like Cade and Stafford will be of interest to Arnold family scholars, the only points to my mind where *Oakfield* becomes really interesting occur in Arnold's description of the fellowship, especially in those scenes when Arnold tests his protagonist's morality against that of his comrades. Like Oakfield, Hugh Stanton and Henry Middleton are "men of character," unafraid to expatiate on moral subjects, and each has experienced disappointment in India which has led to their social isolation. Each feels he has been forced to live among heathen people, charged with completing never-ending and never-appreciated toil – except, in this case, the barbarous heathens who are in want of reform are the officers of the British military.

It would be incorrect to assume that Arnold thinks Anglo-India beyond redemption since through Stanton and Middleton he presents ideals of the *vir bonum* for, respectively, the military and civil branches of the Company's service. Oakfield takes refuge among those friends, telling Middleton after their first conversation that it is "a great help to hear any one talk of this country as one thinks an Englishman should do" (1: 162). But the fellowship is more than a refugee camp for the like-minded and at several points it provides the means for Arnold to illuminate the distinct characteristics of Anglo-Indian culture. Among these cultural practices is the way different characters mediate the effect of alienation. When Oakfield first meets Stanton, for example, the two men bond over Stanton's bitter observation about "how little people at home know or care, what a quantity of unhappiness is shipped off to this country every month":

> They talk of an Anglo-Indian Empire, and the fortunate young lads who get into that glorious service, but they forget that a life of exile is still a life of exile, and as such, to all but the most insensible, more or less a life of pain. (1: 101)

Stanton's assurance, that pain is felt by all who serve in India, becomes the litmus test for a character's membership in the Anglo-Indian community. Stanton, the bona fide graduate of Addiscombe, is much more than a Stoic; he masochistically invites pain and the narrator explains that he "felt, perhaps, a gloomy sort of satisfaction in returning to his duty, and in the very consciousness of his dislike for it he found comfort" (1: 4). Oakfield, in contrast, shares Stanton's belief in doing one's duty but at the same time he neither seeks nor derives any satisfaction from his gloom. For Oakfield, living and working in India is a spiritual calling; he left Oxford to escape the metaphysical hair-splitting that predominated there following the rise of the Tractarians and went out to India for his personal salvation. As Oakfield explains to Stanton, "My whole resolution about India was so sudden, and so negative; to get rid of the present was so much more my object than to arrange a future, that now I find myself actually started on a new reach of life with not even a shadow of an impression, I do not say as to its pains and pleasures, but its dangers and duties" (1: 7). And while there is no doubt that Oakfield encounters his fair share of pain and disappointment during that trial, he endures not because he has become accustomed to take pleasure from it but rather because he thinks himself to be acquiring immortal credit. Stanton's masochistic attitude coupled with his scepticism towards Oakfield's moralizing, alternatively, indicates how effective the corporate apparatuses have been in convincing agents that virtue can be found in the pursuit of an arbitrary and unpleasant task.

Arnold's description of Henry Middleton reflects more generously on the effectiveness of those apparatuses, even if the author and narrator themselves fail to perceive the corporation and its culture as the source. Middleton, who enters the narrative while Oakfield is travelling up-river to meet his new regiment, becomes Oakfield's truest Anglo-Indian friend on the basis of their first conversation, a conversation in which each alludes to and evidently approves of Edmund Burke's critique of empire.[9] Middleton is a man who "had been in India ten years, was fond of his profession, and hard work had greatly raised and improved him" (1: 155). *Oakfield*'s narrator then seizes upon this remarkable man and uses his anomalous virtue to deliver a general exculpation of the one class of "decent" Anglo-Indians:

> It must be allowed, indeed, to the Bengal civilians, that they are for the most part a hard-working set, and it is wonderful proof of the influence work has upon a man, that the young fop of eighteen or nineteen, with no better training than the hybrid half-school, half-college system of Haileybury can give him, is developed mostly into the persevering and sensible, often the zealous and able man of thirty. (1: 155)

The narrator assumes that Middleton, like all other Anglo-Indian civilians, has succeeded despite the hindrance of a Haileybury education, but in having Middleton argue that "much silent toil" is required "to keep the actual machine of government going" (1: 159), Arnold has reiterated the desire expressed by Governor General Wellesley fifty years earlier in his "Notes." Middleton reflects the Haileybury culture when he represents himself to Oakfield as a man who willingly participates in the "silent, unheeded, unthanked toil" of administering power. He realizes that "a good officer … has great power" in a district but nonetheless willingly foregoes the opportunity to "join in a triumphant advance," preferring to liken his task to those who "die in the trench before the successful stormers pass over their dead bodies to the breach" (1: 158–9).

With Stanton the product of Addiscombe and Middleton of Haileybury, Oakfield is the only properly ex-centric member of the fellowship and the reason he does not fit in is because he has been produced by other institutions.[10] Like the late nineteenth-century stereotype of the "globetrotter," Edward Oakfield appears in India as a domestic observer rather than as a professional administrator of the virtuous empire.[11] Uncultivated by imperial apparatuses, it is unsurprising that he is baffled by the actual existing conditions of imperial administration. Committed to the empire in principle, Oakfield never discerns his purpose: "I say to myself, how am I to apply all this [to the] problem? how do you work at it? when? where?" (1: 171). His confusion, I would argue, is a consequence of his institutional conditioning: "Religiously brought up as a child, [Oakfield] had passed a creditable career at Winchester; and, full of hopeful confidence, went up to Oxford as a student of Christ Church" (1: 14). This is a gloss for William Arnold's life under his father, the famous headmaster whose Rugby formed the basis for the modern English public school system. The innovation of Dr Arnold, as anyone who reads Thomas Hughes's *Tom Brown's School Days* (1857) will recall, was to establish character and individual morality as pedagogical objects equivalent in value to intellectual accomplishment and liberal humanism. And so it happens that Oakfield experiences great moral distress when the virtue cultivated by Arnoldian institutions conflicts with the moral virtue of the established Anglo-Indian institutions. Oakfield simply cannot reconcile the two: "I think it a very hard matter to decide … A man certainly owes something to the regiment, and is under a *prima facie* obligation to support its institutions, especially the most important one – the mess; but there are other obligations which outweigh this" (1: 72). This pronouncement typifies Oakfield's future responses to ethical conflict: when in doubt, he gives priority to his "other" obligations.

It might be proposed that those other obligations are simply his personal beliefs and that the narrative of Edward Oakfield shows both how frequent and how serious the conflict between personal and professional ethics can be. Certainly this seems the obvious conclusion based his response in the following exchange with Middleton:

> "As a mere arrangement for preserving the peace ... military law has, I think, a right to prescribe a certain code of manners, even as they, and as colleges, and other public institutions do a certain code of dress, habits, and even diet."
>
> "You cannot mean that a man is bound to submit to a code of manners which his own code of morals rejects." (2: 10)

Convinced that his primary duty is to secure his own soul, Oakfield resolves never to traduce his established sense of what is right. This moral security drives the action of the novel, since it inevitably creates conflict between Oakfield and his less scrupulous peers. He rejects the fraternity encouraged by Company institutions, such as the training colleges and the military esprit de corps, and in fact cares very little for the opinion of his fellow officers. When another friend, Lt Perkins, suggests that "the world" will presume Oakfield a craven if he refuses to duel with Lt Stafford, Oakfield responds that the only opinions which matter are those of his private, sympathetic friends (1: 274–6). His closing speech during his trial makes the same point, but in even stronger terms: "No authority is more usurped and unlawful, none imposes a more degrading and ignominious yoke upon the slaves who yield to it, than Public Opinion, – which is the World, – which is enmity with the one centre of all authority, – God" (1: 331). Public opinion always responds in kind and Oakfield is quickly "cut" by every Anglo-Indian society he visits.

But before we take Oakfield as an example of the tension between the individual and the collective, it is best to recall that in nearly every respect, Oakfield is an atypical Anglo-Indian. His disregard for public opinion startles even his truest friends. The profoundly antisocial Stanton, for one, cannot understand Oakfield's refusal to "round [his] corners off somehow to fit into the state of things we find, and which all our angularity will not alter" (1: 78). Similarly, the open-minded Wykham, who has "all [his] life been taught to respect and to dread" the opinion of the world, thinks Oakfield the expounder of "queer notions" (1: 299). Against such opposition, it is better to read Oakfield's obstinate morality – Forster called it Oakfield's "priggishness" – as his professional rather than his personal concern and the novel's opening pages support this interpretation. There, before Arnold ever indulges in one of this novel's many moral monologues, he reveals that Edward Oakfield's circumstances are very unusual for an ensign in the Company's service. Arriving at the age of twenty-one he is four years older than most ensigns, a sizable gap in a country where ten years of service distinguishes a person as a "veteran, according to Anglo-Indian estimation" (1: 3). Immediately, this sets Oakfield apart from his colleagues who were "sent forth over the threshold of life, at the critical age of seventeen, to make [their] way with such helps as [they] could find" (1: 47).[12]

Also, unlike his peers, Oakfield spent his late teenage years at Oxford. As Arnold's narrator explains, "*In those changing years*, from nineteen to twenty-one, his mind, hitherto quiescent or satisfied by the claims of school and college duty, began to work" (1: 14–15, emphasis added). In other words, Oakfield has reached intellectual, emotional, and moral maturity outside the corporate institutions of the East India Company. Thus it is that the narrator claims of Oakfield what could never be claimed for any true company man: "To tell the truth, [Oakfield] was still stunned by the wonderful change which a few weeks had wrought *for*, but not *in* him. He himself being unchanged, he was perplexed by the entire metamorphose of all his circumstances" (1: 12, emphasis in original). This declaration of internal psychological stability is really unrivalled in Anglo-Indian fiction, a body of texts which takes India's influence on human subjectivity as its sine qua non, the wellspring for the oft-repeated lament that no one in Britain really understands how things must be done in India.

Yet despite Arnold's adamant disapproval of mainstream Anglo-India and his certainty that a man like Oakfield could never fit in, his novel nevertheless testifies to the strength and persistence of corporate culture. Not only are Stanton and Middleton examples of the virtue that can emerge from the preparatory colleges. More significant is the fact that the best solution Arnold can propose for India is to replace a corrupt esprit de corps with another form of corporate membership, the novel's titular "Fellowship in the East." Arnold's fictional coalition is a group of hard-working, misunderstood employees who meet infrequently but never doubt that they know each other intimately. Their membership is open and the elder fellows spend considerable time and effort initiating junior candidates like Vernon, Perkins, and Wykham.

What is more, beyond their conviction that they have exclusive purchase on how things ought to be done (as with Oakfield's moral priggishness, or Middleton's faith in infrastructure projects), the fellows accept and even celebrate the fact that this knowledge will alienate them further from the countrymen whom they nominally represent. If all this sounds like the sociology of a Kipling story like "At the End of the Passage," it is because through his fellowship, Arnold demonstrates a commitment to corporate fraternity that is more Anglo-Indian than the present Anglo-Indian community itself.

The Competition Wallah

If Oakfield is an unrepentant prig who affects to be unaffected by India, then Henry Broughton, the hero of Trevelyan's *The Competition Wallah* (1863), supplies the more orthodox view of India's influence when he writes to his friend in England, "A man gains more new ideas, or, which comes to the same, gets rid of more old ones, within his first month on Indian soil than during any equal period of his life" (21). On the surface it seems strange to have such antithetical views expressed in mid-Victorian novels whose protagonists both claim Oxbridge degrees, especially if, as I have been arguing, it is precisely Oakfield's university experience which inoculates him from Indian influences. However, the contrasting reactions described in *Oakfield* and *The Competition Wallah* can be explained by the change intermediating their publication dates, namely, the substitution of the competition examination for the patronage system. In fact, according to most histories of the early Indian Civil Service, the competition examination was designed explicitly to attract top honours students from Oxbridge.[13] So whereas a university education irretrievably alienates Oakfield from Anglo-India in 1847–8, it becomes a requisite condition of Broughton's initiation in 1863.

With the competition exam, eligibility for an Indian career was extended to every British male. This meant that the relative cultural cohesion guaranteed by selecting candidates from within a small social network – the cohesion that made both William Arnold and Edward Oakfield such standouts – came under great strain. The new generation of civilians, known as the "competition wallahs," changed not only the demography of Anglo-India but also its social landscape. So if *Oakfield* might be described as a lament for Britain's failure to behave honourably as Christian gentlemen, *The Competition Wallah* has no doubt that men of sufficient character occupy the positions of power.

As with *Oakfield, The Competition Wallah* relegates the Indian native to part of the scenery; the real subjects of Broughton's letters are the British in India. Set in 1863, six years after the Indian Mutiny and five after the British Crown assumed direct control of its Indian empire, the novel celebrates the transition to administrative meritocracy. According to Broughton, this fairer system has ensured that the best talents are working in India, with the result that, "the days of corruption have long passed away. The hands of civil servants are as pure and as white as his summer trousers" (242). Comparing Britain to past empires, and indirectly answering Adam Smith's charge that a mercantile corporation is incapable of wielding sovereignty justly, he insists with confidence:

> It is a rare phenomenon this of a race of statesmen and judges scattered throughout a conquered land, ruling it, not with an eye to private profit, nor even in the selfish interests of the mother country, but in the single-minded solicitude for the happiness and improvement of the children of the soil. (149)

This praise of the virtuous empire, full of noble and disinterested administrators, is the apotheosis of the vision expressed in Richard Wellesley's "Notes" to create "a sufficient supply of men qualified to fill the high offices of the State with credit to themselves and with advantage to the public" ("Notes" 723).

Partly, the demise of corruption is attributed to improved methods of passive surveillance which has eradicated the necessity for social pretence. The administrators of India may not naturally be inclined towards honest work, Broughton admits, but its members quickly realize that in such a transparent society honest work is the only option. He cites, among other prudent practices, the positive effects generated by the publication of every official salary and promotion in the annual *Gazetteers*: "There is no temptation to display; for every member of society knows the exact number of rupees which you draw on the fifteenth of each month" (146–7). Such knowledge forecloses the opportunities for social climbing which plague and intrigue the society of contemporary domestic novels like Braddon's *Lady Audley's Secret* (1862) and Dickens's *Great Expectations* (1861); in India no one can inflate his perceived income through fashion, carriages, or parties. Broughton asks, "What well-regulated female can make dress an object in a society of a dozen people who know her rank to a tittle and her income to a pice?" (141). Modes of deception, under whose aegis Broughton includes fashion, gossip, and to an extent even literature, have little practical function in such a world, where work is the single index of social standing.[14] Combined with Broughton's praise for vigorous provincial life – "Where there is so much work to be done by any one who will put his hand to the plough, [that] men have no time to quarrel about the direction and depth of the furrows" (150) – this critique of urban lassitude and fashionable society places Trevelyan as a forerunner of Kipling.

The difference between Trevelyan's vision and Kipling's is palpable in the confidence each holds that Anglo-India is a meritocracy. Kipling obviously held no such faith in the upper-class's ability to discern merit but Trevelyan makes the unqualified assertion that all positions in the Indian administration "are open to every subject of the Queen, though his father be as poor as Job subsequently to the crash in that patriarch's affairs, and though he does not number so much as a butler of a member of Parliament among his patrons and connexions" (147). Proving the existence and virtue of this meritocratic system is the chief object of Trevelyan's novel and, accordingly, he pays particular attention to the principle of open competition. To achieve this purpose, Trevelyan invents a foil for Broughton, an erstwhile college chum. Charles Simkins is meant to be the original recipient of the letters; the conceit for the publication of *The Competition Wallah* is that Simkins has undertaken to forward the letters to the editor of *Macmillan's*.

Along with those letters, Simkins provides a covering letter of introduction and it is there that Trevelyan clarifies how these prizes will only ever be won by men of a particular character, a character wholly consistent with Uncle Macaulay's intention. Simkins establishes the contrast when he describes his friendship with Broughton in terms of the classical fraternity between Damon and Pylades. "Our characters," he explains, "were admirably fitted to supply what was wanting in the other" (2). And so, whereas Simkins calls himself "the more thoughtful and intellectualler of the two," the one who "pondered out in solitude the great problems of existence," Broughton is "the more practical and quick sighted," the one who "lived with the men of action" and "wrote and talked, wielded the oar and passed the wine cup, [and] debated on the benches of the Union high questions of international morality and ecclesiastical government" (2). As Simkins tells it, as their undergraduate days drew to an end both men decided to try for an Indian career.

Through their opposing characters, Trevelyan allegorizes the antagonism between the two dominant forms of imperial desire circulating among the middle classes in nineteenth-century Britain. Simkins represents the idealist reformer, who is "fired at the idea of being placed with almost unlimited power among a subject-race who would look up to me for instruction and inspiration" (3). He thus conceives of India as a laboratory, where one could test the efficacy of Europe's most radical social ideas before importing the successful ones back to England. Such opinions gesture towards the intellectual movements that shaped both the English middle class and its imperial enterprise in the first half of the nineteenth century: utilitarianism and evangelicalism. Simkins makes the association explicit, as he waxes on the prospects for an Indian career: "What a position for a philosopher! What for a philanthropist! Above all, what for a philosophic philanthropist!" (3). As Simkins continues, he alludes to his "advanced opinions on the destination and progress of our race" (4) and the reader familiar with the Company's involvement with India cannot miss this allusion to William Bentinck, the aristocratic utilitarian who, on the commencement of his seven-year tenure as governor general, is supposed to have written to Jeremy Bentham: "I am going to British India, but I shall not be governor general. It is you who shall be governor general" (qtd. in Cohen 8). Likewise, it is hard to dissociate Simkins's humanistic benevolence from that of men like Charles Grant, the long-time director and sometime chairman of the board who advocated the intellectual and religious improvements of the natives in accordance with Christian ideals and who also played an instrumental role in establishing the Christian missions in Bengal.

Broughton, alternatively, represents the new imperial man, the subject whose desire has neither utilitarian nor evangelical motivation. To Simkins's "mission of reforming society by [his] pen," Broughton pronounces "indifference" (18). Throughout his letters, we see that Broughton aspires to secure neither social justice nor civilization for the wretched of the earth. Unlike Oakfield, Broughton is unexcited by the prospects of either improving India or saving his soul. Rather, he aspires to work. Broughton's zeal, if we can call it that, is disinterested professionalism and he chose India, according to Simkins's prefatory letter, simply because he maintains "that the vital object to be looked for in the choice of a line in life was to select one that would present a succession of high and elevating interests" (3). As many Anglo-Indian writers before and after him attest, an Indian career is represented as one of the best guarantees for such variety: "Work in India is so diversified as to always be interesting" (137). Later he will confide to Simkins, "It is a great thing to live in a community where every one has work to do, and where almost every one does it with a will" (236).

The relative fortunes of Simkins and Broughton comprise Trevelyan's judgment as to the best type of character for company service: Broughton places third overall and wins his Indian career; Simkins fails utterly. Yet, even here Trevelyan is careful to ensure that his readers realize that Simkins has not in any way been hard done by and so, after a few more paragraphs Simkins exposes himself as a deluded, idle, and self-important character, the author of useless and unpublished articles, such as "The Subjectivity of Buckle" which lately has been rejected by this particular editor, and verse "in the vein of Browning" (5), which readers should infer will meet the same doom.

The competition exam is designed to exclude men who would be kings like Simkins and to reward instead professionally ambitious men like Broughton. Yet, although it is generally accepted that Trevelyan's opinions on the abstract speculation of utilitarian or evangelical thought varied little from those held by both his father and uncle, it is important to observe that, despite having Simkins fail the competition exam, this author is not disavowing utilitarianism or evangelicalism tout court. Broughton's penultimate letter, which represents how much has changed since his initially disinterested application for an Indian career, affirms the civilizing mission: "To educate, to enlighten, to strike off the fetters of custom and superstitions, this is the grand duty the fulfilment of which we must further by all honest means" (406). Like Arnold's Middleton, Trevelyan's Broughton argues that enlightenment cannot arrive instantaneously. The "battle of Truth," writes Broughton, will likely not be won "in our lifetime, nor mayhap in the lifetime of our sons" and the British in India must simply "labour in the way in which it is given to us to labour, or not at all," by which Broughton means the development of "colleges and railroads, libraries and newspapers, national justice and moderation" – in short, everything that Edmund Burke demanded eighty years earlier in his speech supporting Fox's India Bill (406–7). Answering Burke's charges, Broughton insists, "As far as India is concerned, we do our duty by the commonwealth of nations" (373). So, although Trevelyan pledges allegiance to liberal imperial ideals, his summary dismissal of Simkins demonstrates his belief that the qualities through which Britain claims the virtue of its empire, be they the spread of Christianity or improved governance, are not those the administration must seek in its employees.

Having made this point, Trevelyan allows the Simkinses of the world to slide into marginal oblivion, and Broughton's narrative commences. The first letter begins with an apology for not having written sooner.

He attributes the two-week delay to the "low spirits" brought about by his acute sense of loneliness which he now, with a fortnight's wisdom, understands to be the universal plight of the newly arrived civilian (6–7). This malaise provides an opportunity for Trevelyan's analysis of Anglo-Indian society. In India in 1863, the civil servants are roughly split between two groups: Haileyburians and Competition Wallahs. As Broughton belongs to the latter group and finds himself profoundly unhappy, the Cambridge graduate decides that "the advantages of Haileybury outweighed the defects" (8). The competition process, which determines eligibility for the civil service solely on the basis of exam results, receives harsh criticism, primarily because of its alienating effect. Loneliness, Broughton argues, would not have been as debilitating for previous generations since, back then, every new recruit would arrive already in possession of a two-year acquaintance with his Haileybury cohort. Thus the Haileybury graduate could look forward to the natural hospitality and fraternity extended by the college alumni already established in India. In this way Haileybury could unite all Anglo-Indians irrespective of age, providing a common point of reference and a positive symbol against which all could contrast their negative Indian experiences.

For Broughton, nostalgia for this collegiate esprit de corps is palpable. As the letter continues, Broughton wonders whether the current competition system might be altered somehow so that "a sense of brotherhood would again unite the members of the Civil Service, bound together by the most indissoluble ties" (17). Despite never having attended Haileybury, he feels that he too can commune with its graduates and appreciate the sympathetic homosocial bonds created when they "rowed together on the Lea ... larked together in Hertford ... [and] shared in that abundant harvest of medals which rewarded the somewhat moderate exertions of the reading man at the East-India College" (8). In this way, Haileybury functions as what French sociologist Pierre Nora has called "a site of memory." In his work on memory in late twentieth-century Western culture, Nora elaborates that the *lieux de mémoire* "make their appearance by virtue of the deritualization of our world ... mark[ing] the rituals of a society without ritual; integral particularities in a society that levels particularity; signs of distinction and of group membership in a society that tends to recognise individuals only as identical and equal" (Nora 12). One could argue that Anglo-India after the competition exam was just such a deritualized territory, and looking for evidence, we could point to Broughton's anxiety about his isolated position: "Few of us are lucky enough to have more than two or three acquaintances among the men of our own years; and, while our seniors persist in looking on us as a special class, we have no bond of union among ourselves" (8). For a young recruit, thrown into an Indian career without any cultural or communal support, the idea of Haileybury and its esprit de corps provides security and a common, if imagined, context in which to complete his work.

This desire for an absent fraternity is reinforced institutionally in the new Anglo-India. With Haileybury receding further into the historical background, other modes of unifying diversely spread communities become more prominent. Now, in addition to the publication of employee's salaries, titles, and promotions, the liberal rhetoric of meritocracy, encouraged first in the competition examination, has become a distinct feature of the corporate culture. According to Broughton,

> An Englishman can never be comfortable if he is in a false position; and he never allows himself to be in a true position unless he is proud of his occupation, and convinced that success will depend on his own efforts. These agreeable sentiments are experienced to the full by an Indian civil servant ... He is well aware that his advancement does not hang upon the will and pleasure of this or the other great man, *but is regulated by the opinion entertained of his ability and character by the service in general.*" (143–4, emphasis added)

In this climate, where public scrutiny is universal and omnipotent, where work is the overdetermining facet of life, Henry Broughton represents very nearly the ideal Macaulay had in mind when he first suggested the wholesale reform of civil service appointments.

What is even more interesting is how this unyielding scrutiny and its accompanying compulsion to work has become a source of pride for company men. Broughton, for example boasts, "I know of no better company in the world than a rising civilian ... In most cases, the normal condition of a clever Englishman between the ages of twenty-two and thirty is a dreary feeling of dissatisfaction about his work and his prospects" (142). Service in the Indian civil service is of a different order, he argues, because "there is no career which holds out such certain and splendid prospects to honourable ambition" (148). Keeping in mind Macaulay's intention to attract men psychologically disposed to compete purely for the sake of competition, we might further note how Trevelyan's picture of the modern civil servant pays the ultimate compliment to his uncle's plan. Broughton boasts to his domestic correspondent that he lives, "where intolerance and bigotry are at a ruinous discount; where liberal and unselfish views are as plentiful as blackberries at the bottom of a Surrey valley" (236).

Trevelyan's portrait also suggests that aristocratic virtue has become embedded in Anglo-Indian culture. According to Broughton, the modern company man is impervious to "dissatisfaction about his work and his prospects, and a chronic anxiety for 'a sphere'" (142):

> It is impossible for him to have any misgiving concerning the dignity and importance of his work. His power for good and evil is almost unlimited ... He is the member of an official aristocracy, owning no social superior; bound to no man; fearing no man. (143)

But in that same letter, in a gesture which confirms the ambivalent status of the subject-in-power, Broughton deflates this portrait of unfettered power, as he reveals the full disciplinary effects of the idea of the virtuous empire and the rhetoric of aristocratic virtue. The aristocrat, that is, becomes the (willingly) dutiful servant:

> He never speaks of his duties except in a spirit of enthusiasm, or his profession without a tone of profound satisfaction. He no more dreams of "a sphere" than for a pentagon or a rhomboid. (145)

The picture of a nearly homogenous group of liberally minded administrators who are so satisfied with their occupation that it eliminates the need for all other social groups gives new meaning to the word preoccupied. To use Benedict Anderson's phraseology, if there is an imagined community of Anglo-Indians, then it exists as a community created by dreams of work and fulfilling one's duties.

4 Corporate Culture in Post-Company India

Despite Macaulay's confidence that the competition examination would prevent all but the most incorruptible candidates from gaining a place, the closure of the colleges in 1858, following the Crown's assumption of direct rule in India, renewed the imperial control crisis.[1] For not only did the competition exam open the possibility of an Indian career to any British subject[2] (whereas once it was limited to the social circles surrounding the directors who controlled the patronage) but it also eliminated any opportunity to create the esprit de corps which men like Wellesley and Malthus took as the core of panoptic governance. In 1872 Dr George Birdwood began a campaign to reform the competition exam, arguing that "the present system of competition has necessarily severed the personal tie, which bound the old India House and the servants of the Company together ... the salutary interest in their servants which all masters by nature desire to take and without which it is unreasonable to look for loyalty, independence of spirit, and discipline among men" (10). What is worse, Birdwood explains, is that this new system was failing to draw the crème of Oxbridge, but rather was attracting candidates from much more diverse class backgrounds.[3] It turns out that Birdwood's observations about British India's changing demography did not justify his worries about the civil service infrastructure. When competition exams replaced colleges, Anglo-India did not relapse into corruption, nor did Anglo-Indians cease thinking of themselves as a united community. Fifty years on, Sara Jeannette Duncan could still write a story that unproblematically endorses this view. In "A Mother in India" (1903), Duncan's protagonist describes the scene as she boards a ship bound for Bombay following her husband's furlough:

> I looked up and down the long saloon tables with a sense of relief and of solace; I was again among my own people. They belonged to Bengal and to Burma, to Madras and to the Punjab, but they were all my people. I could pick out a score that I knew in fact, *and there were none that in imagination I didn't know*. (63, emphasis added)

By now, nearly every student of modern literature is familiar with Benedict Anderson's thesis on the relationship between literature and imagined communities, and Duncan's short story suggests that literary texts would be a good place to search for the afterimages of the preparatory colleges and the consolidation of the corporate ethic.

Though the arrival of Kipling is usually taken to inaugurate Anglo-Indian literature, we can see the coincident rise of Anglo-Indian literature in the years following the decline of the collegiate training system. Written in India, often printed at Indian presses or serialized in Indian periodicals, a growing number of poems, short stories, and novels testified to the emergence of an Anglo-Indian voice which speaks in the register of a corporate culture.[4] The preponderance of work and professionalism, of duty and sacrifice in Anglo-Indian fiction confirms that the Company's administrative ethos, the culture developed in its colleges, continued to influence Anglo-Indian society long after the Company itself became irrelevant. In the fiction of Anglo-India, we can trace how colonial texts work to produce and sustain the consent and obedience of the governing classes, incorporating new colonial administrators into a way of living that Pierre Bourdieu would call the colonial *habitus*, that is, into the unspoken habits, bodily skills, styles, tastes, and other non-discursive knowledge that might be said to "go without saying" in a community. In the case of Anglo-India, an administrative society where nearly every utterance was written down, recorded, and archived, the strongest traces of the *habitus* can be found around the second half of the nineteenth century, when the small community of British administrators began exercises in self-representation.

It is important to separate Anglo-Indian literature from the broader and longer tradition of British writing about India. Anglo-Indian literature, as I am using the term, refers to those works written by Britons living in India and so excludes from its canon writers like Elizabeth Hamilton, Wilkie Collins, Harriet Martineau, or G.A. Henty.[5] In addition, Anglo-Indian literature is usually, but not always, less interested in native Indians than in the community of administrators themselves. Even with these restrictive filters, Anglo-Indian literature was so prolific that the editors of *The Cambridge History of English and American Literature* (1907–21) ranked it second among the regional types of English literature (ahead of English-Canadian and behind Anglo-Irish literature).[6] Inevitably, this editorial typology raises a familiar question regarding such bodies of text, namely the degree to which we might classify them as "national" literatures, nascent or otherwise. Nor is this question unimportant since the category of "national literature" implies we take a particular sociological approach to the relationship between authors and their audiences. Since thus far I have suggested that Anglo-Indian literature be read in terms of corporations and corporate ethos while at the same time making recourse to Benedict Anderson's work on literature and the origins of nationalism, it remains to be seen how Anglo-Indian literature of the late nineteenth and early twentieth centuries is not quite national.

The conditions under which Anglo-Indian literature can be called national are different from those for literatures from the settler colonies (like Australia, Canada, and New Zealand) or the planter colonies (like Jamaica and Ireland), if only because British India lacked a regular system of immigration, either voluntary or involuntary.[7] Yet despite the limited routes to India, communities of Europeans did gradually cohere and by the 1870s literary critics began to notice that something distinct from mainstream English culture was being produced in the Indian colonial space. Edwin Arnold, translator of *The Bhagavad Gita*, was one of the earliest to identify this movement. Writing a preface to Phil Robinson's collection of short essays *In My Indian Garden* (1871), Arnold cites Robinson's portrayal of the intimate connection existing between Anglo-Indians and the territory and people they administer as a thing so original as to constitute "the beginnings of a new field of Anglo-Indian literature" (ix). Robinson is a member of what might be called the "first wave" of Anglo-Indian authors, along with Alexander Allardyce (*The City of Sunshine* [1877]) and Iltudus Thomas Prichard (*The Chronicles of Budgepore* [1870]). Each of these authors published his work in India (in Allahabad at the Pioneer Press) before publishing it in Britain, suggesting that Anglo-Indian writers of the 1870s were becoming more concerned about representing themselves within their community than about their reception in the metropolis. What differentiated this group from earlier Anglo-Indian writers, such as Philip Meadows Taylor (*Confessions of a Thug* [1839]; *Seeta* [1873]) or William Browne Hockley (*Pandurang Hari, or Memoirs of a Hindoo* [1826]; *Tales of the Zenana* [1827]; *The English in India* [1828]), is that writers like

Robinson seemed genuinely unconcerned about English audiences; his narrator's unglossed references to "dak bungalow moorghees" and the like suggest he is addressing not the London but rather the Simla and Calcutta set.

Anglo-Indians themselves were soon asserting the character of their distinct society, including among them the young Rudyard Kipling. In one of his earliest contributions to *The Civil and Military Gazette,* Kipling goes further than Edwin Arnold, claiming much more than a field for Anglo-Indian literature. He argues that the consequence of the growing difference between Anglo-India and the "effete civilization" of England will be an Anglo-Indian "poesy ... national and unfettered" ("Music" 44–5). This claim becomes ever more precocious when we recall that it was made in 1884, that is, before Kipling became Kipling and broadened the scope of Anglo-Indian literature, not only personally but through his legion of imitators. Taken together with his habitual claim to be speaking on behalf of "mine own people," Kipling's youthful vision seemingly answers the question of Anglo-Indian nationality in the affirmative. At the very least, if it is not already there, then Anglo-Indian literature soon hopes to be national.

The word "national," however, and Kipling's use of it, should be unpacked and placed in the context of its use in the late Victorian period. Although literary scholars are now inclined to understand the relationship between literature and nationhood through the critical lens provided by Benedict Anderson, to the Victorians of Kipling's era nationality had other implications. Nation assumes its modern aspect in post-Westphalian Europe and as a philosophical category its primary source is found in Johann Gottfreid von Herder's romantic notion of a *volk*. In 1784 Herder theorized nation-ness in reaction to the homogenizing threat posed by French rationalism, especially by the contractual language offered by Jean-Jacques Rousseau. While contract theories saw nations as accumulations of individuals associating because they share common goals, Herder saw a globe populated by nations uniquely determined each by an essential *geist* (Herder 8). In British discussions of nation-ness, it is Herder's romantic racism rather than Rousseau's rationalist definition which was most often taken up.[8]

Given the high value Kipling places on a single drop of "white" blood (as in the short story "His Chance in Life"), it is hard to believe that he thought the community "Anglo-Indian" would ever be a nation racially distinct from the Anglo-Saxons. One way to understand how Kipling meant "national" is to scrutinize his choice of complement, i.e., the word "unfettered," which evokes the strings by which a parent keeps a developing child in order. From this interpretation, the sort of poesy the young Kipling had in mind can be affiliated with that Victorian discourse which argued for the rise of a network called "Greater Britain," with Mother England (or Britain/Britannia depending on your ideological preference) holding together a large and diverse family, united but relating to each other through inflections of the broader, shared semiotics and traditions.[9]

This picture of an organic, developing Anglo-Indian nation evokes the developmental model for decolonization outlined by Bill Ashcroft, Gareth Griffiths, and Helen Tiffin in *The Empire Writes Back* (1989), a seminal text in the area of postcolonial studies. These authors aptly describe the factors behind the emergence of a "national or regional consciousness" when they say that linguistic and cultural difference is produced either by "physical and geographical conditions, or the cultural practices [the colonial people] have developed in a new land" (5, 10).[10] In fact, Kipling himself is cited as an important transitional figure, working at a moment when colonial Anglophones began to assert their "difference from the imperial centre" (5). However, the substance of that difference, and whether it is enough to produce anything resembling a protonation, is debatable in the case of Anglo-India. That is to say, while India's "exotic" geography would (and did, if one considers the first two chapters of any Anglo-Indian memoir) alienate any colonial civil servant from the imperial centre, it is also true that the Indian subcontinent was itself geographically diverse and the colonial agents were spread thinly across it, making it very unlikely that a coherent consciousness could develop around a common geographic experience.

Following Ashcroft, Griffiths, and Tiffin, Anglo-Indian nationality, if it exists, will be found in the second condition, "the cultural practices … developed in the new land"; in this case, even a quick glance will confirm that what distinguishes Anglo-Indian writers from their British contemporaries is the emphasis they place on work and professionalism. Deborah Cohen has persuasively argued that Victorian middle-class identity revolved instead around passionate attachments to (domestic) things (xv). However, while Victorians in England were busy self-identifying through accumulations of things, company men in India were self-identifying through their accomplishments at work. Certainly Victorian fiction ignores neither the working professional nor the effect of that work on an individual's identity. Rather, what characterizes Anglo-Indian fiction is the singular, uniform, and powerful impression that *doing work* has on the structure of society. The Victorian novel may be populated by lawyers, clerks, soldiers, and merchants but very rarely are these characters portrayed actually working.[11] Anglo-Indian writers, on the other hand, seemingly revel in describing the quotidian affairs of civilian administrators. No doubt it is this fascination which led the late Victorian critic Andrew Lang, in his review of Kipling's early fiction, to call all previous Anglo-Indian fiction profoundly dull and boring.[12]

On the basis that work significantly informed the way this colonial community lived and thought, and accepting that employment in British India was overwhelmingly regulated by a single employer, I would submit that it is reasonable to pay close attention to the corporate structure of the British Indian administration. This enables a move away from those understandings of consciousness that take racial nationalism or geographical regionalism as the marker of community. If it is work that determines one's standing in the Indian scheme of things, then by extension it is one's relationship to and within the corporation, not the nation, which should demand our attention when we come to examine their cultural artefacts. Taking a corporate view of Anglo-Indian culture, we can understand why so many of its writers emphasize the inescapability of surveillance; the desire for recognition and the accompanying fatalism when one's toil is unappreciated; and the virtue of fraternity with kindred spirits.

While the 1850s marked the decline of the Company's monopoly in India and though the competition exams destroyed the familiarity bred by the patronage system, the establishment of Indian newspapers, the improved transportation infrastructure, and the rise of Anglo-Indian novels fostered a different sense of belonging, one that increasingly revolved around one's commitment to one's profession. Another way of thinking about this change is to say that fraternity among people who were once *related* (in pre-competition, culturally homogenous Company India) would now (in postpatronage, relatively diverse British India) be *cultivated*. Here we are furnished with a robust example of what Edward Said has called the move from filiated to affiliated communities. In *The World, the Text, and the Critic* (1983) Said uses the concept of affiliation to explain how culture works to repair the alienation that occurs with the turbulence of modernity. Affiliation sutures communities together by showing them not a common biological but a cultural heritage: "affiliation becomes a form of representing the filiative process to be found in nature, although affiliation takes validated nonbiological social and cultural forms" (23). What could once be stated without doubt in early Anglo-Indian memoirs had now become so fragile that it required new forms of institutional support, including especially in the area of fiction. The efficacy of these new institutions can be seen in the fact that for both stages – i.e., for both Company and British India – the coherence of Anglo-India is a fact universally presumed by its membership.

In British India, the security of the empire relied upon the (relatively) faithful and honest service of its (relatively) underpaid and (relatively) underappreciated agents. The crisis of the Indian Mutiny in 1857–8 not only accentuated imperial anxieties at home, but it led some to question the very premises upon which Britain continued to hold India. This chapter considers the affiliative work performed by Anglo-Indian literature in the period 1870–1900. Reading through the fiction of Henry Stewart Cunningham, Rudyard Kipling, and Sara Jeannette Duncan, we observe how the image of the foolishly optimistic colonial agent – the Simkins satirized in Trevelyan's *The Competition Wallah* – is replaced gradually by the grim stoic, the character who somehow draws self-satisfaction from his poorly remunerated and publicly unacknowledged labour. What emerges is the constitutive role literature plays in affiliating individuals. Here we see literature itself providing the substitute compensation – binding Anglo-Indian readers into community by promoting that old canard, that misery loves company.

If I Didn't Laugh, I'd Cry: Resolving Corporate Culture's Broken Promises

The first wave of Anglo-Indian literature engages the peculiarities of its corporate culture humorously. Robert C. Caldwell's collection of comic verse, *The Chutney Lyrics*, published in Madras in 1871, for example, contains among its sketches "Captain Brown of the Police," whose titular captain buffoonishly declares the name of his beloved to be "Sweeter still than breath of lilies, yes than music sweeter yet – / Sweet as when you read PROMOTED to your name in the Gazette" (14). Iltudus Thomas Prichard's *Chronicles of Budgepore* (1870) likewise gently satirizes the "red tape and whitewash" (6) of official life in a small station the narrator insists is "representative" (3) of Anglo-India.

Henry Stewart Cunningham's *Chronicles of Dustypore* (1875) is the first text to engage seriously with, and find grim pleasure in, the conditions of Anglo-Indian service. The novel opens with the claim that only "one Englishman in a hundred thousand" even "knows or cares anything about India" (1), and that the "ninety-nine thousand nine hundred and ninety-nine ... neither know nor wish to know" the particular history of Dustypore's incorporation into the British Empire. Cunningham's Dustypore is a "Miltonic hell" (4) governed and occupied by the British for no economic or military reason. It is a community of masochists, where women insist upon upholding traditions of visiting each other during the hottest two hours of the afternoon and where men labour through "heat, monotony, fatigue, hot hours in sweltering courts, weary struggling through the prose of officialdom, [and] tiresome warfare against sun and dust" (132). Though Cunningham looks benevolently upon his characters, he bemoans the futility of their lives, spent in a climate "breathing sulphurous blasts, glowing with intolerable radiance, [and] begirt with whirlwinds of dust" (126). Yet despite these inhuman conditions, Cunningham's colonial hellscape produces remarkably admirable individuals. The chief official in the district, Mr Strutt, is an ideal company man: one who "had concentrated into his own person the functions and attributes of his employers of the Board" (7). Opposed to this "indefatigable" (7) character are a trio of board members, who know little about the practicalities of administration. Cunningham's narrator observes, "The maxim, 'like master like man,' was as far as possible from being verified in the case of Mr Strutt and his superiors" (8).

Though the *Chronicles of Dustypore* ostensibly follows the romance of the gallant soldier Sutton and the beautiful Maud, it is the anti-hero Boldero who receives the narrator's deepest sympathy. Boldero is a district officer, "one of the Queen's good bargains," whose "mind teemed with schemes for the regeneration of mankind":

> Disappointment could not damp his hopefulness, nor difficulty cool his zeal; he was an enthusiast for improvement and the firmest believer in its possibility. Against stupidity, obstinacy, the blunders of routine, official *vis inertia*, he waged a warfare ... The little bit of the world on which he was able to operate was continually being carved into some improved condition. (141)

Boldero is a paragon of "administrative effectiveness" who feels structural inefficiencies and injustices "as a personal misfortune" and devotes himself to their eradication (142). In short, he is viewed as "a perfect treasure in a land where energy and enthusiasm are hard to keep at boiling heat, and where to get a thing done, despite the piles of official correspondence it gets buried under, is a result as precious as it is difficult of achievement" (144). He also falls in love immediately with Maud, but he is as useless at courtship as he is capable at governing. Supremely worthy, Boldero endures a triple disappointment: first when Maud marries Sutton; later when he watches Sutton's friend Desvoeux seduce her; and finally when he must act as Sutton's nurse while Maud grovels for her husband's forgiveness.

The *Chronicles of Dustypore,* being one of the first celebrations of thankless labour, cannot quite imagine what to do with a character like Boldero. Sutton returns to England a general with his devoted wife, leaving no fixed role for Boldero. Stuck in the conventions of the romance genre, Cunningham contrives a resolution: on the novel's final page, as Sutton receives a hero's parade and the personal thanks of Queen Victoria herself, Maud, basking in the reflected glory "jumps up with an exclamation,"

> for she has recognised a familiar face – it is Boldero, who is making his way to them through the crowd. He brings a blushing lady on his arm, and he is blushing too, and there are introductions and greetings which sound as if his old love-wound had been healed by the only effectual remedy. (374–5)

The fiancée ex machina seemingly resolves the narrative's irresolvable complexities – the thwarted heterosexual desire of Boldero for Maud; the homosexual tension between Boldero and Sutton – in ways that some critics would describe as an author pandering to his audience's expectation for a satisfying ending. However, as Rob Breton has argued, the device of deus ex machina can also "be subversive, undercutting generic conventions, and challenging cultural assumptions" ("Ghosts" 558), opening up new ideological possibilities. The blushing Boldero at the end of the *Chronicles of Dustypore* seems almost embarrassed to be there, out-of-place in a conventional metropolitan narrative where colonial service is duly recognized by the British public – a most unlikely prospect given Cunningham's opening estimate on the number of Englishman interested in India.

Vivat Haileyburia!

As Anglo-Indian literature developed, authors began to find more satisfactory ways of representing the tenets of corporate culture. Consider, for example, how Anglo-Indian fiction sustains one of those Haileyburian objectives, perpetual publicity. We will recall that at Malthus's Haileybury, the detailed publication of a student's results relative to his peers was one of the primary "means of exciting emulation and industry" (*Statements* 49). Through publicity, the Company sought to precondition the ethical behaviour of its field agents by making them think a) that they were always being observed and b) that public opinion was the barrier to promotion. In this feature of the corporate ethic, the Company enjoyed great success since, despite the fact that imperial administrators were spread thinly across the subcontinent, Anglo-Indian diarists and memoirists regularly and unproblematically state that everyone in India knows everything about everyone else. This confidence is quite remarkable given the geographical range of these administrators and the nearly non-existent communication network.

However, because feelings of transparency were initiated at East India College, their continuance was jeopardized in 1853 when the competition examination broke Haileybury's monopoly on training the company men. How then might the panoptic effect, where community members policed and disciplined themselves under a state of permanent suspicion, be preserved? There is no doubt of its continuing necessity since the barriers to the direct management of employee behaviour were not reduced when the Crown substituted for the Company in 1858. Policy was still devised in London and Calcutta, and the progress of communication networks in the latter half of the nineteenth century was not as effective as one might have thought. As Kipling makes clear in one of his earliest stories, even the mighty telegraph, with its promise of instant communication, still in the 1880s failed to overcome the distance between headquarters and field agents. In "His Chance in Life" we see how the responsibility for a riot falls on an isolated clerk in Tibasu, "a forgotten little place" on the east coast telegraph line (1: 88). Despite the presence of that communication network, when an uprising takes place, the clerk receives no orders from his superiors and so must respond independently. While the story is often read today for Kipling's racialized representation of that instinctual response – the native clerk who has "a drop of white blood" (1: 89) in his veins and so is able briefly to assume command and quell the riot – it also discloses the fragility of imperial power in British India.[13] Confronted by a rebellion the imperium conflates on this one agent and "until the Assistant Collector came, the Telegraph Signaller was the Government of India in Tibasu" (1: 90–1).

Yet even in the absence of an effective replacement for college discipline and despite the continuing isolation of agents from the imperial centre, a great deal of late nineteenth-century Anglo-Indian literature continues to insist that India is a transparent social space. Here is the famous opening to Kipling's "The Phantom Rickshaw" (1888):

> One of the few advantages that India has over England is a great Knowability. After five years' service, a man is directly or indirectly acquainted with the two or three hundred Civilians in his Province, all the Messes of ten or twelve Regiments and Batteries, and some fifteen hundred other people of the non-official caste. In ten years his knowledge should be doubled, and at the end of twenty he knows, or knows something about, every Englishman in the Empire. (5: 1)

Nor is this the only Kipling story that develops the idea of Anglo-India as a panoptic space. Even if we limit ourselves to his first collection, *Plain Tales from the Hills*, we gather overwhelming evidence that nothing ever stays private in Anglo-India, especially in that most private of spheres: courtship. "Three and – an Extra" tells of a community's quick divination of a flirtatious relationship between a newly arrived woman and a married man. In "False Dawn," everyone knows Saumarez is romantically interested in one of the Miss Copleighs, even if they mistakenly presume Maud, the elder, to be the object of his affection. "Bitter's Neat" goes even further, almost to the point of caricature, when describing how everyone knows about one woman's desires except for the intended himself. In "Kidnapped," we are told that *affairs de coeur* coterminate with *affairs d'état* since "marriage in India does not concern the individual but the Government he serves" (1: 146). Moving away from romance, the humiliation of the titular hero of "The Arrest of Lt. Golightly" shows how other things are subject to the same immediate publicity. When the vain subaltern trudges home after being caught in a rainstorm that has ruined his raiment, Kipling's narrator gleefully indulges in sartorial mockery, describing how "the tale leaked into the regimental Canteen, and thence ran about the Province" (1: 158).

To understand how literature assumed the mantle of the college in socializing Anglo-Indians into a specific set of habits, it is first beneficial to note that, in Anglo-Indian literature, community is not described in political terms. For instance, in "The Education of Otis Yeere" (1888), Kipling's recurrent character, the redoubtable Mrs Hauksbee, discusses the prospect of a salon in Simla with a Mrs Mallowe. If we follow the work of Jurgen Habermas, we will recognize this as a monumental development, since it would be proof of a political society.[14] However, Mrs Hauksbee's companion warns her off:

> You can't focus anything in India; and a *salon*, to be any good at all, must be permanent. In two seasons your roomful would be scattered all over Asia. We are only little bits of dirt on the hillsides – here one day and blown down the *khud* the next. *We* have lost the art of talking – at least our men have. We have no cohesion – . (6: 9–10)

If a *salon* is to provide a space where opinions may be exchanged and debated en route to the foundation of a rational consensus, and if it is construed as the necessary condition for the emergence of a public sphere, then it is clearly irrelevant in the India of Kipling's stories. As the very public romances conducted in the other stories of this collection attest, the problem is not the creation of a public sphere but the preservation of individuality through the maintenance of a private sphere.

Yet Mrs Mallowe is only half-right in asserting that Anglo-Indians lack cohesion, for their literature demonstrably retains a sense of cohesion long after the closure of the civil and military colleges. The difference, I would argue, is that this society coheres around a corporate, rather than a political, national, or regional culture. To explain, let me consider the aptly named civilian, Orde, who is the deputy commissioner of Amara in Kipling's "The Enlightenments of Pagett, M.P." (1888). Like Mrs Mallowe, Orde admits the absence of a political community. As he explains to a visiting friend, the eponymous Member of Parliament, "the Anglo-Indian is a political orphan," meaning that the Anglo-Indian is an Englishman without a constituency, deprived of representation in the (British) Parliament responsible for developing the imperial policy that affects his livelihood (4: 343). Orde's chief task is to disabuse his old school chum of the foolish theories of imperial governance circulating among metropolitan politicians. The topic of their discussion is the newly founded Indian National Congress, which Pagett celebrates and Orde dismisses. Orde begins by explaining that it is "hopeless to give you any just idea of any Indian question without the documents before you, and in this case the documents you want are the country and the people" (4: 344). When Pagett counters that "the official Anglo-Indian" might be "naturally jealous of any external influence that might move the masses," Orde delivers the first of his enlightenments: that there is nothing "natural" about an Anglo-Indian at all

(4: 345). As he makes clear to his erstwhile schoolmate, Anglo-Indians are still affiliated, nationally, with England:

> "You and I were brought up together; taught by the same tutors, read the same books, lived the same life, and thought, as you remember, in parallel lines. I come out here, learn new languages, and work among new races; while you, more fortunate, remain at home. Why should I change my mind – our mind – because I change my sky?" (4: 345)

Yet, in another sense, Orde changed more than his sky when he took up an Indian career. He also entered into a professional community unconsciously committed to maintaining their particular (corporate) rituals. This explains why, for instance, Orde does not mourn the absence of political society and why he agrees heartily when another character states, "There are no politics, in a manner of speaking, in India. It's all work" (4: 350).

Kipling is not the only author to emphasize publicity or transparency in his fiction but my purpose is not to enumerate the many Anglo-Indian writers concerned with publicity but to illuminate the connection between Anglo-Indian literature and the professional ethic of the East India Company. Previous attempts to chronicle literature of the Raj have often presumed the spontaneous generation of an independent, (post) colonial voice. While recognizing an existing tradition of writing by Britons about India, traditional studies such as Bhupal Singh's *A Survey of Anglo-Indian Literature* (1934) and more postcolonially informed analyses like Shyamal Bagchee's "Writing Self/ Writing Colony *in situ*" (1992) agree that in the second half of the nineteenth century Anglo-Indian literature asserts its independence from the metropolitan centre. A line from Sara Jeannette Duncan's novel *Set in Authority* (1906) describes this development more simply. Huddled in a club, a group of Anglo-Indians are discussing the controversial retrial of a soldier accused of murdering a native. The case has become a scandal in London but, according to Duncan's narrator, "What they thought in London was a matter of great indifference in India. There they were thinking for themselves" (212). To take Duncan's line as a point of departure, the remainder of this chapter constitutes an investigation of what it was that these people thought when they thought "for themselves." The object, to return to the model proposed by Ashcroft, Griffiths, and Tiffin in *The Empire Writes Back*, is to uncover the source of those cultural practices which underpin the nascent Anglo-Indian national literature.

Kipling's Short Stories

Just how this sense of duty was cultivated forms the subject for Kipling's "A Wayside Comedy" (1888), where the narrator prefaces a report of Ted Kurrell's licentious behaviour with the following apology:

> You must remember, though you will not understand, that all laws weaken in a small and hidden community where there is no public opinion. When a man is absolutely alone in a Station he runs a certain risk of falling into evil ways. This risk is multiplied by every addition to the population up to twelve – the Jury number. After that, fear and consequent restraint begin and human action becomes less grotesquely jerky. (6: 115)

Kipling here has stated the basic problem of managing overseas employees: how does one prevent corruption in the absence of public opinion?[15] It is useful to recall Emile Durkheim's answer to just such a problem: in a widely and thinly dispersed population, in a territory without an adequate communication infrastructure, the only thing that will keep professionals honest is the strength of their "ethic" (8). Durkheim is specifically concerned with the manufacture of professional ethics by social institutions. According to him, when individuals are deprived of the traditional immediate and frequent solidarity with other members of the group, collective consciousness can only emerge through a stable and organized corporate structure, which meant either a profession or a state. The great puzzle for Durkheim is how organization and discipline emerge in the economic sphere, which at once dominates all aspects of modernity and simultaneously operates without a professional ethics or, at least, operates such that "the ideas current on what the relations should be of the employee with his chief, of the workman with the manager, of the rival manufacturers with each other and with the public ... are so slight that they might as well not be" (9–10). Economists, operating where Durkheim feared to tread, have theorized the problems of employer-employee relations in terms of what is called "reservation utility." A relationship begins when an agent agrees to represent the interests of the principal who in turn agrees to compensate the agent for this service. That relationship, however, is dynamic, meaning that at any time an agent might choose to pursue alternative activities that offer greater remuneration. As Herbert Gintis and Tsuneo Ishikawa explain, "The employee, while receiving a specific wage, does not guarantee the delivery of a specific bundle of labor service" (196).

Reservation utility is the "value" of these alternatives and, in terms of the employer, disobedient options. Thus, while "the evil ways" pursued by Kipling's Ted Kurrell are limited to adulterous womanizing, the menace of unsupervised individuals evokes the more material threat at the core of British imperialism.

The connection between Kipling and Durkheim was first made by Noel Annan, who argued that Kipling saw society as a nexus of groups regulated by "religion, law, custom, convention, morality – the forces of social control – which imposed upon individuals certain rules which they broke at their peril" (331). More recently, John Kucich has explored the sadomasochistic dimension of these secret, "magical" groups in Kipling's fiction (*Imperial Masochism* 139). For Kucich, magical groups, operating under a calculus of pain and shame, were an important tool as Kipling attempted to restructure imperial hegemony around proficient, technocratic, lower-middle-class professionals. I want to consider the limits of Kucich's model later, but for now, let me restrict my attention to the claim he shares with Annan that Kipling's sociological approach to imperial society acknowledges the productive function of groups in producing collective discipline.

In Kipling's stories, not only do characters' social statuses depend on the discharge of administrative duties, but characters can also be assured that each transgression or failure will be universally disseminated. As we read his fiction, we witness work and transparency calcifying into an imperial ethic which overrides personal interest. It may be suggested by some, taking a page from D.A. Miller, that the appearance of these topoi heralds the triumph of imperial discipline, the product of circulating micropowers which panoptically compel the social body to self regulate. Continuing in this vein, the conflict between private and public selves can then be reconfigured as the confrontation between the romantic individualist and the homogenizing and totalizing impulses of modern social networks. Zoreh T. Sullivan argued this much when she described Kipling's short stories of the 1880s as testaments to "the world's greatest imperial power collaps[ing] at its human joints" (80). Her *Narratives of Empire* (1993), an exemplary piece of postcolonial criticism, weaves together the theories of Edward Said and Homi Bhabha to demonstrate how Kipling's representation of ethical crises illuminates the ambivalent nature of colonial discourse.

However, by examining the special circumstances of the ethical crises in Kipling's fiction, I would suggest that we play the part of Sporus in the case of the butterfly if we resort to micropowers in our explications.

Miller, we should remember, defines Foucauldian discipline as, among other things, "an ideal of unseen but all-seeing surveillance, which, though partly realised in several, often interconnected institutions, is identified with none" (viii). Patently this is not the case in Anglo-India where there is practically only one institution: the government. Transparency is directly and intentionally produced by the state since India, if we are to believe the narrator of Kipling's "William the Conqueror" (1898), is "a land where each man's pay, age, and position are printed in a book, that all may read, [so] it is hardly worth while to play at pretences in word or deed" (13: 226). The circle can be drawn tighter still, for the Indian government of Kipling's day was not really a government at all but a corporate administration created by the East India Company. Whereas Trevelyan's *Competition Wallah* might be thought to describe an India in transition between corporate and Crown rule, Kipling's short stories reveal the persistence both of the Company's original logistical problem and the complex cultural discourses developed to resolve it. In those short stories Kipling reproduces the control crisis at the heart of the East India Company's administration. On the one hand, Kipling is keen to consign "John Company" to history, transmogrifying it into the sublunar deity Kumpani in "The Bridge-Builders." On the other, he continually confronts its social architecture in his anxious return to issues of duty, sacrifice, and matters of conscience.

The society presented in Kipling's Anglo-Indian short stories is structurally unchanged from the days of Company rule. The supreme power continues to operate from afar, ignorant of the reality in the field. The gap between the authority and its agents has not, if we again trust the portrait in "William the Conqueror," been reduced by the advances in communication networks, "for the Government held the Head of the Famine tied neatly to a telegraph-wire, and if Jimmy had ever regarded telegrams seriously, the death-rate of that famine would have been much higher than it was" (13: 244). In nearly all his early stories, Kipling burdens the proficient technocratic officials of Anglo-India not only with the impossible task of making "two blades of grass grow where there was but one before," ("Only a Subaltern" 3: 416) but also with the cumbersome expostulations of abstract thinkers in the central government. Such obstacles are numerous and are frequently a source of humour in Kipling's stories. The most familiar is probably the inept Bengali, Grish Chunder Dé, the man appointed to run a district by a viceroy seeking to satisfy his liberal sentiments ("The Head of the District"). Dé succeeds Yardley-Orde, a man who is either a caricature or an apotheosis of Anglo-Indian fortitude. On his deathbed, Yardley-Orde utters what are surely two of the most unintentionally comic lines in Kipling's fiction: "'Sorry to be a nuisance, but is – is there anything to drink?'" and "'It isn't that I mind dying,' he said. 'It's leaving Polly and the district'" (6: 123). Against such a hero, Dé fails spectacularly, conforming to the stereotype of the Bengali Babu, fleeing from the terror of manly Indian tribesmen in revolt. So cowardly is Dé that he cannot even die with honour; it is his brother who supplies Dé's proficient (white) replacement with the titular "head" of the district.

However, before attributing this ineptitude entirely to Kipling's racist opinion and/or fear of educated Indians, we should note that Grish Chunder Dé has plenty of European counterparts in Kipling's short stories. The gamut of characters runs from Aurelian McGoggin ("The Conversion of Aurelian McGoggin"), the naive disciple of Comte and Spencer, dubbed the Blastoderm by his fellows, who becomes Kipling's first eponymous hero to suffer an aphasiac collapse, through Pinecoffin ("Pig"), the earnest official driven to madness by writing reports on the essence of a pig, right up to the quintessence of bureaucratic madness, the accounts clerk ("The Pit That They Digged") who denies the vitality of man, who has recovered from his death-bed, and now finds himself asked to pay for the costs of his mistakenly dug grave. Even the Carlylean Yardley-Orde expires before completing his day's work. It is certainly not for lack of effort, but it remains a curious fact of Kipling's fiction that few if any of his characters ever finish their job. Repeatedly, we see independent thought swamped by the pressure to complete the work at hand and we begin to perceive why the narrator of "A Germ Destroyer" (1888) states that "as a general rule, it is inexpedient to meddle with questions of State in a land where men are highly paid to work them out for you" (1: 134); or why in "Kidnapped" (1888) the best praise we hear of Peythroppe is that "all his superiors spoke well of him, because he knew how to hold his tongue and his pen at the proper times" (1: 143). The path is cleared for the encounter between the London-based Member of Parliament and an ex-Radical now employed by the Indian government. When Pagett asks the former agitator about the rise of the Indian National Congress, he is told simply, "There are no politics, in a manner of speaking, in India. It's all work" ("The Enlightenments of Pagett, M.P." 4: 350).

Some might argue that this image of an overworked administrative corps invariably doomed never to finish their jobs underwrites Kipling's defence of a permanent British presence in India. Others, taking the long view, could see it as a continuation of an institutionally cultivated sense of failure, deliberately encouraged to stunt the ambition of company agents who, were they so inclined, could easily take advantage of their unchecked power. We could argue, following John Kucich, that masochism makes for the best colonial administrators; at the very least we can assert that those administrators most conscious of their inability to succeed in full would be most likely not to fail in total. To confirm this attitude in Kipling's fiction, consider the crisis experienced by Findlayson, the civil engineer who sees his bridge swept away by a spectacular Ganges flood: "For himself, the crash meant everything – everything that made a hard life worth the living" ("The Bridge-Builders" 13: 24).

Yet to get a sense of the limits of Kipling's masochistic tendencies, it is better to consider his description of a self-denying character who, technically, is not connected to the government at all. "A Bank Fraud," tells the story of Reggie Burke, a commercial bank manager and overseer of London-based colonially invested capital. Kipling's narrator opens with a salacious promise:

> If Reggie Burke were in India now he would resent this tale being told; but as he is in Hong Kong and won't see it, the telling is safe. He was the man who worked the big fraud on the Sind and Sialkot Bank. (1: 206)

Given such an introduction, we might quite reasonably expect an adventure similar to Conan Doyle's contemporary story of a bank fraud, "The Red-Headed League" (1891). *Sans* Holmes, we might think Reggie Burke succeeded and absconded to enjoy his fortune in foreign climes. For several pages, the narrator sustains such expectations, introducing Reggie Burke as a well-liked branch manager for a bank whose directors "had tested Reggie up to a fairly severe breaking-strain. They trusted him just as much as Directors ever trust their Managers" and Kipling invites his readers to "see for yourself whether this trust was misplaced" (1: 207). Burke's life is disturbed with the arrival of a new assistant, an accountant named Riley who is introduced as a Yorkshireman full of "savage self-conceit … wonderfully narrow-minded in business, and, being new to the country, had no notion that Indian banking is totally distinct from Home work" (1: 208). Burke and Riley "failed to hit it off" but Burke's chance appears on the day when Riley is pronounced terminally consumptive; the same day a message arrives informing the manager that Riley will be fired in thirty days.

Anglo-Indian history provides a legion of opportunistic precedents for Reggie Burke, including most notably Robert Clive, the clerk-turned-general who in the mid-eighteenth century saw in the coincidence of the Seven Years War and internal Indian political instability the chance to make his fortune. But Kipling did not name his hero haphazardly and, following his eighteenth-century namesake, Burke rejects the opportunity for personal enrichment, turning "A Bank Fraud" into an allegory for the ideal company man. We discover that Burke's "fraud" is the net of lies woven to provide palliative care for his assistant, and this humanitarian fortitude symbolizes the transition Anglo-India has made since the days of Clive's nabobs. He chooses to ignore the orders of the head office and withholds the termination letter, forging in their stead praiseworthy despatches. He sustains the illusion by paying Riley's salary out of his own pocket and even contrives at one point, "contrary to all the laws of business and finance" to give Riley a 25 per cent raise (1: 215). Riley, the directors, and (until the narrator chooses to disclose it) the public remain ignorant and ungrateful to the end and when Riley expires, Burke's only consolation is that he has sustained the man for one month in excess of the doctor's prediction.

In the end, Reggie's "big fraud" affects three parties. First are the bank directors, who are told neither of Riley's condition nor of the sacrifices their branch manager is making on his behalf. The centre of power is at an unbridgeable distance, and the manager never once considers the possibility of appealing to the directors for intercession. Second is Riley, the portrait of the ignorant Englishman in India, who presumes the universal applicability of his customs and culture and so completely misunderstands the Anglo-Indian society that he repays heroic charity with ungrateful moral sermons. The third victim is the perpetrator himself, Reggie Burke, a representative member of the Anglo-Indian class described in "The Phantom Rickshaw" as "the men who do not take the trouble to conceal from you their opinion that you are an incompetent ass ... [yet who] will work themselves to the bone in your behalf if you fall sick or into serious trouble" (5: 2).

The sacrifice of Reggie Burke is typical of the painful and putatively noble sacrifice made by the heroes of Kipling's early fiction. John Kucich has identified these moments of futile self-sacrifice as the key component of the "virulent class politics underlying Kipling's consolidation of middle-class ideological systems" (188). Kucich positions Kipling as an author who was critical of upper-class mores (and Toryism in general) as they represented themselves in both domestic and colonial societies.

Building on Kipling's evident support for technocratic professionalism, Kucich sees Reggie's self-defeating use of his privileged knowledge as an act of "a self-martyring moral despotism," one of the many instances of "masochistic self-glorification" in the early stories (175, 177). By refusing to take part in regular social practices (by telling Riley that he has been sacked), Reggie Burke's affective transaction takes place in a secret social economy, one that runs parallel to the official chain of command. The new economy is structured by one's access to knowledge, rather than one's rank, which enabled Kipling to create a symbolic order whereby the lower middle-classes could be incorporated into, and indeed feel that they were in control of, imperial culture.

The value of this argument is its correction of Kipling's conservative rehabilitators, who have celebrated the author's classlessness.[16] Kucich is also absolutely right in insisting that Kipling's work conveys "a remarkably unilateral class politics" (138). But this argument loses some of its traction when it proposes that this unilateral politics is an expert synthesis of "the ideological languages of distinct metropolitan middle-class constituencies" (139). Searching for the source of Kipling's alienated suffering and, to use Kipling's favoured adjective, "grim" characters, Kucich suggests an "imaginative fusion" of evangelical, utilitarian, and professional values, the preferred formula for most twentieth-century studies of Victorian colonial culture.[17] However, it is not clear that any imaginative fusion of metropolitan Victorian ideologies was necessary in the Anglo-Indian case, where a corporate ethic dominated. To be clear, I am not dismissing the influence of either evangelicalism or utilitarianism on the rhetoric of Anglo-Indian colonial discourse (whether Kipling's or anybody else's) as much as I am suggesting that neither generated it. The consistent emphasis on these ideologies overvalues the influence of vague metropolitan culture at the expense of the structures of feeling produced by one specific colonial institution.

One of the strongest proofs that Kipling was more interested in Anglo-Indian cultural practices than in synthesizing metropolitan middle-class ideologies is the nature of his early audience. As one Edwardian chronicler of Anglo-Indian literature puts it, while Kipling was the first Anglo-Indian author to write for two audiences (one colonial, the other metropolitan), his art remained great because he *refused* to play the part of a Janus-faced intermediary between colony and metropolis. Kipling, according to Edward F. Oaten, knew he must write "primarily for his own people, who possess [his] sympathies and point of view" (142). More recently Stephen Arata has come to a similar conclusion when he argues that the fiction and poetry of the 1880s and 1890s "explicitly rebuffed the English reader" through their copious use of "the untranslated phrase, the unglossed allusion, the in-joke, the unapologetic gesture towards structures of feeling and experience which had no counterpart outside the enclosed world of Anglo-India" (154–5). Kipling wrote his early stories, including "A Bank Fraud," for the *Civil and Military Gazette*, hoping no doubt that they would eventually be published widely but intending them presumably for immediate consumption by an audience of Anglo-Indian professionals. Andrew Rutherford notes that the third edition of *Plain Tales from the Hills*, the first to be published in England, contained many revisions to make the stories more intelligible to a domestic audience.[18] Kipling did not earn his metropolitan fame until 1890 and so whatever effect this celebrity had on his art and ideology, in the case of the stories written in the 1880s, the class, *pace* Kucich, was already consolidated. Thus when Kipling's narrator says of Reggie Burke, "You must see for yourself whether this trust was misplaced" ("Bank Fraud" in *Writings* 1: 207), he does not so much modulate, following Kucich's argument, the "ambiguous affective positioning" (55) of the bystanding reader. Instead, the narrator appeals to a readership preconditioned to recognize Reggie Burke as one of their own and, moreover, to take grim pleasure in the revelation of his secret heroism. Reggie Burke's sacrifice confirms their sense that they serve an ideal rather than an inefficient and uninterested employer. As opposed to the conventional lenses of evangelicalism or utilitarianism, it might be better to read scenes like these in terms of the parallel economies of inevitable shame and impossible ambition. We need only return to Oakfield's fellowship to see that what Kucich recognizes as the "sadomasochistic logic" (35) original to Kipling's sociology might better be understood historically as the *already existing* products of Anglo-India's corporate culture.

Sara Jeannette Duncan's *Set in Authority*

The masochistic corporate fraternity is hypostasized in much of fin de siècle Anglo-Indian fiction, and nowhere more than in the work of Sara Jeannette Duncan. Duncan was born in Canada but, while stopping in Calcutta on a globetrotting world-tour, she met and married Everard Coates, superintendent of the city's museum. Though she was certainly a supporter of the British Empire, Duncan's Canadian heritage provided her with a non-metropolitan perspective and in India she occupies the vantage point of an intimate outsider, someone who is almost but not quite the same as her Anglo-Indian colleagues. Like William Arnold, Duncan came to India having been influenced by other, non-corporate institutions and so the degree to which her narrative voice is alienated or surprised at the behaviour of Anglo-Indians registers the presence of the "cultural practices" predicted in the model proposed by the authors of *The Empire Writes Back*. Unlike Arnold, who was concerned more with morality and the path to the good life, Duncan shares with Kipling a journalist's eye and she has a professional inclination towards recording the quirks, faults, and trivialities of society. All this places Duncan in a position to interrogate rather than affirm or deny the principles which structure Anglo-India's corporate culture.

The novel I want to consider in detail, *Set in Authority*, is a social drama that focuses on the reaction of several different communities to a murder trial. The proverbial stone in the pond is Henry Morgan, alias Herbert Valentina Tring, a private British soldier accused of murdering the husband of his Indian mistress. Morgan's trial receives more than the usual attention because it is scheduled to take place in a district where a Muslim has just been appointed as magistrate. The consequent prospect of a British subject being judged by a native in a capital case causes a scandal that tests the limits of fin de siècle liberalism in both India and England. The historical context for this examination is the controversy surrounding the Ilbert Bill, Lord Ripon's attempt in 1883 to place European subjects under the jurisdiction of native Indian judges.[19] In both real and Duncan's fictional India, the popular reluctance to exclude magistrates from cases purely on the basis of race contradicted one of liberal philosophy's first principles.

Though some minor characters represent the entrenched conservative position, all the major characters in this novel are liberals, but Duncan is less interested in identifying their hypocrisy than in exploring the gap between principle and practice. This means that issues of ethical balance, conscience, and duty are foregrounded as honest liberals debate between themselves how best to handle the Morgan case. For the most stubbornly principled (the group we might call the descendants of Edward Oakfield), this means absolutely disregarding the likely effects of their decisions and committing to the principles of governance instead of the pragmatics of governing. For the more politically astute, it means striking a balance between competing sets of interests. While this second group would never deny the abstract right of a qualified native to preside in a capital case, they also recognize that the judge is not the only person whose civil rights are in jeopardy in the trial.

The action of the novel takes place partly in London and Calcutta, but mostly in Pilaghur, the district where the crime allegedly occurred. It is in Pilaghur that Duncan scrutinizes the bonds tying a community of Anglo-Indian officials to each other and to the wider imperial administration. To that community's consternation, the Calcutta-based viceroy has insisted that the Muslim judge remain in place. When this judge surprises his racist opponents and actually acquits the soldier, the viceroy turns consternation into apoplexy by ordering a retrial. As the news of the affair reaches London, the liberal set describe it in Kiplingesque terms as "a soldier tragedy from India, one of those 'Without Benefit of Clergy' things" (171). Unable to decide whether to praise or disavow the viceroy, the elderly liberal members of London's Aganippe Club appeal to one of the younger generation. Victoria Tring gives a measured response: "I should like to know more about it first, but on the face of it, it looks to me very like one of those matters in which it would be wise to trust the man on the spot" (135). Victoria Tring presumes the man on the spot to be the viceroy, the man who will eventually become her fiancé. But Duncan makes it clear that the real man on the spot is not the aristocratic viceroy, but the company man, Eliot Arden, who is the chief commissioner of the district. Duncan introduces Arden as a paragon of virtue. Pilaghur's supreme civilian authority, he is articulate, charming, cultured, sympathetic, and liberal: in all respects the incarnation of Richard Wellesley's hope – expressed a century earlier in the college of Fort William's first prize-winning essay – that company men would be "valuable and ornamental members of society" (Martin 6).

By its very title, the novel announces its intention to explore the nature of colonial power. To be set in authority is, of course, to be an agent and Duncan repeats the familiar view that administrators like Arden exercise a circumscribed despotism: "The Chief Commissioner has the glory and responsibility of power … Both garland and rein lie upon his neck" (76). Arden, then, belongs to the tradition of educated middle-class men who find themselves asked to embody, represent, and exercise imperial power on behalf of a metropolitan authority. However, at the outset Arden is described as one who has overcome the psychological ambivalence that paralyses so many other characters in his position, and he fluently negotiates between centralized imperial policies and the particular demands of his district. As a result, he is admired not only by the local community of Anglo-Indians, but also by the colonial Indians and, most importantly, by the viceroy. The affection between the viceroy and this commissioner is an important narrative point since all the other Anglo-Indian officials in this novel see their viceroy in more orthodox terms, i.e., as a metropolitan politician who knows nothing of India but has been parachuted into power because of his London connections. However, because the viceroy thinks Arden is "a type of man in some ways rather like himself" (79), Duncan is able to isolate the systemic problems of colonial governance. As one character observes, it is "curious ... that Lord Thame should have been predestined to persecute Morgan, and you [Arden] predestined to protect him, from exactly the same motive – what you believe to be right" (156). Both Arden and the viceroy subscribe to liberalism and so without the potential distraction of political partisanship, Duncan can explore the problematic position occupied by a moral man who has been set in authority.

The moral dilemma occurs after Morgan's initial acquittal when Arden receives a dossier of testimony from Indian witnesses that apparently confirms Morgan's guilt. The officer responsible for collecting the dossier is akin to Kipling's Riley or Aurelian McGoggin, someone newly arrived with his metropolitan sensibilities still intact and unable to understand the customary application of imperial power. When Arden mentions the dossier to his confidante, Ruth Pearce, she asks:

> "Do you find anything in it?..."
>
> "It's the usual thing – a little truth and a great deal of lying, constructive lying, after the event, it seems to me. It's cleverly put together."
>
> "Does the truth in it bear at all importantly?"
>
> "Not importantly enough to justify a second trial. But you mustn't pin me down like that. I speak of only what I conceive to be the truth. The Viceroy, no doubt, will believe much more of it; because it is in the line of what he wants to prove." (187)

Arden apprehends that many "truths" can be derived from the dossier. As a local expert, familiar with the land and its people, he recognizes it as "the usual thing." He also perceives that the viceroy, a man of policies and principles, will be more susceptible to the half-truths of a cleverly crafted dossier.

Knowing that the dossier, if forwarded to the viceroy, would condemn the soldier, Arden here literally holds a life in his hands. He also acknowledges his discretionary authority when he tells Ruth that he "*need* not do it … They *might* override me – the law provides for it; but practically they couldn't" (156, emphasis in original). Here is a clear opportunity for heroic action, to take advantage of the power invested in his position and, by obeying protocol, withhold the dossier from the viceroy. Such an act would not only satisfy his conscience but also serve principles of justice. But for Arden, what exists de jure does not exist de facto and when Ruth "wildly" suggests that he follow this path, Duncan describes how he, "took with some eagerness the *moral upper hand*. 'You can't mean that … It went on at once'" (187, emphasis added). Now unless we are willing to understand Arden as a disciple of a perverted form of Kantian deontological ethics, for whom following procedure is the only possible path to the good, then it is hard to understand how his choice to send a fatal dossier which, in his opinion, is "a great deal of lying … cleverly put together," could be construed as the moral upper hand. It is hard, that is, unless we admit as an ethic that of the professional bureaucrat, the functionary who, recalling Richard Wellesley's vision, is "properly qualified to conduct the ordinary movements of the Great machine of Government" ("Notes" 731). Later in the novel, when Arden realizes that indeed the soldier will be convicted and executed, he absolves himself from personal responsibility because once the matter passes out of his hands, "he did not see it to be a doubt in which his conscience was sole and predestined arbiter" (202). In another context, Hannah Arendt has shown this to be the ethics shared between imperialism and the concentration camp.[20] Arden justifies his action because he has taken the idea of the virtuous empire as the supreme good and has accepted the system of administrative power as its legitimate worldly institution.

This scene with Ruth is one of many in the novel where Duncan elaborates Arden's corporate ethic through dialectical conversations. Ruth provides the antagonistic position because, like Duncan herself, she is not fully a member of Anglo-Indian society. Furnished with all the capabilities of a late-Victorian New Woman, including a profession and a fierce independence, she interrupts the established order of corporate Anglo-India. As the narrator explains when introducing the guests at a dinner-party, "Miss Pearce properly comes last, because she had no quotable position. The table of precedence does not provide for demi-official lady-doctors" (85). This demi-official status enables her to take liberties denied to (or is it repressed by?) Anglo-Indians. For example, she has comfortable social relations with the local elite of Pilaghur's native population.[21] Likewise, she has formed an unusually strong bond with Arden, who admits that it is precisely the lack of an official relationship which enables their confidence: "From the first he had felt himself with Miss Pearce essentially the man and but incidentally the Chief Commissioner; he who was so universally the Chief Commissioner that he might hardly have claimed any other identity" (185).

A confident and quick-witted character who shares Arden's liberal predilections, Ruth serves partly as Arden's conscience but she also represents transgressive desire. Officially, Arden is a married man with a duty to obey the directives of his superior. Yet he is intrigued by Ruth's argument that action should be dictated by conscience. As they discuss the dossier, she insists that "one isn't bound by the beliefs of others. One is bound by one's own" (157). At this point, the narrator makes a general comment on the nature of their relationship:

> They came back so constantly, these two, to the question of conscience, duty, right. It seemed always just below the level of their thoughts; the least reference disclosed it. They were for ever inciting one another to this abstract consideration; if it lurked under any aspect of any subject they would have it out, and fling it back and forth between them. One would say they drew a mutual support and encouragement from the exercise; one might go further and say that one offered it to the other. (157)

This passage illuminates the subconscious function of ideology – the lurking thing just below the level of the characters' thoughts – but we should also notice how that other subconscious discourse makes ideology perceptible.[22] The co-presence of sexuality and thought forces the moral and the romantic plots to intertwine, with Arden finding his path to personal pleasure doubly thwarted by his obligation to the institutions of administrative power and marriage.

Like the speaker in Kipling's poem "A Song in Storm," Arden believes that the game is more than the player of the game and the ship is more than the crew. To show how effectively the corporate ideology has reduced personal agency in Anglo-India, Duncan contrives circumstances that would completely exonerate either the official or the marital transgression. In the case of the former, I have already noted that Arden is perfectly within his rights to withhold the document; he is officially bound to screen everything submitted to the viceroy and in his expert professional opinion, this dossier is rubbish. In the case of the latter, Duncan sends Mrs Arden back to Europe where she contracts tuberculosis and dies, leaving Arden free to pursue his affection for Ruth. Yet even in these conditions, Arden is incapable of heroic action. It might be helpful to contrast his behaviour with that of William Arnold's Oakfield. Whereas the son of the Rugby headmaster insists that his personal morality is the last bastion of his subjective integrity, Arden, the corporate employee, says he finds satisfaction in being a component in "the machinery of the best-oiled bureaucracy" (204).

Duncan seems determined to press this point for, while Arden and Ruth wrestle over matters of conscience in India, back in London, the viceroy's mother relates an illustrious moment in the family history:

> "There was once a dispute between a Thame and Cromwell," said Lady Thame. "My son's ancestor had his conscience behind him and Cromwell gave in ... [Henceforth] in personal matters we have always felt it a point of honour, to put it on no higher ground, to defeat our Cromwells." (229)

Such agency is denied the servants of the Indian government. Arden derives his virtue from sources other than his conscience. He is a man who "had made it a point of honour for twenty years never to protest, and he did not protest now" (218). When Arden meets his Cromwell in the guise of Viceroy Thame, the result is a retrial where the soldier is convicted and sentenced to death. In his "failure to keep covenant with his opinion," Arden alienates Ruth and, according to the narrator, grows "a little more formal and official, a little greyer and sadder" (218).

I should make it clear that Arden's failure to act is not the result of a personal weakness. He is, as I have said, consistently described as the paragon of Anglo-Indian virtue. In fact, what little resistance he does put up against the viceroy's will is seen by the Anglo-Indian community as foolishly courageous. His colleagues presume he has ruined his prospects and his assistant eulogizes him as "a pyrotechnic sacrifice to an opinion" (162). The disciplined community of officials thus described cannot entertain the possibility of real heroic action since they are more automatons than autonomous. Similarly, the love-story of Ruth Pearce and Eliot Arden collapses because at the decisive moment, neither character is capable of decisive action. This is not to say that they do not recognize or value heroism. Far from it. For instance, when Ruth compares the opinions of Arden and the viceroy she admits she admires the latter: "The Viceroy's is the more heroic attitude because it is the more unpleasant" (156).

The difficulty for characters like Arden and Ruth is that they have been conditioned to live and work in the shadow of the viceroy, finding their virtue not in their own agency but in his magnificence. As the narrator describes it:

> [The Viceroy] stands for the idea, the scheme, and the intention to which they are all pledged; and through the long sacrifice of the arid years something of their loyalty and devotion and submission to the idea gathers in the human way about the sign of it. (84)

At first it might seem odd that I have included Ruth among those under the viceroy's symbolic influence. After all she has no official position in and therefore no direct obligation to Anglo-Indian society. She is additionally the most assertive character in the novel, a woman who speaks "fearlessly, with [a] disregard of everything but the issue." As proof, when Arden asks, "You think there is no room for the speculation how far one is entitled to come between the ruler and his conscience?" Her reply is decisive: "None at all" (185).

One might presume that the free-thinking Dr Pearce is capable of independent action but at the end of the novel when, in an echo of the dossier scene, she has the fate of the viceroy literally in her hands, the distant notes of "God Save the King" induce a curious response. This faint pageant is enough to convince her to withhold the letter that would otherwise reveal to Victoria Tring that the man condemned to death by her fiancé is, in fact, her estranged brother Herbert in disguise. So what do we make of Ruth's final act? Why does the woman with no official obligation, and with better reason than most for discrediting the viceroy, why does this woman throw the letter of a dying man into the fire? She burns it without hope of recognition or satisfaction. Having never expressed any loyalty to the empire in the first place, having always insisted on the significance of one's conscience, she breaks a deathbed promise and consigns a condemned man's last words into oblivion. In the end, she sacrifices "her sense of duty" in a "curious little holocaust" to preserve the honour of the Indian empire (271). If nothing else, her Pavlovian defence of the chief executive triggered by the distant trill of the national anthem confirms just how deeply Duncan thinks corporate discipline has sedimented in Anglo-Indian society.

I would like to conclude by returning to Victoria Tring's suggestion in the Aganippe Club, that liberals should trust "the man on the spot." The problem is that in India, the man on the spot is a colonial agent whose trustworthiness his employers have systematically presumed negligible. Trust is the radical singularity which the East India Company could not confront when it designed the corporate discipline for Anglo-Indian society. Instead, it carefully crafted the illusion of agency, including especially the secret heroism of the romantic Anglo-Indian novels that Duncan so clearly distances herself from. When Arden yields to the viceroy's will he becomes "aware of a loss of significance; a familiar deadly conviction overcame him that he was a convention of the Indian Civil Service, and nothing more" (190). What I hope to have shown is that Duncan's novel reveals a society whose ethics have been overdetermined by a sense of duty to an idea. The idea is noble, to be sure, but for Anglo-Indians it is not a source of strength; rather, its pursuit cripples the novel's central characters by stripping them of individual agency. The pathetic, anti-romantic fate of the protagonists, who surrender both justice and their consciences to duty, testifies to Duncan's dissatisfaction with existing imperial structures. So often, Anglo-Indian writers, just as Wellesley, Malthus, and Macaulay before them, describe individual agents as cogs in a machine. In failing to indulge in rage against the machine, the middle-class agents of empire concede that they have invested too much of themselves in corporate structures. Thus, whether through caricature, satire, or melancholia, the fiction of Anglo-India anticipates modernity by circulating among its readership what would become the defining feature of middle-class employees of large modern organizations: self-pity.

5 Unmaking a Company Man in Rudyard Kipling's *Kim*

The game is more than the player of the game,
And the ship is more than the crew

– Rudyard Kipling, "A Song in Storm"

In relation both to Kipling's oeuvre and to the conventions of Victorian fiction, *Kim* (1901) is an exceptional text. Edmund Wilson called it Kipling's "only successful long story" (113). Kipling himself seemed unsure what to think of it; in his autobiography he described it as plotless, adding that managing the narrative required an author with the skill of Cervantes. Elaborating the idea of *Kim* as a work of picaresque, he even suggests that the eponymous hero practically wrote the novel himself. "The only trouble," Kipling confesses, "was to keep him within bounds" (*Something of Myself* 82). This fantasy of limitlessness requires qualification, however, because it is important to remember that in Kim's travels, the *tour d'horison* is not a *tour du monde*: the novel remains firmly bound within the sociological unity of British India.

Because of these bounds, criticism has taken *Kim* to be deeply invested in the idea of empire more broadly, and one of the archetypal novels in the canon of colonial literature. Edward Said places *Kim* alongside Conrad's *Heart of Darkness*, *Nostromo*, and *Lord Jim* as the primary texts of imperialism "render[ing] the experience of empire with such force … [bringing] to a basically insular and provincial British audience the color, glamour, and romance of the British overseas Empire" (*Culture* 132). Less often studied is the effect of *Kim* upon Anglo-India. In his portrayal of Kipling as the "master stylist" of empire, Said notes that "Kipling not only wrote about India but was *of* it" (*Culture*

132, 133; emphasis in original). Bart Moore-Gilbert, in one of the early and incisive responses to Said's panoramic vision, plumbs the depth of Kipling's affiliation with the group he affectionately named, in the subtitle to his collection *Life's Handicap*, as "Mine Own People." Reconstructing, through Anglo-Indian newspapers, periodicals, and fiction, an already vibrant Anglo-Indian culture, Moore-Gilbert explains how "the discourse of the exiles in India characteristically tended to consider itself as different to that emanating from Britain" (5). His purpose is to excavate an Anglo-Indian version of "Orientalism" distinct from Said's general model and so to name the characteristically Anglo-Indian ways that Kipling stereotyped colonial relations of power.

This chapter follows Moore-Gilbert's insistence that we read a text like *Kim* for its Anglo-Indian particularities, but with a different aim in mind. As the previous chapter has argued, the typical features of Kipling's Anglo Indian fiction – the continual representation of a transparent society where the sole index of social status is professional proficiency – coincides with the tropes of a corporate culture. My intention is to read *Kim* as both a product of that corporate milieu and as an attempt to reify and so to distribute the Anglo-Indian solution to the problem of colonial agency across the empire. Written years after Kipling left India, at the height of his international literary celebrity, *Kim* is, for all its Anglo-Indian debts, undoubtedly a broadly imperial text.[1] If the short fiction of the 1880s and 1890s addressed the tastes and reading habits of the Anglo-Indians, *Kim* was written for the empire by a man increasingly interested in Britain's place in the world, the author of, among other things, the nationalist hymn "Recessional" (1897) and the poem written to encourage the United States to intervene in the Philippines, "The White Man's Burden" (1899).

In adopting the novel form, Kipling positioned *Kim* in the tradition of the dominant literary genre of the Victorian period, a genre that scholars like Ian Watt and Nancy Armstrong have argued coincided with and shaped the tastes of the rising middle class.[2] For Armstrong, the novel serves particular ideological purposes with regard to both the development of individual identity and a consolidated vision of wider social reality.[3] Said speaks to this latter project when he argues that *Kim* naturalizes British hegemony in India by suggesting that colonial order possesses a "timeless, unchanging, and 'essential'" quality (*Culture* 134). Said is one of many to question the accuracy of Kipling's representation; naming the text as "Orientalist," he argues that *Kim* does not describe India as it actually was but rather as Kipling would like it to be seen. Crucial to Said's analysis is the preternaturally skilled Kim, whose mutability is understood as a colonialist's fantasy: a white man who can think, speak, and act like a native.[4]

Since Said's path-breaking argument, most have agreed that *Kim* is a colonial bildungsroman, a novel organized around the maturation of an orphaned bazaar boy into a potential colonial agent.[5] The emphasis here needs to be on the word potential, because the novel famously ends with its protagonist on what can only be described as a cosmic threshold, with the whole world (or, at least the Indian subcontinent) laid out before him. The question of what happens at the end of the novel is one that I will – as invariably all analyses of *Kim* must – return to later in the chapter. First it is necessary to engage Kim's powerful, if arrested, development by distinguishing *Kim* from the conventional bildungsroman. For, despite containing a series of adventures relating the moral, spiritual, intellectual, and physical growth of a young man, *Kim* defies those conventions because the protagonist's journey from innocence to experience is incomplete. The novel ends with Kim yet to announce whether he will follow as the lama's disciple or serve as an agent in Creighton's surveillance network. That indecision is emphasized in the novel's structure as well, since at the last moment, the narrator shifts his attention from Kim to the boy's spiritual mentor, Teshoo Lama. In the final scene, the Buddhist monk, having reached enlightenment and merged with the Great Soul, has returned to the earthly plane so that his disciple, Kim, will not miss the Way: "Son of my Soul, I have wrenched my Soul back from the Threshold of Freedom to free thee from all sin – as I am free, and sinless. Just is the Wheel! Certain is our deliverance. Come!" (240). Other novelists would proceed to a resolution, an answer to the call either through direct speech or indirect narratorial comment, but Kipling pushes Kim away. The next and final line – "He crossed his hands on his lap and smiled, as a man may who has won Salvation for himself and his beloved" – speaks only of the metaphysical satisfaction of an old man who has always been secure in his identity and purpose (240).[6]

Critics have cited this awkward ending as proof of Kipling's own divided loyalties.[7] The lama, as Mark Kinkead-Weekes imagines in his formalist reading, would have initially been "a personality almost at the furthest point of view from Kipling himself" (215), but in an instance of the triumph of artistry over intention, the lama's "negative capability" overwhelms even Kipling himself, preventing the author from giving the last word to his intended (221). Edmund Wilson argues the ending represents the only possibility remaining to an author who throughout the novel has refused to allow his primary antagonists to come into conflict. Because Colonel Creighton's benevolent imperialism never clashes with the lama's benevolent mysticism, Wilson says we should be unsurprised that no "final victory or synthesis [is] allowed to take place" (114). Whereas Wilson argues that Kipling's traumatic childhood left the author disinclined towards confrontation, Said's interpretation of *Kim* against contemporary imperial politics contends that the conflict is unresolved "not because Kipling could not face it, but because for Kipling there was no conflict" (146). For Said, the strange conclusion is not so much a fault of Kipling's aesthetic but of his politics, a symptom of "a great artist blinded by his own insights about India, confusing the realities that he saw … with the notion that they were permanent and essential" (162). Zoreh T. Sullivan picks up these critics' shared theory of Kipling's involuntary incapacity by focusing on the aesthetic paralysis produced by "Kipling's divided sense of self, its multiple loyalties to the power of empire … and his love for a lost India" (148). Thus Sullivan critiques Kipling's "final evasion" as "a luminous freeze-frame" which "leaves Kim and the reader hanging in mid-air" (177–8). Like Wilson and Said, Sullivan chides Kipling for allowing "all that has been solid" to melt "into the air of visionary illusion and prayer" (177).

Critical interest in the ideological consequence of Kim's indecision is prompted by the fact that this character is otherwise an icon of imperial fantasy, a colonial Proteus, able to assume many shapes, speak many languages, and perform many cultural identities on a whim. Scholars fascinated by Kim's radical subjectivity argue that Kipling has deliberately fashioned a boy with no history other than a few papers asserting his parentage, a boy who belongs to no country or creed and so is seemingly able to permeate all. Noel Annan said it was Kim's "vocation … to find his niche on earth and to discover what he really is" (343). The postcolonial reading advanced by Anne McClintock uses Kim's fluctuating personae to provide an analogy for understanding the hybridity of colonial discourse.[8] Likewise, John Kucich's attempt to push Kipling studies in a class-focused direction takes a fascination with Kim's ambivalence as its point of departure.[9] Jed Esty calls *Kim* an "antidevelopmental bildungsroman" which "literalizes the problem of colonialism as failed or postponed modernization" (14).[10]

Yet for all this interest in Kim's ambivalence and its consequences, these scholars have disregarded the fact that Kim himself seems awfully aware of his own predicament. This seems strange since it is difficult to think of a character in Victorian fiction more explicitly conscious of his subject formation than Kimball O'Hara. After all, there are few bildungsromans which prompt their heroes to ask, on three separate occasions, "Who is Kim?" (101, 156, 234). This self-knowledge, that despite all his powers he remains subject to the influence of unknowable forces, is what separates Kim from the protagonists of the colonial bildungsromans.[11] In other words, while Kim may never grow into possession of his self, he is acutely aware that there are forces beyond his individual will which are vying for that self. As he admits in transit between the military camp and St Xavier's school, "I go from one place to another as it might be a kick-ball. It is my Kismet. No man can escape his Kismet" (111).

Here, Kim's critical self-consciousness of his being supremely powerful yet supremely powerless ties the novel to the agency crisis of the colonial subject-in-power, the company man. It is too much to accept Kim as the colonialist fantasy for a pure subject; he is not Defoe's Crusoe, a character capable of fashioning a world through his industry and wit. Even as Kipling insists that *Kim* is "nakedly picaresque," we must also recognize the limits to Kim's putatively raw and uninhibited subjectivity are not simply, as Said argued, the geography and society of colonial British India. In other words, while Kim is "vagabonding over India," it is not of his own accord; rather, his mobility is managed and his access to India is contingent upon his submission to other authorities. The infrastructure of British India, and the Malthusian imperial necessity generate the action of the novel. The lama puts him on the Grand Trunk Road to Benares; Mahbub Ali commissions him with the secret message which brings him into contact with the colonel; the colonel intervenes to allow Kim his wandering holidays; and employment in the government's Indian survey – the euphemism for the British secret service – shuttles him across India. Without any of this, Kim might still lay claim to the cosmopolitan title of "Little Friend of all the World," but his cosmos would be limited to the environs of the Lahore bazaar.

What I am suggesting is that Kim's loose sense of identity and the equally loose structure of the picaresque are tied to the problem of colonial agency, more specifically the way that power is organized, distributed, and curtailed in British India. *Kim* cannot be disentangled from Kipling's Indian heritage and experience. In *Something of Myself*, Kipling describes how "in a gloomy, windy autumn *Kim* came back to me with insistence and I took it to be smoked over with my Father" (82). Kipling credits these nostalgic conversations with his father as the origins of the novel: "Between us, we knew every step, sight, and smell on [Kim's] casual road, as well as all the persons he met" (140). This romantic recollection of an India perfectly remembered by stories told between father and son, closes the referential loop started when Sara Jeannette Duncan conjoined imagination with "my people" in her short story "A Mother in India": "They belonged to Bengal and to Burma, to Madras and to the Punjab, but they were all my people. I could pick out a score that I knew in fact, and there were none that in imagination I didn't know" (63). My purpose in this chapter is to place Kipling back among his own people and resituate *Kim* as a colonial novel which, despite its metropolitan attachments, cannot ultimately escape the corporate world view of Anglo-Indian society. I will do this by revisiting Kipling's mediation of the paradoxically powerful protagonist finding himself unable to make a decisive choice and reading him, to switch to the vocabulary of the previous chapters, as a plenipotentiary colonial official in the midst of an agency crisis.

Agency Crises

The critical response to Kim's famous question furnishes an excellent opportunity to demonstrate my point. Here is Kipling's opening to the eleventh chapter:

> Followed a sudden natural reaction.
>
> "Now am I alone – all alone," he thought. "In all India is no one so alone as I! If I die today, who shall bring the news – and to whom? If I live and God is good, there will be a price upon my head, for I am a Son of the Charm – I, Kim"
>
> A very few white people, but many Asiatics, can throw themselves into a mazement [*sic*] as it were by repeating their names over and over again to themselves, letting the mind go free upon speculation as to what is called personal identity. When one grows older, the power, usually, departs, but while it lasts it may descend upon a man at any moment.
>
> "Who is Kim – Kim – Kim?" (156)

In her analysis of the novel, McClintock characterizes this incident as "ethnic vertigo," a part of Kipling's attempt to represent and thereby manage the threat of racial crossings (71). For McClintock, "On the cusp of cultures, denizen of the threshold zones of bazaar, rooftop and road, Kim is both cultural hybrid and racial mimic man" (69). This choice of modifiers (cultural, racial) in this argument indicates the mainstream of Kipling criticism. To date, nearly all critics of *Kim* read his ambivalence as a function of the struggle between, in Patrick Williams's words, Kim's "culturally Indian and naturally British" identities (50).[12] Deanna K. Kreisel, for example, links this persistent struggle for a stable, national identity to the novel's trance scenes, "which are always occasioned by a sudden confrontation with [Kim's] own 'hybridity,' the fact that he is not fully European and not fully Indian" (32).

Against these tendencies, however, it might be better to reread this crisis-of-identity scene within the context of the novel and ask why Kipling would choose this particular moment to cast his protagonist into uncertainty. To begin, we could casually observe that Kim asks similar questions and confronts his hybridity elsewhere in the novel, without succumbing to either magical trances or ethnic vertigo. Similarly, there is nothing in or around this particular scene to suggest that Kim has been "explicitly … confronted with emblems or reminders of racial crossings" (Kreisel 33). On the contrary, this crisis-of-identity scene immediately follows the conclusion of Kim's institutional training, understood dually as his matriculation from St Xavier's school and his subsequent initiation into the fraternity of native secret service agents known as the Sons of the Charm. Moreover, this is the moment where Kim has been unbound and let loose upon India by Colonel Creighton, who has decreed, "For six months he shall run at his choice … [and be paid] twenty rupees a month" (148). Up until this point in the novel, Kim has been described as a free agent, a bazaar boy who distinctly dislikes being ordered about. Thus it seems strange that at this moment, the day of Kim's greatest freedom, Kipling deflates the hero's agency by describing instead how Kim falls "rapt" into a trance-like state where, instead of going where he pleases, he sits still and contemplates "the tremendous puzzle" of his life.

In this case, the novel gives very little suggestion that Kim's crisis is prompted by cultural, racial, or national hybridity. Rather, what we have is an adolescent boy thrust out of his training college and enduring the anguish of isolation for the first time in his life. In short, we have a fictional reworking of the experience of just about every newly trained civil servant in Anglo-Indian history. As I elaborate these historical echoes, I am less interested in refuting Kim's ambivalence than in asking whether a new set of questions might direct our attention away from the dialectic of cultures (British/Indian) and races (European/native) and towards the Anglo-Indian community of colonial administrators. Instead of reading *Kim* as a novel of ethnic or cultural crisis written, as Said has ruled, just as Britain's hegemony was beginning to feel the pressures from below that would culminate in Indian independence, I want to suggest that it should also be read as a reworking of the issues, ideas, and ethics which over the course of the nineteenth century became the constituent elements of what I have been calling Anglo-India's corporate culture.

Orphans and Pure Subjectivity

Any discussion of Kim's subjectivity must begin with his orphan status, a pedigree disclosed in the opening chapter but also recalled, lest we forget, halfway through the narrative (3–4, 139). Following Nancy Armstrong's point about the "constitutive relationship" between the novel and the modern subject, it is easy to see how orphans – raw subjects uninterpellated by domestic institutions – provide deep reservoirs of potentiality out of which novelists might fashion their social message (3).[13] Unencumbered by the accidents of birth, they are excellent subjects for authors seeking to represent the effects of institutions on the soul or character.[14] Of course Victorian novelists were not alone in recognizing the use-value contained within the radical potential of orphans. As figures who were not quite fully English, orphans have always made ideal candidates for imperial service.[15]

Kipling scholars have not ignored the significance of Kim's orphan background. Teresa Hubel argues it is this, just as much as his Irish working-class heritage, that places Kim outside the community of middle-class Anglo-Indian colonial administrators. Hubel argues that, as an alienated orphan, Kim serves as a vehicle through which Kipling can fantasize about cultural combination without threatening the middle-class British imperium (235).[16] Her argument dovetails nicely with Edward Said's characterisation of Kim as, in anthropologist Victor Turner's phrase, liminal. Said asserts that "by holding Kim at the centre of the novel … Kipling can *have* and enjoy India in a way that even imperialism never dreamed of" (*Culture and Imperialism* 155). Both Hubel and Said see Kim as a marginal yet safe, almost-but-not-quite-white figure who, through a series of minor transgressions followed by an assimilation, helps to maintain the established order of a society.

But any service an orphan might render in the elaboration of an ideology or social order is limited by the orphan's willing participation. In the final analysis, orphans are beholden to nobody and are thus free agents. For novelists, muting this agency is usually a rather simple task, since the author exerts total control over what a character says and does, and can thus suppress any rebellion. It is very peculiar then to see Rudyard Kipling, that apparently most ideologically committed imperialist, do precisely the opposite by allowing his protagonist to comprehend his independence. We can now return to the crisis-of-identity scene and recall that before asking his existential question, Kim laments that "in all India is no one so alone as I! If I die today, who shall bring the news – and to whom?" (156). Remember that this alienation, which Kipling calls "a natural sudden reaction," paradoxically follows the two great initiation rituals of the novel (joining the Great Game and becoming a Son of the Charm). The moment when Kim has acquired more friends and colleagues than this bazaar boy has ever had becomes the first point in the novel when Kim is aware of the full significance of his free agency. Likewise at the end of the novel, after foiling the Russian plot, the horizon of possibilities opens up once more for Kipling's hero. Here again, instead of looking to his colleagues for support or validation, Kim considers the startling power of his independence.

In both scenes, Kim's glimpse of his radical power is swiftly followed by psychological disturbances: a trance and aphasia, respectively. Both might be understood as anxiety attacks which occur when Kim feels himself separated from an ordered system. They appear to contradict our received portrait of Kim's ability to do and succeed at whatever he pleases. If Kim is meant to be read as an ideal colonial servant (and I think he is) then it is surely significant that his agency is curtailed and his potency diminished on the threshold of his greatest successes. I would contend that Kipling grants Kim these moments of insight in order to represent his more general concern over the potentially radical agency of colonial administrators. By making Kim confront the scale of his individual power – a scale so awesome that it literally overwhelms his consciousness – just after his entry into and successes in the corporate structures of power, Kipling acknowledges the tenuous hold that the idea of the virtuous empire exercises over the activity of company men.

To appreciate what Kipling is working towards in this representation, it will be helpful to recall the misadventures of Peachy Carnehan and Daniel Dravot, the protagonists of Kipling's "The Man Who Would Be King." Like Kim, these characters are of lower-class origins and have received a degree of basic training from imperial institutions. Peachy and Dravot use these skills to set up an independent enterprise with a view to making themselves kings in an Afghan province. In doing so, they act out of personal interest, which Kipling, ever the disciple of Carlyle, imputes as lust for power, riches, and sexual conquest. Kim, alternatively, is more public-minded. For example, he willingly tosses the seized Russian equipment, worth in excess of "a thousand rupees" (212), into a gorge, reasoning that "a Sahib cannot very well steal" (211) and later chastely refuses the Woman of Shamlegh, who offers her kingdom, saying, "Shamlegh is thine: hoof and horn and hide, milk and butter. Take or leave" (214).[17] What is more, in refusing her, Kim speaks and acts like an English sahib, kissing her on the cheek – something the narrator says is "practically unknown among Asiatics" – and holding "out his hand English-fashion" (435). Where the pursuit of personal interest leads Carnehan and Dravot to disaster, Kim's ability to regulate, even repress, his passions assures his success.

School and Training: Establishing a Self-Perpetuating Corporate Ethos

Kim suppresses his urges because, despite the novel's picaresque qualities or Kim's own boundless freedom and power, *Kim* is a novel overwhelmingly concerned with the problem of agency and man-management. And in this, Kipling's description of Kim's education, strongly echo the ideals for colonial training established by previous generations of colonial authorities and policy makers for the training and selection of new recruits. That is to say, Kipling in this novel suggests a model of surveillance where not only intruding Russians or the potentially seditious Five Northern Kings but also colonial agents find themselves under perpetual scrutiny.

To understand the behaviour of company men like Kim, it is helpful to think of how Kipling represents Kim's relationship to rules and the law in this novel. Kipling's self-described problem of keeping Kim "within bounds" suggests a relationship between the colonial writer and the colonial agent as each sets out to impose an imperial order amid a turbulent and dynamic colonial subject. Part of Kipling's charm is the way he permits his protagonists to transgress the established regulations in order to assert a new level of control. Recalling the adventures of his fictional antecedents in Kipling's *Stalky and Co.* (1899) Kim seems constantly to be adventuring out of bounds.[18] The opening image of the novel – "He sat, in defiance of municipal orders, astride the gun Zam-Zammah" (1) – conveys Kipling's sense of both Kim's power and his disregard for formal rules. The key for Kipling's imperial ideology is striking a balance between these antagonistic positions, of attaining a sort of regulated anarchy. To slip into the eighteenth-century register of Edmund Burke, it is about cultivating men who will implement the spirit rather than the letter of the laws. In this context, philosopher Peter Winch's analysis of how humans understand and follow a rule is instructive. Winch argues that *understanding* denotes that an agent possesses the ability to apply a rule appropriately.[19] Following Heraclitus's principle that no two situations are equivalent, Winch argues that precedence alone is insufficient for our evaluation of what or when is appropriate. Competent agents must in the end intuit their actions based on their subjective understanding of the rules. (Winch speaks of the similar phenomenon where competent speakers within a language community know how to form intelligible, grammatical, yet unique sentences.) In the case of company men, where the novelty of India meant that appeals to tradition and precedence would likely be less frequent than that of, say, a London magistrate, this intuition or character becomes especially important. A professional company administrator cannot know how to perform his duties by reference to a set of instructions or imperial policies, nor is the situation improved much by appeals to personal, informal experience. This was, of course, Edmund Burke's point when he argued that intuition, which he understood as British character, rather than British institutions, should form the basis for colonial ethics. In *Kim*, all the company men adhere to a set of rules, which they seem to apply intuitively. Their judicious sense of what must be done in a given situation contrasts with the pedantic application of regulations by administrators such as Aurelian McGoggin.

The way Kim acquires his knowledge emphasizes Kipling's belief in the continuing importance of socialization in the manufacture of imperial consciousness. Kim's maturation, guided as it is by the advice he receives from his many father-figures, constitutes an exploration of how those rules are acquired. As first presented, precocious and impish, is Kimball O'Hara anything but pure intuition? At the beginning, his lack of interest in worldly affairs is partly a product of his natural inclination towards boyish games, the precursors to the colonial service known throughout the novel as "the Great Game."[20] Developing this image, the coded conversations between Mahbub Ali and Colonel Creighton see the boy as a young horse, as when Mahbub recommends Kim to Creighton as an ideal candidate for the secret service: "When a colt is born to be a polo-pony, closely following the ball without teaching – when such a colt knows the game by divination – then I say it is a great wrong to break that colt to a heavy cart, Sahib" (98). However, wiser men like Creighton are careful not to send a rough character, however naturally adept, into the field without a sense of the rules. Thus while Kim is chela to the lama, he is also variously apprenticed to experienced practitioners of the Great Game, men who teach him its rules. Creighton also adds that his informal tutelage must be augmented by a proper disciplinary atmosphere and so he insists that Kim attend a school.

In Kipling's India, school may take three forms: the military and Masonic orphanages initially favoured by Father Victor and Reverend Bennett (82); the barrack-school for children of enlisted soldiers (91); and St Xavier's, school for "the sons of subordinate officials in the Railway, Telegraph, and Canal services; of warrant-officers ... of captains of the Indian Marine, Government pensioners, planters, Presidency shopkeepers, and missionaries" (106). Of these three, St Xavier's (by its name presumably run by Jesuits) is acknowledged as "the best schooling a boy can get in India" (155) and its positive influence on Kim has been greatly underestimated by critics. Perhaps because of Kim's restless nature elsewhere in the novel, manifested especially in his desire to escape from the "three days of torment ... in the big echoing white rooms" of the Irish Mavericks' regimental school house, Kim is presumed to be disposed against all types of formal instruction (91). Despite puzzling claims by Edward Said that St Xavier's imposes a "useless authority" (*CI* 137), and by John Kucich that Kim alternates between feelings of "condescension" and "contempt" (190) towards its schoolboys, Kipling makes it clear that St Xavier's is a special type of school. His approval of its methods reflects the fact that, with the exception of school dinners, Kim enjoys his time there.

Primarily this is expressed through the image of the school as a collection of similarly disposed but unrelated trainees who build their community through storytelling. At St Xavier's, Kim develops a fraternity with his schoolmates as they relate "their adventures, which to them were no adventures, on their road to and from school that would have crisped a Western boy's hair." On occasion, listening to these incendiary tales involving tigers, floods, and elephant-requisitions,

> Kim watched, listened, and approved. This was not the insipid, single-word talk of drummer-boys. It dealt with a life he knew and in part understood. (106)

This is not the first instance in Kipling's fiction of bonds being formed through storytelling. "At the End of The Passage" (1891) sits in on one of the periodic meetings of four civil servants who "were not conscious of any special regard for each other," but who cling to each other, swapping stories, rather than confront the abyss of their isolation. In both this story and *Kim*, the community of autobiographical storytellers establishes a standard for behaviour through their shared experiences. In this environment Kim "quietly ... measured himself against his self-reliant mates" (106). The narrator confirms Kim's favourable reaction to life at St Xavier's: "The atmosphere suited him, and he throve by inches" (106–7).

Appropriately in this novel so concerned with fashion and dressing-up, Kim's favour is expressed in the form of sartorial approval. On the one hand, back in the barrack-school Kim must dress as a "little scarlet figure" and he feels that "trousers and jacket crippled body and mind alike" (91). On the other hand, when St Xavier's issues him "a white drill suit ... he rejoiced in the new-found bodily comforts as he rejoiced to use his sharpened mind over the tasks they set to him" (107). The joys are limned when Kim, nearing his first set of holidays, thinks that "a barrack-school would be torment after St Xavier's" (107). On another occasion, following Kim's summer of training with Lurgan, the narrator observes, "Of all the boys hurrying back to St Xavier's ... none was so filled with virtue as Kimball O'Hara" (137).

St Xavier's thus represented is an uncommon Indian school. The flourishing of knowledge, the sensitivity of the teachers, and the affability of the cohort make it seem closer to a Haileybury than the barrack-school where Kim "much disapproved of the present aspect of affairs, for this was the very school and discipline he had spent two-thirds of his young life in avoiding" (86). For the superior school, alternatively, Kim harbours only fond reminiscences. During his summer of vagabonding he cannot help "thinking of the neat white cots of St. Xavier's all arow under the punkah," a memory that "gave him joy" (116). Later, as he dreams of his future in the secret service, of being "almost as great as Mahbub Ali," and stalking "Kings and ministers," Kim remembers that "meantime, there was the present, and not at all unpleasant fact of St Xavier's immediately before him" (137). Kim even goes so far as to apologize to Mahbub for having earlier doubted the sense in sending him to school: "I say now, Hajji, that it was well done; and I see my road all clear before me to a good service. I will stay in the *madrissah* till I am ripe" (115).

Part of Kim's affection for his alma mater derives from its institutional ethic; whereas at the barrack-school young boys are drilled in

Gradgrindian facts, at St Xavier's aristocratic virtue is conspicuously cultivated. Its students are told "never [to] forget that one is a Sahib, and some day, when examinations are passed, one will command natives"; according to the narrator, this promise inspires Kim to learn, "for he began to understand where examinations led" (107). Like the students at Malthus's Haileybury or the candidates of Macaulay's competition examination, Kim understands that the primary purpose of schooling is not to acquire knowledge but habits of industry, organization, and a desire to compete against his peers (he took a biography of Lord Lawrence as a prize for his proficiency in mathematics). He also begins to learn the proper codes of conduct befitting a secret service agent, as he explains to Mahbub:

> The Colonel is the servant of the Government. He is sent hither and yon at a word, and must consider his own advancement. (See how much I have already learned at [St Xavier's]!) (115)

The parenthetical boast confirms that the teachers at St Xavier's do much more than train boys in facts. They seem also to have read their Burke, for Kipling represents them as having uncommon sensitivity towards the geographical and cultural specificity of India. "The country-born and bred boy has his own manners and customs," Kipling writes of the typical Xavier's student, "which do not resemble those of any other land; and his teachers approach him by roads which an English master would not understand" (105). So whereas Kim's "quickness would have delighted an English master," the teachers at St Xavier's "know the first rush of minds developed by sun and surroundings" (107). Nevertheless, the education is not fully Oriental but rather a fusion of English character and Indian forms since, at the end of his time there, when he is about to undertake his appointment as a chain-man Kim receives, like Thomas Malthus's Haileybury graduates, stern paternal warnings. In Kim's exit interview, the head cautions that there "is a great deal of hard work before you," and the narrator describes (sincerely) how Kim receives "much good advice as to his conduct, and his manners, and his morals" (149).

It is also clear that St Xavier's creates a strong sense of esprit de corps, since nowhere else in this novel does Kim respect boys of his age group. From Abdullah and Chota Lal toppled from Lahore's Zam-zammah cannon in the novel's opening allegory of imperial conquest; through the stereotypical regimental drummer-boy of the Irish Mavericks "loathed … from the soles of his boots to his cap-ribbons" (86); to the skilled Hindu boy apprenticed to Lurgan "cuffed" in anger (127); the boys who appear in this novel as rivals to Kim are as deeply loathed as they are eventually defeated. Not so the St Xavier's boys who are never criticized and even reappear later in the novel, in connection with Kim's pride in his accomplishments during his adventures. As Kim tramps through the hills with the lama, Kipling describes a process of physical maturation: "The hills sweated the *ghi* and sugar suet off his bones; the dry air, taken sobbingly at the head of cruel passes, firmed and built out his upper ribs; and the tilted levels put hard new muscles into calf and thigh" (194). Most important, though, as Kim endures this punishing regimen, he takes masochistic pleasure from it: "Then did Kim, aching in every fibre, dizzy with looking down, footsore with cramping desperate toes into inadequate crannies, take joy in the day's march – such joy as a boy of St. Xavier's who had won the quarter-mile on the flat might take in the praises of his friends" (194). On one level, this description of Kim's masochistic pleasure is a piece of exemplary exposition on the Carlylean faith in the gospel of work. Kim signals his maturation by deriving manly satisfaction from private accomplishment where once, as a schoolboy, he would have sought the external validation of his peers. On the other hand, when Kim invokes the admiration of the St Xavier schoolboys as the vehicle for his metaphor, the passage reveals the extent to which Kim has internalized the ethic cultivated at St Xavier's.

Admittedly, St Xavier's comprises only a part of Kim's formal training; the other half occurs at Lurgan's curiosity shop in Simla. Yet consistent with St Xavier's, Lurgan's more irregular institution registers the traces of Anglo-India's corporate culture. Known as the Healer of Sick Pearls (with pearls and jewels being a codeword for students), Lurgan is responsible for preparing Indian natives for fieldwork in the Great Game; among others, the famous E23 is his protégé. On the first morning of their acquaintance, Lurgan tests "to see if there [is] – a flaw in the jewel" (131), by forcing Kim to look closely at the shards of a broken water jug and to describe what he sees. In Kipling's stylized vision, this involves Lurgan encouraging Kim to see something that is not there, namely a reassembled jug, through the application of a mysterious pressure to the back of Kim's neck. Lurgan's grip is a "light touch" which paradoxically held "like a vice" so that Kim's "blood tingled pleasantly through him" and "wave[s] of prickling fire raced down his neck" (130). Though Kipling never elaborates on what Lurgan has done to Kim, except to have Lurgan say that it is "not magic" (131), we know that with "each beat of his pulse" (130), Kim sees the jug coming back together. Should he believe the illusion, this would be a sign of his susceptibility to temptation and corruption. As Lurgan explains, "Sometimes very fine jewels will fly all to pieces if a man holds them in his hand, and knows the proper way" (131).

However, Kipling proves Kim's incorruptibility through a trick that would have pleased Edmund Burke greatly. Kipling informs us that throughout this trial "Kim had been thinking in Hindi" and that when he takes "refuge in – the multiplication-table in English," Kim can extricate himself from Lurgan's illusion:

> The jar had been smashed – yess [*sic*] smashed – not the native word, he would not think of that – but smashed – into fifty pieces, and twice three was six, and thrice three was nine, and four times three was twelve. (130)

From this passage it is clear that it is not only the practical and mechanical multiplication-table which saves Kim but "the multiplication-table in English." In other words Kim's escape is not simply the victory of (Western) scientific rationality over (Eastern) spiritual mutability but rather the assertion of the relative practical values of different cultures. Without Kim's decision to use the word "smashed" in place of its Hindi analogue we cannot know whether he would have broken the spell. Just as Edmund Burke insisted that baptism in English character could inoculate company men against the temptations and vice of Oriental despotism, so Kipling suggests that by judicious and timely appeal to English character Kim becomes "the first who ever saved himself" from Lurgan's illusion (131) – Kim is also, of course, the first European ever to be trained by Lurgan and the first who could ever use his Englishness as a defence.

English- or British-ness? The Location of Corporate Culture

By bringing Burke back into this discussion, I hope to do more than trace one line of continuity across the nineteenth-century imperial discourse. It is also to remind ourselves of the arbitrary nature of the English (or British) identity itself, and especially its contingency on cultural institutions. Thinking once more of the energy expended by administrators and educators like Wellesley, Malthus, and Macaulay in the direction of cultivating a particular character, and their attending confidence in the disciplinary apparatus of their choice, enables an interpretation of Kim's success which moves away from the simple conclusion that Kim's Englishness is something essential, natural, or bred in the bone. But this would seemingly run contrary to Kipling's insistence on the first page that, despite his many "native" affectations, "Kim was white – a poor white of the very poorest" (3). As much as the Zam-zammah allegory, this opening declaration of Kim's race has characterized recent approaches to the novel. McClintock, for instance, reads this scene as exemplary proof both of Kipling's fascination with cross-cultural knowledge and understanding and of his simultaneous anxiety over the threat that the pure play of mutable imperial identities poses to the stability of imperial order (69–71). Endowing Kim with a British core, Kipling can allow his protagonist to immerse himself in all kinds of Indian practices, knowing that they are only temporary, idle performances.

If we probe a little deeper into McClintock's argument, it becomes less clear that Kipling places any virtue in essential racial identities. To begin with the contrary position, it is curious that despite McClintock's interest in the collusion of transvestism and colonial surveillance that she does not even once mention the definitive cross-dressing scene in the novel. I refer here to the evenings of leisure in Lurgan's shop:

> After dinner, Lurgan Sahib's fancy turned more to what might be called a dressing-up, in which game he took a most informing interest. He could paint faces to a marvel; with a brush-dab here and a line there changing them past recognition … Lurgan Sahib had a hawk's eye to detect the least flaw in the make-up; and lying on a worn teak-wood couch, would explain by the half-hour together how such and such a caste talked, or walked, or coughed, or spat, or sneezed, and, since "hows" matter little in this world, the "why" of everything. The Hindu child played this game clumsily. That little mind, keen as an icicle where tally of jewels was concerned, could not temper itself to enter into another's soul; but a demon in Kim woke up and sang with joy at the changing dresses, and changed speech and gesture therewith. (134–5)

Aside from the masculine image of the hawk's eye, this scene is as close as one can imagine a Tory imperialist like Rudyard Kipling ever gets to a high camp style. More pertinent, at least to McClintock's argument if she had used it, is Kipling's clear assertion here that the racialized Hindu boy lacks the ability to complete such a complicated trick. Only

Lurgan and Kim, both of whom are described as sahibs who are anything but sahibs, are permitted by the anxious Kipling, the argument could be made, to pass.

However, against this position, we can observe that the nameless Hindu boy is not the only native who dresses up in the service of Her Majesty. More proficient and experienced is the Bengali babu, Mookerjee, who first meets Kim in Simla and is praised before Kim by none less than Lurgan, the master of disguise, deception, and detection:

> From time to time, God causes men to be born – and thou art one of them – who have a lust to go abroad at the risk of their lives and discover news … These souls are very few; and of these few, not more than ten are of the best. Among these ten I count the Babu, and that is curious. How therefore great and desirable must be a business that brazens the heart of a Bengali. (263)

The "thou" is Kim, the boy whose natural suitability for the service Mahbub confirms elsewhere when he confides to the colonel that "only once in a thousand years is a horse born so well fitted for the Game as this our colt" (274). Yet Mookerjee contradicts the equivalence of extraordinary talents with (British) racial background.

The standard view of Mookerjee is that he represents Kipling's caricature of what the Russian spy calls "the monstrous hybridism of East and West" (199), the Anglicized native whose origins are usually traced to Macaulay's "Minute on Indian Education." The stereotypical figure has appeared before in Kipling's fiction (most famously in "The Head of the District") and has more recently been denoted by postcolonial theorist Homi Bhabha as a "mimic man," the necessary historical product of ambivalent colonial discourse (87). For example, McClintock sees Mookerjee as "a risible mimic man … mimicry gone wrong" (70); Abdul JanMohamed calls his situation one of "absurdity" (69); Said says he is "the grimacing stereotype of the ontologically funny native, hopelessly trying to be like 'us'" (153). None of these critics, whose work is ostensibly directed towards identifying moments of native resistance and agency within overwhelming structures of imperial power, is willing to attribute to Mookerjee the talents that they readily identify as part of Kipling's idealization of the proficient white male. That is to say, they refuse to consider the possibility that Mookerjee is faking it.

To evaluate this possibility, consider the public performance of the other characters who perform an uncharacteristic identity in order to achieve their true objectives. Colonel Creighton, the man who commands armies in secret, is in public a man "easily cheated about a horse," a man who "is madder than most other Sahibs" (100). The same holds for Strickland, whom E23 calls "not less than the greatest" player of the Great Game, yet who appears in public as an "angry, stupid Sahib" prone to "strutting and twirling his dark moustache" (174–5). Kim, like the postcolonial critics, learns to see through these public facades, and even describes Creighton as "a man after his own heart – a tortuous and indirect person playing a hidden game" (100). It is baffling, therefore, that no one has yet thought Mookerjee capable of the same feat, that Mookerjee plays the part of the cowardly Bengali babu just as easily and for the same ends as Creighton or Strickland play the part of the foolish sahib.

There is plenty of textual evidence to support this view. Consider how the stereotype enables this Bengali to ingratiate himself into the hunting party of the Russian and French spies. Consider too how easily Mookerjee shrugs off the stereotype when necessity requires it. Remember that Lurgan's celebration of Mookerjee's talents is said in retort to Kim's impression of the "hulking obese Babu whose stockinged legs shook with fat" (135). Kim admits he does not "understand how *he* can wear many dresses and talk many tongues" (135). Yet Mookerjee consistently exceeds expectations. In the house of the Kulu woman, for instance,

> Kim looked on with envy. The Hurree Babu of his knowledge – oily, effusive, and nervous – was gone; gone, too, was the brazen drug-vendor of overnight. There remained – polished, polite, attentive – a sober, learned son of experience and adversity, gathering wisdom from the lama's lips. (189–90)

Furthermore, though Mookerjee may insist to Kim that he is a "Bengali – a fearful man ... awfully fearful" (187), the statement is later ironically undermined. Chasing the Russian and French spies through the hills, the narrator describes how "Hurree Babu, that 'fearful man,' had bucketed three days before through a storm to which nine Englishmen out of ten would have given full right of way" (196–7). Kim too finds his initial stereotypical assessment thwarted when he considers the peril Mookerjee undertakes by remaining with the Russian party after their documents have been stolen: "He makes a mock of them at the risk of his life – *I* never would have gone down to them after the pistol-shots – and then he says he is a fearful man" (234).

If we consider that Kimball O'Hara is a Celt who has learned the rule of strategically deploying (Anglo-Saxon) English character to his advantage, then we apprehend Mookerjee's strategic manoeuvres. This Bengali differs from the stereotypical portrait painted in Kipling's early fiction (an exemplary case being "The Head of the District") because, like Kim, he has learned not simply the British forms but also the British character. Mookerjee knows the proverbial rules of the game, and has enough intuition to apply his knowledge judiciously. I am thinking in particular of the scene following Kim's graduation, when Mahbub and Mookerjee arrange for Kim to have his "colour" changed by Huneefa the prostitute. There, just as Kim appealed to his multiplication-tables and English lexicon to diffuse Lurgan's illusion, Mookerjee refutes the devils invoked in the ceremony by calling them "dematerialised phenomena," quoting Herbert Spencer, and "talking English to reassure himself" (152). In another important way, Mookerjee copies Kim's strategic essentialism. Just as Kim negotiates his identity through a series of positive statements – "I am a Sahib" (185) later becomes "I am not a Sahib. I am thy *chela*" (225) – Mookerjee vacillates between his allegiances.

Mookerjee's proficiency evokes the moral of Kipling's "The Ballad of East and West," a poem remembered today for its opening couplet: "Oh, East is East, and West is West, and never the twain shall meet, / Till Earth and Sky stand presently at God's great Judgment Seat." That moral is actually contained in the next, less-well-remembered couplet: "But there is neither East nor West, Border, nor Breed, nor Birth, / When two strong men stand face to face, tho' they come from the ends of the earth!" Britons and Indians may be irreparably separated, but Kipling's poem develops a space where profession and talent (in the poem it is horsemen; in the novel it is secret service agents) can override the affiliations of, in the poet's list, geography, nation, race, and class. Mahbub affirms this cosmopolitan and meritocratic sentiment when he tells Kim that "this matter of creeds is like horseflesh. The wise man knows horses are good – that there is a profit to be made from all" (121–2). But better still is the distinction Mookerjee draws between *English* and *British* as he briefs Kim on the Russian mission. The difference is drawn as Mookerjee explains his frustration that Creighton would not simply "issue demi-offeecial orders" to poison the intruding spies: "And Colonel Creighton, he laughed at me! It is all your beastly English pride. You think no one dare conspire. That is all tommy-rott." Here not only does Mookerjee use English idioms to critique English behaviour but, in the next instant, both the case of the possessive pronoun and the modifier change as Mookerjee speaks of civil hospitality as "our British pride" (187). This switch, from yours to ours and from English to British, indicates an expansion of possible collaboration as in the community of accomplishment outlined in "The Ballad of East and West," appears in *Kim* as a collective of cooperating colonial subjects (Anglo-Saxons, Celts, Muslims, and Hindus) working together in the service of the British Empire.

Controlling the Radical Free Agent

Identifying Kim O'Hara as a restless seeker and wanderer, Edward Said includes *Kim* within the late-Victorian aesthetic of disillusionment, noting that *Kim* is only separable from novels like *New Grub Street*, *Middlemarch*, and *Jude the Obscure* because of its optimism and its confidence. Unlike Gissing's Edwin Reardon, Eliot's Dorothea Brooke, or Hardy's Jude Fawley, Kim successfully overcomes the obstacles which threaten his morale and his ability to progress in the existing social order. Said understands this success as a function of *Kim*'s imperial setting. Unlike domestic Britain whose green and verdant hills – the site of many a declaration of romantic subjectivity – were by the fin de siécle experiencing the full force of industrial capitalism, Kipling's India, argues Said, continued to provide a practically limitless imaginative and geographical space:

> For what one cannot accomplish in one's own Western environment – where trying to live out the grand dream of a successful quest means coming against one's own mediocrity and the world's corruption and degradation – one can do abroad. Isn't it possible in India to do everything? be anything? go anywhere with impunity? (159)

What Said seems to be saying is that where external circumstances cause other Victorian protagonists to slip into a crisis which leads, at best, to a compromised faith in their ability to fashion the world, Kim O'Hara is always, in Said's final analysis, master of his fate, his *kismet*.

Kim's mastery, his ability to penetrate Indian communities and geographies as and when he pleases, should on the one hand be interpreted as a pure colonialist fantasy but it is equally important to consider how his agency is curtailed within the structure of administrative power. Sara Suleri advances this opinion by identifying "the terrifying absence of choice in the operations of colonialism" and diagnosing Kim as "an imperial casualty of more tragic proportions than he is usually granted" (116). In her reading, Kim's Indian freedom is conditional on his submission to a higher order, the English set of practices regulated by Creighton. Yet I am not so sure that Creighton's supervening authority is as secure as this since Kipling himself devotes a good deal of this short book to scenes where the proverbial rules of the Great Game are disseminated. Kim consistently thinks of his relationship to Creighton in terms of a civil contract, a conception which differs strongly from the filial devotion he lavishes on the novel's other two father-figures, Mahbub and the lama. We can appreciate Creighton's relationship more clearly by comparing the official secret service with the unofficial fraternity of native-born agents known as the Sons of the Charm. The former is what Ferdinand Tönnies would call a civil society, something structured by artificial and soluble contracts; the latter a community, something tied by stronger bonds of fellow-feeling. In a civil society, a contract first presupposes parity between negotiating parties and second it confers the ability to withdraw if the other party has violated the terms. Kim confirms the first presumption when he negotiates with the colonel in Urdu and "actually dare[s] to use the *tum* of equals" (102). For the second part, we might look to Kim's reaction when the colonel encroaches on his holiday time; his enjoyment of a perilous adventure with Mahbub Ali is curtailed "because – in defiance of the contract – the Colonel had ordered him to make a map of that wild, walled city" (143). Mahbub Ali warns the colonel of the consequences: "If permission be refused to go and come as he chooses, he will make light of the refusal. Then who is to catch him?" (141–2). In short, the narrator suggests if Creighton fails to live up to Kim's expectations, it follows that Kim will simply opt out of the contract and pursue other amusements and interests.

Creighton's difficulty here is not dissimilar to the reality faced by the London directors of the East India Company trying to manage their field agents. Both are aware that they exercise little direct control over their employees and so must resort to more indirect forms of man-management. This is why, despite his evident importance and influence in Kim's life, the colonel only speaks to the boy once after their initial meeting, and that is on the train to Lucknow where Kim will enrol in St Xavier's. Here he dispenses advice on what not to do (i.e., sell information or act disrespectfully towards the natives), praises the boy's "good spirit," and promises him that if he diligently completes his duties, they shall meet again (101–2). Otherwise, though Creighton looms large, his influence on Kim is indirect. We know that he discusses Kim's future with other members of the secret service and we also know that "often in the past few months" he "had caught himself thinking of the queer, silent, self-possessed boy" (109). Yet despite his alienation from his agent, it is hinted throughout the novel that he has intervened to save Kim from punishment, an intervention which Kipling metonymizes as the unseen "hand of friendship" which averts the "whip of calamity" (111). In this sense, like Miss Havisham of Dickens's *Great Expectations*, Creighton is the absent authority under whose suspected scrutiny Kim regulates his behaviour. (For a Magwitch, Kipling gives us Teshoo Lama, the surprisingly resourceful mendicant who provides the funds for Kim's excellent schooling at St Xavier's.) Like Pip, Kim cannot prove whether Creighton is indeed the silent hand of friendship, but he is nonetheless convinced that this man knows everything about his life and has taken an active interest in monitoring its progress. Creighton haunts Kim's thoughts and his conversations with Mahbub, Lurgan, and Hurree, with Kim always fearful that Creighton will "cast him off" (137).

Creighton metonymically stands for panoptic surveillance, the man who has rendered India transparent. In Said's reading, this transparency is deployed to police India and its imperial subjects and, as such, "Creighton embodies the notion that you cannot govern India unless you know India" (*Culture and Imperialism* 153). Colonel Creighton, the "ethnographer-scholar-soldier," becomes the focus of Said's analysis because he represents the "union of power and knowledge" (183, 184). Said is certainly right that Kipling's India appears as an impossibly complex social space put into order by colonial administrators committed to the Orientalist acquisition of knowledge about the land and its people.[21] At times, as in the descriptions of the Grand Trunk Road, Kipling presents India as a teeming, incoherent mass of diverse humanity, structured with innumerable languages, cultures, and caste divisions. This is best shown as Kipling describes Kim's first journey on the road. At one point, Kim feels the road rises a little, "so that one walked, as it were, a little above the country, along a stately corridor, seeing all India spread out to left and right" (56). From this slight vantage point, Kim apprehends briefly the Indian sublime but at this stage in the novel he is but one of many travellers on the road, a part of but unable to critically reflect on its meaning. The boy, as yet untutored, "felt these things, though he could not give tongue to his feelings" (56). After his training, however, Kim acquires the critical perspective which enables him both to survey and to know India and so he will become the author of incredibly detailed, secret reports of cities like Jeysulmir (144). When he has been trained by Lurgan's jewel game, Mookerjee's rosary-bead division, and St Xavier's course in elementary surveying, Kim joins the fellowship of colonial administrators who study, know, and then manage the jumble with a combination of rationality and respect for its diversity.

However, even more closely scrutinized than the India policed by the ethnographer-spies who "know the land and the customs of the land" (67) is the smaller community of ethnographer-spies themselves. And whatever desire critics might have to label *Kim* a novel about colonial surveillance, we have yet to take a full reckoning of the true object of their surveillance. I think this is something that Said hints at, but never explores, in his passing question on the fantasy of passing: "Was there ever a native fooled by the blue- or green-eyed Kims and T.E. Lawrences?" (*Culture and Imperialism* 194–5). Said's question is taken up more fully by Parama Roy in her study of the relation between "passing" and colonial surveillance. By considering the case of Richard Burton among others, Roy convincingly demonstrates that "going native" was successful only as an imperial fantasy; in fact, the natives always knew when an Englishman stained with tamarind juice was in their presence (20–1).[22]

There are even suggestions in *Kim* that Kipling was aware of this impossibility since we should not overlook the fact that, on at least two occasions, Kim forgets which type of native he is impersonating and speaks incorrectly (157; 233). Elsewhere, though Kipling insists that Kim "found it easier to slip into Hindu or Mahommedan garb when engaged on certain businesses" (5), the novel gives no definitive indication that the natives are truly fooled by his costumes. On the contrary, when Kim asks Mookerjee how he was tracked from Simla to the house of the Kulu woman, the Bengali replies, "Oah. Thatt was nothing … all the common people know what you do … they know about you and the lama for fifty miles – the common people" (185). Indeed whether by his good looks or his actions, nearly every male native and certainly all the females seem to *notice* Kim.

I want to introduce Slavoj Žižek's discussion of totalitarianism at this point because it helpfully points towards the true object of these exercises in "passing." In associating Kipling with totalitarianism, I am exploring the lapsus in George Orwell's 1942 essay, "Rudyard Kipling," which considers "the shallow and familiar charge the Kipling was a 'Fascist'" (75):

> The "Fascist" charge has to be answered, because the first clue to any understanding of Kipling, morally or politically, is the fact that he was *not* a Fascist. He was further from being one than the most humane or the most "progressive" person is able to be nowadays. (75)

Orwell does not propose to canonize Kipling, or to celebrate his politics, but rather chooses to identify "his confidence, his bouncing vulgar vitality," in empire as a basically liberating (i.e., enlightenment) project:

> Imperialism as he sees it is a sort of forcible evangelizing. You turn a Gatling gun on a mob of unarmed "natives," and then you establish "the Law," which includes roads, railways and a court-house. (78)

Žižek similarly identifies totalitarianism as a product of the Enlightenment, in his proposal that totalitarianism liberates human subjects by transforming duty into pleasure. The difference between an authoritarian power and a totalitarian power, according to Žižek, is that the former imposes on its subjects, saying "you must do this thing" while the latter adds, "you must do this thing *and you must enjoy doing it*!" Citing the bizarre fact that "on Stalin's birthday, prisoners would send him congratulatory telegrams from the darkest gulags," Žižek explains how totalitarianism presupposes "a space in which the leader and his subjects could meet as servants of Historical Reason" (4).

In a similar way we might understand Kipling's affectionate rendering of Kim's interaction with native Indians *qua* imperial agent. Mookerjee, as it were, answers Said's rhetorical question: yes, all the common people know about you, and not only do they permit your (invasive and surveilling) masquerade but they actually enjoy it. If we continue with Žižek's analogy, we will see that the true purpose of going native is to deceive other members of the elite, the players of the Great Game rather than the "common" colonized natives. This is the case when Kim disguises E23 as a *saddhu* in the train compartment, to avoid both a gang of police led by "a hot and perspiring young Englishman" and the rivals for E23's packet of letters (173). In similar fashion Kim's native mimicry fools a treasonous English Commissariat sergeant as well as the Russian and French spies.

The most illuminating feature of the totalitarian analogy is its emphasis on the purge, the self-cannibalization of the party. Indeed, I would argue that however flawed or efficient "passing" may be as a method for gathering or delivering information about your subjects and the enemies of the state, in *Kim* nothing compares to self-imposed transparency under which the players of the Game toil. Appropriately in this libidinal economy, the transparency carries both positive and negative connotations. When Mookerjee informs Kim that his "extraordinarily effeecient performance" in the case of E23 is already well-known and that "we are all proud of you," Kim is delighted:

> For the first time in his life, Kim thrilled to the clean pride (it can be a deadly pitfall, none the less) of Departmental praise – ensnaring praise from an equal of work appreciated by fellow-workers. Earth has nothing on the same plane to compare with it. (184)

In a similar scene Lurgan, Kim's tutor in the arts of espionage, anticipates following Kim's progress via the unofficial interdepartmental social network: "He foresaw the honour and credit in the mouths of a chosen few, coming to him from his pupil" (148).

The negative effect of this publicity is more keenly felt. At the crucial stages in his education, when he is learning from St Xavier's and from Lurgan, Kim is taught, twice, the consequences of betraying his official trust. When Kim asks Mahbub what might befall a boy who sold the information he was entrusted to convey to Creighton, Mahbub simply replies that "Then thou wouldst have drunk water twice – perhaps thrice, afterwards. I do not think more than thrice" (219). Similarly, when he asks Lurgan about the price on Hurree's head and is told that he might earn himself "a belt full of rupees," by selling certain information, Kim follows up by asking, "How long might such a boy live after the news was told?" Lurgan replies, "Perhaps if he were very clever, he might live out the day – but not the night. By no means the night" (262–3). It is as if by their very power, colonial agents have become entrapped in a cycle of paranoid anxiety which they know can only result in their arbitrary destruction.

In *Kim*, characters ostensibly on the same "team" in the Game expend considerable energy surveilling and tricking each other. Consider Mookerjee's appearance as a "Dacca drug vendor" in the house of the Kulu woman. Dacca being a city in Bengal, we can reasonably conclude that Mookerjee's costume cannot have been put on for any purpose other than to fool Kim. The effect of the trick is registered in Kim's reaction. At first the narrator assumes a first-person intimacy with the protagonist, who is projecting his ideal sense of self: Kim feels "annoyed ... that he had been hoodwinked." But shortly thereafter the narrator pulls back from Kim and adopts a more objective journalistic style, which reveals that even while the boy affects unflappability he has been deeply disturbed: "He chewed leisurely upon a few cardamom seeds, but he breathed uneasily" (184). Elsewhere Kim is twice unnerved by Mookerjee's ability to vanish as "noiselessly as a cat" (138, 155).

We can see here in operation a process whereby the initiates are made aware of their inability to disguise themselves or to detect a disguise. Kim's inferiority becomes apparent when we compare his nervous reactions with those of two other proficient secret service agents. The first incident occurs early in the novel as Kipling introduces the character of Mahbub Ali. Though Kim wants to surprise Mahbub by appearing as a Hindu beggar, and though Mahbub entertains this folly while Kim is "in character," when Kim reveals himself by speaking in English, "the trader *gave no sign of astonishment*" (33, emphasis added). Similarly, lest we attribute this placidity to the horse-trader's sanguine character, we should note Mookerjee's response on his visit to Lurgan's shop, where he sees Kim sitting in the corner in the disguise of "a certain caste of *faquir*" (260):

> "I think," said the Babu heavily, lighting a cigarette, "I am of the opeenion that it is most extraordinary and effeecient performance. Except that you had told me I should have opined that – that – that you were pulling my legs." (261)

This praise for Kim's performance is qualified not only because it is delivered in front of both the performer and his teacher, or because it is delivered among a fraternity of Game players, but also because Mookerjee, elsewhere so excitable and garrulous in the novel, here speaks heavily, slowly, and languidly, taking the time to pause before carefully delivering the final compliment.

If we consider, as I think we should, *Kim* to be a novel about education and maturation, then Mookerjee's performances teach through example and shaming. Kim's failure to detect Mookerjee, coming so soon after his training in espionage with Lurgan in Simla, reminds both the boy and the reader of the cost involved in this fantastic totalitarian vision. And this proves Suleri's point: Kim can "play" the Game and exercise colonial power only when he agrees to play by its rules. In the same way, the reader can have India, but only when it has been mediated by a colonial agent. Suleri, however, sees only the tragic consequence for this entrapped subject when she puts forward a teleology of disenchantment. In her withering assessment of the effects of colonial education, Suleri sees the magical, mercurial, and innocent bazaar-boy as one who receives the power to know and make meaning, but only at a mortal price. The cost of his critical perspective is an inability to participate freely in Indian life and so, Suleri reasons, the conclusion is Kipling's elegiac fashioning of his admission that "posteducated Kim … must be killed" (130).

Yet this bleak account leaves little room for the pleasures of imperialism, the love and fellow-feeling which courses through the novel between the principal characters. Mahbub, in particular, finds his parental affection for Kim increase as the boy progresses in the secret service. Consider also Kim's satisfaction when he experiences the incomparable clean pride of Departmental praise. The positive effect spurs him actively to seek further missions. "Well is the Game called great!" he exclaims when Mookerjee recruits him to help foil the Russian plot as he considers the value of "my share and my joy [in it]" (188). We should also recall that this novel ends not with suffering or death but in terms that suggest spiritual redemption. The lama tells Kim, "I [have] freed thee from all sin … Just is the wheel! Certain is our deliverance! Come!" (240).

At the same time, there can be no doubt that this last and greatest mission, which began with Mookerjee's Dacca deception, extracts a severe physical and psychic toll. Throughout its progress, Kim is described as a beleaguered agent, struggling to balance his official responsibility and his filial duty to the lama: "Kim's shoulders bore all the weight of it – the burden of an old man, the burden of the heavy food-bag with the locked books, the load of writings on his heart, and the details of the daily routine" (224). But it seems that, consistent with the views expressed in Kipling's early short stories, Kim takes pleasure from this self-sacrificing toil. At the climax of the mission, "Kim shivered with cold and pride. The humour of the situation tickled the Irish and the Oriental in his soul" (207).

But carrying the weak body of the lama and the heavy package of documents nearly kills the young man. Kipling reminds us, "Their weight on his shoulders was nothing to their weight on his mind" (228). But rather than choose between one or the other, Kipling allows his hero to indulge in a radical pleasure that is denied to most agents. When he finally descends from the Himalayas to the home of the Kulu woman, Kim shrugs off *both* his responsibilities: to personal conscience, represented by the lama, and to his duty, represented by the package. In this scene, the ultimate in pleasure-through-pain is represented when Kim's agony is "relieved" by a massage which is described in terms of dismemberment:

> [The two women] took him to pieces all in one long afternoon – bone by bone, muscle by muscle, ligament by ligament, and lastly, nerve by nerve. Kneaded to irresponsible pulp, [and] half hypnotized ... Kim slid ten thousand miles into slumber – thirty-six hours of it – sleep that soaked like rain after drought. (229)

Arguably, this is the novel's most controversial scene since it is here that the handsome and proficient masculine agent, who has hitherto rejected the affections of females in favour of homosocial affiliation, surrenders his agency to two women who render him irresponsible. The absence of a resolution in *Kim* shares coordinates with a corporate *Gemeinschaft*. What the critics have called the novel's "failed" conclusion now seems appropriate for a novel fashioned out of a culture that valued work in itself, rather than work as a process towards some objective goal. Kim's greatest joys in this novel do not come from private reflection on the significance of his efforts but rather from his expectation that his efforts will be acknowledged and appreciated by his peers.

In his decisions and indecisions, then, Kim is not unlike Henry Broughton, the character from George Otto Trevelyan's *Competition Wallah* viewed to possess the ideal psychological demeanour for imperial service. Broughton, we will recall, insists that he chose to apply for an Indian career not because he was interested in civilizing India or in making a name for himself but because, for him, "the vital object to be looked for in the choice of a line in life [is] to select one that would present a succession of high and elevating interests" (Trevelyan 3). This principle could very easily describe Kim as well, since he is introduced as someone who will "use his properties" (i.e., his skills) only when "there was business or frolic afoot" (7). Personal advancement or profit hardly ever enters his mind. More to the point of Kipling's novel, Broughton's description of his career aspirations, in its refusal of a teleological goal in favour of a succession of diverse interests almost uncannily predicts Kipling's decision to adopt the style of the picaresque in *Kim*. The ideal style for the novel of corporate colonial culture turns out to resemble and work to reproduce the ideal corporate character.

Kim's Dream

By way of conclusion, I would like to take advantage of the novel's ambivalent ending to indulge in one possibility. As Kim lay in the home of the Kulu woman, blind and silent, he must have seemed to those around him to be dead already. Yet perhaps in the depths of that subconscious escape, he had real thoughts too. Perhaps like the lama, he transcended the nets of earthly desires, achieving the perspective to see all India as it really was. But what if he trained his focus not on India but on corporate Anglo-India? Perhaps then he saw not only the Sons of the Charm leaving behind empty categories of nationalism in preference for professional fraternities. Rising further, perhaps he also perceived Henry Broughton's smug confidence in competition and Edward Oakfield sneering at the moral inferiority of his peers. Perhaps Kim even reached such heights as to pierce the veil shrouding fiction from reality and saw precocious Macaulay devising the reform of British society, saw Malthus writing from his small cottage on the Haileybury grounds, saw even imperious Wellesley in the moment he decided to defy his masters for their own good. And finally, just at the horizon of the universe which contained his being, the universe of aristocratic virtue, perhaps there Kim caught a fleeting glimpse of the terrible Irishman who sought to save the British from their imperial selves, and the spectacular stage which inaugurated the idea of the virtuous empire.

Conclusion: Out of India

In William Arnold's *Oakfield*, aboard a ship bound for India, the veteran Anglo-Indians have a hard time believing that a fellow Briton could surrender so much for so little: "Well, old fellow," says Stanton to Oakfield, "you know best why you came out. I tell you candidly I can't comprehend it … Why you, at one and twenty, should have voluntarily abandoned a respectable university career to come to this wretched country, I cannot conceive" (1: 2). This book began as an attempt to explain why so many middle-class men took up the opportunity to enter the colonial service, but I soon found Victorian culture to be full of Oakfields and their Stantonian critics. For every dubious questioner, there appears yet another hopeful volunteer of empire. Stanton's challenge, for example, echoes Jane Eyre's assessment of her cousin's missionary zeal, when she predicts that in India, St John Rivers will lay "his genius out to wither, and his strength to waste, under a tropical sun" (Bronte 372). Francis Hutchins has studied this paradox comprehensively and characterizes India's "attraction" for Victorian Englishmen in these brutal terms: "India came to be valued not for its pleasures, or promise, but precisely because it was possible to be desperately unhappy there" (29). Like so many who have studied imperial culture and its attitudes, however, Hutchins takes a top-down approach. His basic thesis is that as reform ideologies like utilitarianism and evangelicalism took hold in Victorian society, perceptions about empire's usefulness changed accordingly; since Victorian society was becoming progressively more interested in conduct, moral rectitude, and character, this argument goes, an Indian career attracted a certain kind of middle-class aspiration (Hutchins 8–11).

This study has not only elaborated the "coming to being" of this imperial attitude, from the glory days of the nabob to the self sacrificing company man, but grounded that analysis in the material world. My research on the East India Company, its internal policies, and its external critics, has convinced me that this top-down approach repeats the mistakes identified by Karl Marx and Freidrich Engels in their satire of the Young Hegelians. In *The German Ideology*, Marx and Engels trumpet the claims made by the philosophers who have attributed the problems of humanity to the "false conceptions about themselves, about what they are and what they ought to be." Eliminate this bad ideology, replace it with a good one, and mankind will liberate itself: these "innocent and childlike fantasies," say Marx and Engels, misunderstand the relation of ideology to the material world (1).

Corporate Character takes a Marxist approach to ideology and links the culture of British India to the structure of its administration. In pairing disobedience with self-sacrifice, I have proposed a psychosocial framework for understanding how the risks of radical agency were *culturally* managed. By examining novels, short stories, poems, essays, memoirs, personal correspondence, and parliamentary speeches related to the East India Company and its bureaucratic after-image, the Indian civil service, I hope to have filled part of the scholarly lacuna identified by David Cannadine when he insisted that we are still very far from understanding the British Empire "as a social organism, or construct, of any kind" (9).

The major claim of this book is that the corporation, as a social institution, has influenced the development of colonial culture in ways that have yet to be appreciated in scholarship. Following Antonio Gramsci, I have built on the insight that human subjects and human institutions are mutually constructed. More broadly, my findings help extend the emerging field of posthegemony studies, where scholars led by Jon Beasley-Murray, are challenging conventional Gramscian notions of the relation between power and order. "Social order was never in fact secured by ideology," Beasley-Murray insists, but rather by "habit and affect" (ix). Posthegemony calls attention to the active and constitutive role of institutions on an individual's thoughts and feelings. My point is that a corporation is a sociological unit whose unique constitution and organizational aims encourages a particular set of practices, codes, and behaviours among its membership. While my arguments for the existence of a corporate culture may seem unremarkable for a twenty-first century in the age of globalization, in the context of the Victorian period the concept was still undeveloped. In 1847 Charles Dickens could still plausibly imagine a world spanned by the family firm Dombey and

Son. It is only with the expansion of empire and capitalism in the 1850s that commercial organizations became complex enough to be said to acquire a distinct culture. Here, I defer to the insight of a Victorian commentator who observed a "great resemblance" between individuals within corporations and concluded that "corporations produce a general likeness that cosanguinity cannot always attain" (Blanchard 6). This likeness is a consequence of what I call a corporate culture.

Although this book has restricted itself to the corporate culture of nineteenth-century Anglo-India, my discussion of the visibly gentle ways that otherwise free-thinking British subjects were incorporated within empire's social organism need not be confined to the Victorian period. Sara Jeannette Duncan's critical account of claustrophobia in a sphere where administrative rank is the solitary index of social standing seems, for example, extensible to E.M. Forster's *Passage to India* (1922), and also to Paul Scott's melancholy set of postimperial novels, *The Raj Quartet* (1966–75) and their coda, *Staying On* (1977). Likewise, while I have argued that the structural transformation of the East India Company into a governing agency is an unprecedented event in the history of modern empires, its influence in the British case extended well beyond the Indian sphere. In fact, the reformed Company and its notion of "covenanted civil servants" would provide a model for the governance of all Britain's subsequent colonial acquisitions. The Colonial Service, which administered all territories excluding India and the settler colonies, explicitly copied not only the structure and internal regulations of the Indian civil service, but also its training program and entrance exam. Similarly, Haileybury and Addiscombe would, as the empire expanded, inspire other schools designed explicitly to train young Britons to serve overseas. These included the Imperial Service College, and Kipling's alma mater, the United Services College, whose disciplinary regime is chronicled in his *Stalky and Co.* (1899).

Given the Company's influence on the daily lives in other colonial spaces, we should not be surprised to see corporate culture's motifs of unheralded toil, shame, duty, and honour carry over into colonial fiction more broadly.[1] Among the works of Joseph Conrad, for instance, "Nigger of the *Narcissus*" (1897) can be read as a reflection on the tension between official duty and private sympathies; *Nostromo* (1904) as a warning against the perpetual threat of corruption in colonial territories; and "An Outpost of Progress" (1897) as a register of the effects on ethics imposed by extreme isolation. But Conrad's *Lord Jim* (1900) is perhaps the best representative of this trend. The novel is organized around an infamous dereliction of duty, where Jim, a young merchant mariner, abandons his severely disabled ship and so consigns the lives of the eight hundred pilgrims on board to fate. Conrad's narrator attributes this cowardice to Jim's fundamentally weak character. He is a boy who had enlisted in the merchant marine and had risen to a respectable rank on a ship that ran the "home service," the routes between England and its colonies. There Jim "had to bear the criticism of men, the exactions of the sea, and the prosaic severity of the daily task that gives bread – but whose only reward is the perfect love of the work. This reward eluded him" (8–9). Thus Jim exchanges "the home service, with its harder conditions [and] severer view of duty," for the country service where Englishmen "shuddered at the thought of hard work, and led precariously easy lives" (12). As occurs in Kipling's universe, a character who fails to derive pleasure from hard work is doomed in a Conrad novel. Following a trial and a public humiliation, Jim resolves to remake his life in another venue but the rapidity of colonial gossip is such that he cannot ever quite outrun his reputation. Like Kurtz in *Heart of Darkness*, he follows the practice of Kipling's men who would be king, and establishes a modest but ultimately pyrrhic empire on the fringes of Britain's. Stein declares him "romantic" (153); Marlow can neither admire nor abandon him; and Jim himself attests to be "satisfied … nearly" (222).

Beyond Conrad, authors such as H. Rider Haggard, Robert Louis Stevenson, or, alternatively, phenomena like the "Boys' Own" movement might, following this book, have their representations of imperial ethics re-evaluated, and my hope is that by illuminating how corporate ways of thinking and feeling influenced the development of nineteenth-century British imperial culture, we might reconceptualize our reception of colonial literature. Previous works in this area, from Said's *Culture and Imperialism* (1993) to McClintock's *Imperial Leather* (1995) to Kucich's *Imperial Masochism* (2007), have consistently interpreted colonial texts within a national paradigm, a choice that renders it difficult to understand colonial subjectivity or to read colonial literature as anything other than derivatives of a British source. *Corporate Character* has challenged this assumption by asking what, if anything, was British about the British Empire? What were the rules by which colonial administrators governed their activities? From where did those rules originate and how were they disseminated and sustained over the nineteenth century?

By focusing on the role of the East India Company in the appointment, training, and management of Britain's colonial agents, I have argued that what we have been calling colonial culture might equally be understood as a corporate culture, one whose internal coherence had less to do with national characteristics than with institutional habits. Thus this book contributes to the ongoing efforts by Victorianists to develop new and robust ways to explain how communities grew and represented themselves. The variety of nineteenth-century subjectivities was never contained within the horizon of the nation-state and here I have tried to position the East India Company not as an adjunct to the British nation but as a discrete institution, one whose culture requires separate analysis. The result is an account of colonial consciousness as a subjectivity uniquely articulated by the contingent and often improvisational responses of an institution plagued by an irreducible logistical challenge: how best to manage the actions of one's overseas agents. Kimball O'Hara is as wild and as free as any figure in colonial literature; the way the British Empire adapted to the fact of his freedom – making work seem fun, making the sympathy and respect of one's work colleagues the object of one's desire – not only anticipates the sociology of twenty-first-century corporations but it also suggests how deeply capitalism and governmentality interpenetrated each other in nineteenth-century Britain.

Notes

Preface: The 8,000-Mile Screwdriver

1 Kipling, "To the Duchess of Sutherland" 10 October 1900. *Letters*, III: 35.
2 Kantorowicz, *The King's Two Bodies*.
3 According to Stjepan Meštrović, an American sociologist who served as an expert witness during the Abu Ghraib trials, the presiding judge supported the prosecution by insisting that the army was not on trial, and that attempts to tie the case to the White House be avoided. In *The Trials of Abu Ghraib* (2007), Meštrović claims that the prosecution even suppressed testimony which corroborated theories that the crimes at Abu Ghraib were part of the United States's widespread pattern of abusing detainees captured during the War on Terror.

Introduction: Empire's Corporate Culture

1 The history of the imperfect consolidation of "British" identity during the late eigteenth and early nineteenth centuries is well documented. Linda Colley's *Britons* (1992) remains the best account of the invention and dissemination of "Britishness" in the eighteenth century. Katie Trumpener's *Bardic Nationalism* (1997) describes Irish, Scottish, and Welsh resistence to the homogenizing tendencies of those moderninzing, anglicizing cultural initiatives. Both Colley and Trumpener identify imperial expansion as a key contributor to the invention of Britishness. And since the tension was never fully resolved, with many Victorians interchanging English and British depending on the context, there is an alarming amount of slippage in the archival record. Scholars of imperial identities accordingly have a choice: use only one of the terms consistently (a flattening which

is unfaithful to the historical record); or navigate carefully between them. This book, which adds the notion of a corporate identity to the nationality debates, will attempt the latter.

2 J.A. Hobson, the radical counterpart to Seeley's Whig historiography, makes precisely the opposite argument in *Imperialism: A Study* (1902): that empire *was* a conspiracy of financiers and capitalists to secure new overseas markets for the investment of surplus capital. Labelling these "certain sectional interests" as the "economic parasites of imperialism," Hobson concludes that "[w]e must put aside the merely sentimental diagnosis which explains wars or other national blunders by outbursts of patriotic animosity or errors of statecraft. Doubtless at every outbreak of war not only the man in the street but the man at the helm is often duped by the cunning with which aggressive motives and greedy purposes dress themselves in defensive clothing" (51). Several years earlier, George Bernard Shaw made a similar point in *The Man of Destiny* (1896), explaining that imperialism was merely a means for finding "new market[s] for … adulterated goods" (658).

3 The penchant of W.E.H. Lecky, Thomas Macaulay, and other Victorian commentators for celebrating the rectitude of colonial officials has since been replicated by many of empire's chroniclers, including David Gilmour, whose *The Ruling Caste* (2005) argues that Indian service was part opportunity and part calling.

4 Unless otherwise noted, all references to Kipling's fiction and prose are taken from the "Outward Bound" of Kipling's works, published by Charles Scribner in 36 volumes from 1897–1937. This is one of only four sets authorized by Kipling himself. Parenthetical references indicate volume and page number.

5 Bayly calls the changes following the transfer "tiny," adding that "Parliamentary and ministerial control … had been gradually creeping up on the Company since the Indian Act of 1784" (195).

6 "On the City Wall" provides as good a place as any to register the antipathy Kipling felt towards anglicization, the educational policy synonymous with Macaulay and articulated in his "Minute on Indian Education" (1835). The main character in Kipling's story is Wali Dad, "a young Mohammedan who was suffering acutely from education of the English variety and knew it" (4: 303). Wali Dad ends up in this story as the key figure in the plot to free a rebel leader from a British prison.

7 Macaulay was hardly alone in this feeling by the 1840s. In the inaugural issue of the *Calcutta Review,* the founding editor and journalist J.W. Kaye in 1844 described Anglo-Indian life as an exercise in humble moderation,

reporting that "comfort and respectability seem to be aimed at, and attained. There is little licentiousness to shock and less poverty to distress" (20). One recently returned Anglo-Indian, Kaye adds, "once complained pathetically to us that the English were 'magnificently selfish'" (11).

8 Other than Suleri's *The Rhetoric of English India* (1992), few studies give sustained consideration of Kipling's historical antecedents.

9 For a detailed history of the nabob, in relation both to imperial and domestic politics, see Nechtman's *Nabobs* (2010), especially chs 3 and 4. A less scholarly history is supplied by Edwardes, *The Nabobs at Home* (1991).

10 For discussions of national character coeval with Macaulay's speech, see Trumpener's *Bardic Nationalism* (1997). In particular, Trumpener's reading of Charles Maturin's *The Milesian Chief* (1812) shows how the broad acceptance and understanding of a cultural category such as "national character" meant that romantic national tales had to become "increasingly sophisticated in representing the link between cultural/character formation and a complex historical temporality" (147). For a broader discussion of the Victorian faith in the existence of national character, see Varouxakis's *Victorian Political Thought on France and the French* (2002), especially pp. 105–16.

11 See Bayly's *Indian Society and the Making of the British Empire* (1988), 79–106; and Marshall's *Problems of Empire* (1968), 50–177.

12 After the Battle of Plassey, the stockholders of the East India Company demanded an exponential increase in the annual dividend while, at the same time, the British Crown extracted greater tributes (Lawson 35–7).

13 For details of how the East India Company managed its agency relationship as a strictly mercantile relationship, see James H. Thomas's "East India Company Agency Work in the British Isles, 1700–1800," 33–148.

14 Macaulay, for example, argued, "I will not, therefore, in a case in which I have neither principles nor precedents to guide me, pull down the existing system on account of its theoretical defects. For I know that any system which I could put in its place would be equally condemned by theory, while it would not be equally sanctioned by experience" ("Speech on the Government of India" 153).

15 One of the best and most accessible studies into the nature of modern corporations is Bakan's *The Corporation* (2004), which provocatively (if problematically) invites readers to consider the full implication of our modern conception of corporations as legal persons.

16 Accounts of this transformation are supplied by Keay (1994); Lawson (1993); Philips (1961); B.B. Misra (1959); and Carlos and Nicholas (1988).

17 Tönnies, in fact, speaks of "the joint-stock-company – which is liable only for itself, and limited almost exclusively to making a profit – [as] the

perfect type of all possible social and legal constructions based on rationality. This is precisely because, even in its origins (which can sometimes be misleading about the real nature of things), it is a *Gesellschaft* association without any admixture of the elements of Community" (209).

18 David Gilmour has argued persuasively that this belief is much more applicable to African imperialism than to Indian, where relatively few upper class families served (*The Ruling Caste* 33).

19 See Hyam's *Empire and Sexuality* (1990). See also Young's *Eros Denied* (1969).

20 For studies of the complex ways that women writers and conceptions of feminity variously critiqued and supported imperialism, see Sharpe's *Allegories of Empire* (1993), David's *Rule Britannia* (1995), and Joseph's *Reading the East India Company, 1720–1840* (2004).

21 Samuel Rutherford Crockett, reviewing Kipling in *The Bookman* in 1895, for example, celebrated the marked improvement Kipling's fiction offered over its predecessors, noting how for the first time "the East spoke to us authentic, every man in his own tongue" (140).

22 Both E.P. Thompson and Peter Earle foreground this process in the titles to their respective books, *The Making of the English Working Class* (1963) and *The Making of the English Middle-Class* (1989).

1. Corruption and the Corporation: The Impeachment of Warren Hastings

1 Holden Furber was the first historian who attempted to quantify the drain on the national income imposed by the East India Company's administration (310). For a more comprehensive account of how shareholders responded variously to the Company's changed responsibilities, see Bowen's *The Business of Empire* (2006), 84–117. For examples of moral criticisms, consult Dirks's *The Scandal of Empire* (2006), 7–36.

2 In 1779, for example, the Committee of British Subjects Residing in Bengal petitioned Parliament to intervene against the recently established Supreme Court, under whose jurisdiction "the inhabitants of these Provinces, as well natives as British subjects, have suffered severely" (Committee 65).

3 Mickle's *Candid Examination of the Reasons for Depriving the East-India Company of Its Charter* (1779) makes such a prophesy on pp. 19–20.

4 See Clark (2003); Dirks (2006); and Marshall (1965).

5 See Macaulay, "Warren Hastings" 230–2.

6 Chatterjee's *The Lineages of Political Society* exemplifies the endurance of this new antagonism, using Burke and Hastings to make a point about

how liberal imperialism must necessarily incorporate two senses of normative historical time (6–7).

7 For details of Burke's parliamentary career, and his abiding interest in Indian affairs, I rely on F.P. Lock's definitive two-volume biography, *Edmund Burke* (1998–2006).

8 Yet, as P.J. Marshall observes, "Burke's writings and reported speeches on India are given little attention in most studies of his thought" ("Burke, Hastings and the Higher Law" 31). Fredrick Whelan's study, *Edmund Burke and India* (1996) provides the authoritative account of Burke's Indian activities, seeking to understand them within the context of political principles evident elsewhere in his public life. His purpose, which is not mine, is to reconcile the Indian Burke with the American Burke, the Irish Burke, and the English Burke.

9 Even Pitt's biographers are at a loss to explain why he threw his support behind Burke. For example, the Victorian biographer Philip Stanhope can only guess that something in Pitt's "lofty mind" stirred when he finally reflected on the Hastings case (1: 241–4).

10 According to Bonar's *Catalogue of the Library of Adam Smith*, Smith owned a copy of Bolts's essay (15). Burke too had read Bolts's *Considerations*, and remarked that "it certainly has the merit of being the first that turned the national attention to the state of our affairs in the East Indies" (*Correspondence* 5: 263–4).

11 Ricoeur first makes this argument in "The Model of the Text" (1973), but elaborates it more fully in his 1975 *Lectures on Ideology and Utopia*. Mario J. Valdes explains that Ricoeur makes this connection on the grounds that "ideology is constructed socially on the basis of infinite layers of narrativity" (Valdes 34).

12 Whelan 2–3.

13 "He has revealed quite clearly to everybody the plans and schemes by which he aims at corrupting his judges"

14 See Canter, "The Impeachments of Verres and Warren Hastings." For a more recent reckoning of the relation, consult Carnall's "Burke as a Modern Cicero" (1989).

15 Uday Singh Mehta's study of liberalism and imperialism comes to the same conclusion, stating that "much of what [Burke] says about British rule in India is squarely within the framework of a plea for good government; none of it is a plea for Indian self-government" (158).

16 Burke elaborates this concept, declaring that "we are all born in subjection ... to one great, immutable, pre-existent law, prior to all our devices, and prior to all our contrivances, paramount to our very being itself, by which

we are knit and connected in the eternal frame of the universe, out of which we cannot stir" ("Opening" 350).

17 Beginning roughly with the ascension of the evangelical Charles Grant to the chairmanship of the East India Company and fuelled by James Mill's chauvinist *History of British India* (1817), the rhetoric of the nineteenth-century civilizing mission presupposes the incontrovertible superiority of British culture and Christian thought and denigrates Indian culture as irredeemably backwards. By depicting India as an easily corruptible state, Burke's rhetoric inadvertently prepared the ground for later utilitarians and evangelicals. Likewise Burke's insistence on a universal "natural law" became a supporting pillar for those liberals who presumed that all humans were basically equal and could therefore benefit equally through the application of rational administrative reform. I discuss this idea in more detail in the next chapter. For the connections between utilitarians and evangelicals in Indian policy making, see Hutchins's *The Illusion of Permanence* (1967).

18 Hume expands this thought in a footnote to the second part of the fifth section of his *Enquiry Concerning the Principles of Morals*: "It is needless to push our researches so far as to ask why we have humanity, or fellow-feeling with others. It is sufficient that this is experienced to be a principle in human nature. We must stop somewhere in our examination of causes; and there are, in every science, some general principles, beyond which we cannot hope to find any principles more general" (*Enquiries* 219–20n).
For more on the relationship between Burke's political thought and the moral philosophy of Hume, see Watkins's dissertation "Politics *in medias res*."

2. How the Civil Service Got Its Name: India as a Noble Profession

1 In their thorough discussion of eighteenth-century perceptions of the nabob, Philip Lawson and Jim Phillips maintain that nabobs "appeared to threaten established moral values, the security of imperial interests, and the sanctity of the constitution" (226).

2 Tillman Nechtman's history of the nabob notes that London newspapers in 1786, in a campaign against the nabobs, began listing the personal wealth of the East India Company's wealthiest retirees. These ranged from £120,000 to £350,000 (13–14).

3 As far as I know, there is no record in the India Office archives of such a despatch. While there is no doubt that Napier defied London's instructions and indeed waged a rogue campaign to conquer Sindh and bring it under

British hegemony, the witty exculpation "Peccavi" probably originates in the *Punch* cartoon of 18 May 1844.

4 Agency theory entered into economic analysis in the 1970s, beginning with Stephen Ross's claim that agency relationships "are universal. Essentially all contractual arrangements, as between employer and employee ... contain important elements of agency" (134). Ross then applies the principles of game theory to propose models in which the principal might maximize, through economic compensation, the utility of the agent. Ross notes, though, that even when that optimal outcome is known to the principal, and communicated clearly to the agent, "the difficulty [for the principal] arises in monitoring the act that the agent chooses" (138). Contributions to economic agency theory that have worked to refine Ross's position include Jensen and Meckling (1976); Jensen (1983); and Eisenhardt (1985). Kathleen Eisenhardt (1989) summarizes the need for a robust understanding of agency because "much of organizational life, whether we like it or not, is based on self-interest" (64). Since the mid-1980s, scholarship on agency theory has developed along two lines: principal-agent theory, which relies extensively on mathematical models and "ideal" markets; and positivist agency theory, which more specifically concerns situations of conflict between the goals of principal and agent and is hence interested in describing the governance or disciplinary mechanisms that limit the agent's selfish behaviour. It is this latter strain which is of more interest to my own cultural analysis of the agency crisis.

5 See Hutchins (1967) and Patterson (2009).

6 In the early nineteenth century, one could use the word liberal to name groups as diverse as utilitarians, evangelicals, dissenters, aristocratic Whigs, Peelite Tories, radicals, and classical political economists.

7 See his *The English Utilitarians and India* (1959).

8 Indeed the purpose of that letter from the court to the board is to justify the founding of a company college at home in England.

9 Wellesley's vision of a permanent empire was quickly taken up, unsurprisingly, by members of his staff. George Barlow, speaking at the public disputation for the first class of Fort William College's graduates, estimated that the students could now "enjoy the grateful and animating prospect of being eminently useful to their country ... by aiding it in fulfilling the high moral obligations attendant on the possession of its Indian Empire, on the discharge of which the prosperity and permanency of that Empire equally depend" (xii–xiii). The theme of service in aid of a permanent empire became a continuing theme at end-of-term speeches at the East India College. Member of Parliament James Weir Hogg one year warned that the

Indian empire "will pass away with a rapidity equal to that with which it was acquired, if not sustained and rendered permanent by the pure but firm administration of justice and appropriate laws ... These are the means alone whereby that mighty empire can be rendered permanent; and you, my young friends, have the proud consciousness of being the instruments whereby we hope to accomplish an end so beneficial to your country, and so honourable to yourselves" (24).

10 For an account of how professions were represented in Victorian fiction, see Ruth (2006).

11 In "Reification and the Consciousness of the Proletariat" (1923), Georg Lukacs argues that reification "requires that a society should learn to satisfy *all its needs* in terms of commodity exchange" (91, emphasis added). In this sense, abstractions like the (recognition of and/or adherence to) rule of law are reconceived as commodities. The degree to which one possesses these commodities determines the degree of prestige one has within the community.

12 Warren Hastings, on the other hand, has been recuperated by postcolonial scholars interested in his influence of the promotion of cross-cultural studies via the (later Royal) Asiatick Society in Calcutta in 1784. See, for example, Ahmed (2009).

13 This kind of self-fashioning, of course, operates to normalize an otherwise complicated history. Ronald Hyam has estimated that while 90 per cent of Britons in India in the mid-eighteenth century entered into marriages with native women, the increased professionalization of the administrators, coupled with the arrival of missionaries and British women, changed the dynamics of sexual interaction between the British administrators and their colonial subjects (*Empire and Sexuality* 115–36).

14 These complaints, however embellished, were grounded in fact and attributable largely to the court of director's bizarre choice of the college's first principal. Samuel Henley was a one-time professor of moral philosophy at William and Mary College in Virginia but is better known as the notorious translator of William's Beckford's *Vathek* (1787) (notorious because Henley's English translation was published a full year before Beckford's French "original"). At the outbreak of the American revolution, Henley returned to England and taught at Harrow; when appointed to the East India College, he was sixty-six years old. According to H. Morse Stephens's definitive history of the East India College, "How he obtained his appointment is nowhere stated ... but it may be asserted with confidence that he was not the right man for the place" (272). In Stephens's judgment, Henley's inept and irregular system of discipline directly inspired two great student rebellions in 1813 and 1816.

15 The challenge faced by Reverends Malthus and Walter is not dissimilar to the one faced by Tennyson's Ulysses, the heroic king who resigns his throne to Telemachus, the methodical son who is

> discerning to fulfil
> This labour, by slow prudence to make mild
> A rugged people, and through soft degrees
> Subdue them to the useful and the good.
> Most blameless is he, centred in the sphere
> Of common duties ("Ulysses" 35–40)

16 To appreciate how "conspicuously" predominant the feelings of an imperial sovereign were at the college, consider that the following was listed as "the most popular and enduring" college song:

> The Romans were a knowing race,
> Vivat Haileyburia!
> They made a road down to this place,
> Vivat Haileyburia!
> Romans came and passed away;
> Normans followed; where are they?
> But we are here, and here to stay!
> Vivat Haileyburia!
> Then close your ranks and lift your song,
> Vivat Haileyburia!
> That life is short, but love is long;
> Vivat Haileyburia!
> And all through life, where'er we be,
> School of our hearts, we'll think of thee,
> And drink the toast with three times three,
> Vivat Haileyburia! (Wright 4)

17 Especially appropriate here is Hanuman's observation, in Kipling's "The Bridge Builders" (1898) that the Anglo-Indians are "the men who believe their God is toil" (13: 42). Elsewhere, consider "The Conversion of Aurelian McGoggin" (1887) whose titular character is struck by aphasia after attempting to apply Comtean positivism to the administration of British India.

18 It is worth mentioning that, aside from the extension of the franchise, few topics animated these liberals as much as administrative reform. Mill, for instance, confessed in a letter to Harriet Mill, "The mere attempt to make patronage go by merit and not by favour seems to me to be a revolution in English society and likely to produce greater effects than any reforms in the laws" (148).

19 *India Office Records: Revenue, Judicial and Legislative Committee Miscellaneous Papers*: PC 1828, L/P&J/1/92.

20 I have in mind Homi Bhabha's chapter on mimicry in *The Location of Culture* (1994), which reads the "Minute" as a symptom of fetishes for fixity, stability, and transparency, yet simultaneously as a document which annihilates the possibility that these fetishes will ever materialize. When narcissistic desire strives to reproduce its image on the colonial subject, colonial discourse confronts the reality that there are no essential identities, no "*presence[s] Africaine[s]*" (88). The anxiety engendered by such an acknowledgment, Bhabha concludes, undermines the monologic aspirations of colonial discourse and explains the high frequency of repeated stereotypes and truth statements within it.

21 See Eagleton's *Literary Theory* (1983) and Palmer's *The Rise of English Studies* (1965).

3. Representing Working Conditions in Company India

1 See, for example, Leask (1992); Marshall (1990); and Crane (1992).

2 Marshall reports that in 1830 there were 36,409 Europeans in the king's and Company's armies in India; in 1827, the number of civilians employed by the Company amounted to 3,550; as late as 1852 the number of private individuals outside offical employment was listed as 2,149 ("The Whites of British India" 26).

3 In fact, because of the 1839–42 Afghan War (Britain's first major overseas campaign since the end of the Napoleonic Wars), Anglo-Indian histories and biographies were particularly popular in the late 1840s and early 1850s.

4 The connection between author and protagonist deserves elaboration because *Oakfield* not only mirrors Arnold's Indian experience but also uncannily predicts his demise. Like Oakfield, Arnold went up to Oxford (although the author never completed his degree) before obtaining through patronage a cadetship in the Company army; like Oakfield, Arnold was generally appalled by the moral quality of his regimental fellows in India; like Oakfield, Arnold found solace in a small fellowship of kindred spirits; like Oakfield, Arnold switched to the civil service and became less dissatisfied; and like Oakfield, Arnold died shortly after taking sick leave from India. *Oakfield* was published shortly after Arnold's return to England in 1853. In 1855 he was invited to go back to India as the Director of Public Instruction in the Punjab territory. He lived through the Mutiny of 1857–8 but became ill in 1859. Unlike Oakfield, William Arnold never reached home and instead died in Gibraltar on 7 April 1859, on his thirty-first birthday.

5 Here is Arnold's description of Arthur Vernon's demise, whose tones recall Edmund Burke's Indian speeches:

> Alas for those who come year by year from home to India without even the experience of school or college life to assist them, are thrown into society, to the evil and low-principled tone of which no college or school furnishes a parallel; and, borne down, not only by weight of superior age, but of military seniority, force back all ebullitions of tender feeling, learn to be ashamed of affection, ashamed of industry, ashamed of common honesty in money matters, ashamed even of professional duty, ashamed of all that is softening, strengthening, humanising, till all that is noble in them shrinks and withers before the overbearing, coarse, animal, worldly existence which they obey; – which they obey till it enslaves them; and the boy of seventeen who suppressed love's workings, becomes the man of five and twenty who has no such workings to suppress. (1: 69–70)

6 Kenneth Allott's modern edition is thus very Forsterian when it suggests that *Oakfield* should be read now as "a spiritual autobiography" since it is "hardly more than accidentally an Anglo-Indian novel" (30).

7 In 1972 D.C.R.A. Goonetilleke recovered *Oakfield* as a piece of "forgotten" nineteenth-century fiction, an oversight redressed when Kenneth Allott edited a reissue of the novel in 1973. *Oakfield* was further buoyed during the "Raj revival" in British popular culture in the 1980s following the post-Falklands nationalist upswing. Udayon Misra devotes a full chapter of *The Raj in Fiction* (1987), and most studies after that of British Indian literature have given *Oakfield* at least a modicum of attention (e.g., Chakravarty 100–3).

8 See Spivak's castigation of Michel Foucault and Gilles Deleuze in her essay on third-world representation, "Can the Subaltern Speak?" (1988).

9 Middleton lays down the Burkean gauntlet by suggesting that the physical development of India is paramount: "A few thousand miles more of Grand Trunk Road, ditto of Canals, and people will no longer be able to say, that if the English were swept off the face of Hindostan to-morrow, the only trace they would leave behind would be the broken tobacco-pipes of their soldiers" (1: 157). Oakfield in reply worries whether "the English message to India is civil engineering simply," and confesses that he has "been disgusted to find how many speak of [India] as though it were no more to them, than that carcase floating along there is to the vultures feeding on it" (1:162).

10 And in this, Edward Oakfield anticipates E.M. Forster's character, Cyril Fielding, who also stands outside the colonial bureaucracy not only in his profession but also in the sense that he arrived in India when he had already past forty.

11 The globetrotter is the species of Englishman described by Kipling in "Letters of Marque" as "the man who 'does' kingdoms in days and writes books upon them in weeks" (7: 12).

12 The allusion to Burke's parliamentary speeches on both Fox's India Bill and the impeachment of Warren Hastings clearly identifies Arnold's dissatisfaction with the moral character of the Company's officers.

13 J.M. Compton argues that the committee which drew up the examination anticipated that successful competitioners would be top Oxford and Cambridge honours graduates. "But," he continues, "as the years went by, the Civil Service Commissioners had to be content with, first, any men from Oxford and Cambridge, and, finally, men from any university at all. Yet they were still manipulating a system drawn up expressly for a high proportion of high honours graduates from the two older universities" (267). R.J. Moore attributes this pride of place to the self-interested political machinations of Benjamin Jowett. The original plan for the competition examination did not entail the closure of Haileybury, according to Moore, but Jowett lobbied heavily for amendments. Jowett seems to have been particularly effective in influencing Gladstone, member for Oxford, and concluded one letter, dated 23 July 1853, with an excellent example of Victorian pork barrelling, pleading that "you love Oxford too well not to do what you can for it" (qtd. in Moore 251).

14 In this, Trevelyan anticipates Kipling's antipathy to the artifice of the Indian government's headquarters in the hill-station of Simla, "the seething, whining, weakly hive, impotent to help itself, but strong in its power to cripple, thwart, and annoy the sunken-eyed man who, by official irony, was said to be 'in-charge' of it" ("The Education of Otis Yeere" 6: 23).

4. Corporate Culture in Post-Company India

1 Though closed in Janaury 1858, Haileybury reopened in 1862 as a public school.

2 In fact, the 1853 Indian Civil Service Act opened the ICS to anyone who could pass the exam, including most controversially, Indians themselves. Satyendranath Tagore, brother of Rabindranath, was the first Indian to enter the ICS, travelling to England and passing his exams in 1863. That it took nearly ten years following the Indian Civil Service Act of 1853 for a native-born Indian to win a place suggests some of the hypocrisy behind the universally open gestures of the exam. Mrinlani Sinha supports this when she observes that in 1883 – thirty years after the Act – only eleven Indians had passed the exams in London (37).

3 Birdwood cites Matthew Arnold complaining about the effects of the competition exam, noting that "the candidates to whom I gave the highest marks were almost without exception the candidates whom I would not have appointed. They were crammed men, not formed men; the formed men were the public school men" (qtd. in Birdwood 7). The historian J.M. Compton's more scholarly account supports Birdwood's observations about the demographic shifts, if not the moral decline, prompted by the competition system (267–71).

4 Bhupal Singh's *A Survey of Anglo-Indian Fiction* (1934) remains the best catalogue of nineteenth- and early twentieth-century Anglo-Indian literature. For a detailed study of Anglo-Indian newspapers and periodicals, see Chandrika Kaul's *Reporting the Raj* (2003).

5 For studies of British writing about India, see Teltscher's *India Inscribed* (1996); Rajan's *Under Western Eyes* (1999); and Leask's *British Romantic Writers and the East* (1992).

6 Singh's *Survey* lists over a thousand works on India published prior to 1933.

7 Until it transferred power in 1858, the East India Company strictly regulated access to the subcontinent. The propriety of the Company's effective monopoly over immigration was regularly debated. Most famous is their prohibition of non-Anglican missionaries in the early 1800s, a ban that was only lifted when Charles Grant, a member of the Clapham Sect, became chairman of the board. There were also, in the 1850s, vigorous debates as to whether India could follow the path taken in New Zealand and establish a settler colony. See, for example, Campbell's *A Scheme for the Government of India* (1853), especially pp. 123–4.

8 Eric Hobsbawm confirms the ascendancy of Herder over Rousseau when he argues that, although the terms "race" and "nation" have since acquired a plurality of complicated denotations, in the period 1870–1918 they were used "as virtual synonyms" in discussions about the character or traits of a given community (*Nations* 108). It will be unsurprising that Herder's romanticism appealed to British conservatives like Edmund Burke and William Wordsworth. Burke, for example, roused "a Spirit (I mean a National Spirit)" to head off the threat of revolutionary France and Wordsworth spoke of "the solemn fraternity which a great Nation composes – gathered together ... under the shade of ancestral feeling" (qtd. in Cobban 99, 147). Less expected is the respect accorded by liberal thinkers such as John Stuart Mill, who clearly alludes to the Herderian *volk* when he comes to consider how nationalism affects representative democracy. In *Considerations on Representative Government*, Mill cites class interests as the primary

obstacle to effective representation but warns that class antagonism can be further problematized by "strong antipathies ... of nationality" (255). Thus he concludes that, ideally, states should be mononational since "free institutions are next to impossible in a country made up of different nationalities" (361).

9 At the fin de siècle, many influential Victorians – politicians like Charles Dilke, Joseph Chamberlain, and Alfred Milner; historians like James Froude and John Seeley; romance writers like H. Rider Haggard, G.A. Henty, and (to an extent) Robert Louis Stevenson – were in the process of imagining, to use Dilke's phrase, a "Greater Britain." John Plotz has recently argued that this idea of Greater Britain inaugurated a form of cultural portability: a way for colonial figures to defy their assimilation into a colonial landscape or a colonized culture by consuming products invested with the aura of Englishness. The iconic example, for Plotz, is the consumption of strawberries in India (45). For a broader study of the Greater Britain movement in Victorian culture, see Bell (2007).

10 This argument is not without its problems. By reading nineteenth-century colonial literature as the necessary (flawed or incomplete) precursor to today's literature, Ashcroft et al. betray their Whiggish prejudice. Consider, for example, how their condemnation of the literature and culture of colonial administrators, a body of work that remains forever compromised by the idea of Home; it "can never form the basis for an indigenous culture nor can [it] be integrated in any way with the cultures that already exist in the countries invaded" (5). The authors consider this type of writing to be only the first in a series of steps towards a liberated, decolonized, and (presumably) authentic postcolonial voice.

11 For recent discussions of the place of work in Victorian fiction, see Breton's *Gospels and Grit* (2005) and Lesjak's *Working Fictions* (2006), both of which theorize the aesthetic of work and its shadowy, unromantic double, labour. The former achieves this through a close attention to the way work appears in the fiction of various classes in the nineteenth century; the latter through a sustained engagement with those Marxist Arnoldians, the thinkers of the Frankfurt school. For an account of work as it relates specifically to the intellectual labour of the professions, see Ruth's *Novel Professions* (2006).

12 In 1891 Lang wrote that "the wind of literary inspiration has rarely shaken the bungalows of India ... With a world of romance and of character at their doors, Englishmen in India have seen as if they saw it not. They have been busy in governing, in making war, making peace, building bridges, laying down roads, and writing official reports. Our literature from that

continent of conquest has been sparse indeed, except in the way of biographies, of histories, and of rather local and unintelligible *facetiae* ... we might almost say that India has contributed nothing to our finer literature" (198–9).

13 For examples of this type of critique, see Arata's *Fictions of Loss in the Victorian Fin de Siècle* (1996), 161–2; McBratney's *Imperial Subjects, Imperial Space* (2002), 26–7; and D'Cruz's "My Two Left Feet" (2003), 108–10.

14 Habermas's study of the development of a public sphere in eighteenth-century Western Europe, argues that "*salons* ... were centres of criticism," providing a neutral space where "sons of princes and counts associated with sons of watchmakers and shopkeepers," engaged in "economic and political disputes" with the guarantee "that such discussions would be inconsequential, at least in the immediate context" (*Structural* 32, 33).

15 Nor was Kipling the only Anglo-Indian to realize that corruption would spread without the countervailing influence of public opinion. Here is an excerpt from Henry Cotton's 1911 memoir *Indian Home and Memories*:

> At that immature age I was, like all other members of the Civil Service – and as they still are up to the present time – vested with magisterial powers beyond comparison greater than those possessed by young men of the same age under any civilised Government. Uncontrolled by public opinion and from the nature of the case with little judicial experience, it would have been strange if I had not been led into occasional errors and sometimes into abuse of power. That must be the obvious result of a system which is to blame. (79–80)

16 Kucich names Christopher Hitchens and Andrew Rutherford as two of the more prominent proponents of this view (137).

17 For other discussions of evangelicalism and utilitarianism in relation to Anglo-Indian culture, see Stokes's *The English Utilitarians and India* (1959); Viswanathan's *Masks of Conquest* (1989), especially p. 77; Suleri's *The Rhetoric of English India* (1992); and Hutchins's *The Illusion of Permanence* (1967).

18 Rutherford explains how "the phrase 'out here' is replaced by 'in India' throughout; and, not surprisingly, there is a further reduction in the use of Indian vocabulary. Thus 'a *memsahib*' becomes 'a white woman'; 'the *shroff*' becomes 'the bankers'; 'dead on the *charpoy*' becomes 'dead on the bed.'" (xxvii). Rutherford continues for about a page in this vein, citing many other emendations.

19 Ripon cited John Stuart Mill among others in arguing that the race of a candidate was immaterial to his qualifications. However, many Anglo-Indians feared that native judges would be hopelessly prejudiced against

European defendants and would abuse their positions to redress the colonial imbalance. The reaction against the Ilbert Bill was so strong that it was soon characterized as the "White Mutiny." For an analysis of the historical reaction to the Bill, in both Britain and in India, see Kaul's "England and India: The Ilbert Bill, 1883" (1993). Jenny Sharpe, in *Allegories of Empire* (1993) and Nancy Paxton, in *Writing under the Raj* (1999) have separately argued for a correlation between anxiety surrounding the Bill and the contemporary revival of "Mutiny novels."

20 See Arendt's meditation on the connection between racism, imperialism, and bureaucracy in *The Origins of Totalitarianism* (1968) and her apt description of institutional men in the South African context: "They were nothing of their own making, they were like living symbols of what had happened to them, living abstractions and witnesses to the absurdity of human institutions" (189).

21 If all this sounds like a premonition of E.M. Forster's description of Adela Quested, it should be remembered that Duncan hosted Forster for a while on his first trip to India.

22 More generally, Julia Kristeva has argued that the frequency of these intersections in literature and culture is what makes psychoanalysis such a radically useful form of ideology critique. See "From Symbols to Flesh."

5. Unmaking a Company Man in Rudyard Kipling's *Kim*

1 John McClure makes this point when he distinguishes between Kipling's realistic (albeit ironical) short stories of "official" Anglo-India and the mythic fantasy operating in *Kim*.

2 See Watt (1957) and Armstrong (2006).

3 In *How Novels Think* (2006), Armstrong suggests that certain forms of fiction created an empowered subject – a witty, wilful, or energetic character – who was able to change the existing social order and acquire the social credit commensurate with his or her talents. Once the novel had created this figure, readers understood their own identity in terms of narrative that worked towards the production of a self-governing, self-aware subject.

4 For a history of the colonial fascination with passing, see Roy (1998)

5 Scholars following Said, including Sara Suleri, Zoreh T. Sullivan, Don Randall, Kaori Nagai, and John Kucich, have thoroughly analysed the effects of a text like *Kim* in maintaining the breadth of public consent in Britain for empire in an age of domestic turbulence.

6 Compare this to the final line of *David Copperfield*, spoken of course by David, which reveals the culmination of the protagonist's moral, emotional, and spiritual development: "Oh Agnes, oh my soul, so may thy face be by me when I close my life indeed; so may I, when realities are melting from me like the shadows which I now dismiss, still find thee near me, pointing upward!" (877). Similarly, consider the conclusion of *Wilhelm Meister's Apprenticeship*: "'I know not the worth of a kingdom,' answered Wilhelm; 'but I know I have attained a happiness which I have not deserved, and which I would not change with anything in life'" (542).

7 For what it is worth, Kipling gave his own measure of the conclusion in a letter dated 11 November 1902: "As to *Kim*, I don't see myself that the Lama died, nor do I see any sign of the old man's dying. My own idea is that in the fullness of time we may learn how Kim went on with his somewhat unusual career" ("To Edward Lucas White" *Letters* 3: 111).

8 See McClintock's discussion of *Kim* (66–72). For McClintock, through Kim, Kipling can maintain that the colonial agent and writer remain in control of dynamic situations, when they are in fact neurotically struggling to stamp an order on an object that is, ultimately, ambivalent.

9 Kucich argues that Kim's "sadomasochistic omnipotence" helped Kipling "underwr[i]te a remarkably unilateral class politics, which accommodated contradictory attitudes to imperialism" (138).

10 Esty's claim resembles that made by Don Randall about the "predicament implied by Kim's truncated Bildung, his insuperable adolescence, mirrors the problem of imperial consolidation," or of "an empire that has not discovered … its appropriate coming of age" (158).

11 The genre of colonial bildungsroman has been studied extensively in Esty (2011).

12 This is the case not only for postcolonial critics but also for earlier respondents. Here is Edmund Wilson's assessment of the (in his opinion, flawed) conclusion: "Now what the reader tends to expect is that Kim will eventually come to realize that he is delivering into bondage to the British invaders those whom he has always considered his own people, and that a struggle between allegiances will result" (113).

13 Certainly if we are looking for confirmation that the Victorians were deeply interested in how material conditions affected the development of human beings, one could do worse than observe the frequency of orphans in the major novels of the period. Heathcliff, Jane Eyre, Pip, Oliver Twist, Marian Halcombe, and Daniel Deronda: all are orphans and each is the subject of intense psychological scrutiny by their respective creators and readers.

14 Thus it is unsurprising to see orphans predominate in novels concerned with social reform. However, the case of the Victorian orphan supplies a cautionary tale for those who celebrate radical potentiality as the only path to liberation. According to Laura Peters, precisely because they lacked families, orphans (both real and fictional) also threatened the established socio-economic order. This placed orphans at the mercy of the most intense institutional forms of discipline and punishment. Using Jacques Derrida's illumination of Plato's *pharmakos* as an analogue, Peters emphasizes the ambivalent position of orphans in Victorian society. The orphan, she insists, "plays a pharmaceutical function in Victorian culture," a surplus that acts as both poison and cure (18).

15 For example, in the years before it acquired territorial power in India, the East India Company was a prominent patron of Coram's Foundling Hospital, from whence it recruited many of its writers. In the age before Clive, life in India was not unlike that imagined by Hobbes regarding man in the state of nature. Young boys without family connections made attractive candidates for a life that was nasty, brutish, and short. What is more – and here the Company exceeds Hobbes – orphans were less likely to complain about being poorly remunerated. We could also note that the policy of recruiting orphans into Her Majesty's Service also extends well into the twentieth century (at least in fiction). Ian Fleming's MI6 agent, James Bond, is one of the more famous orphan agents.

16 Hubel's argument, which more generally proposes that Kipling symbolically appropriated the working-classes in order to fantasize about intercultural mingling, is not without its problems, however. For example, Hubel insists that "it is extraordinarily meaningful that in Kipling's poetry and prose about the East, white working-class people are the only characters and speakers who ever suggest that the East is equal to the West – even that the East is better than the West" (246). Yet we need go no further than Kipling's famous "The Ballad of East and West" (1889) to find a counterexample. Though it is granted that the opening lines insist that there will never be a true meeting of cultures, this poem is not written in Kipling's working-class vernacular (like, say, "Gunga Din"). Moreover, the equality proposed in the poem is between a (Western) cavalry officer and an (Eastern) horse thief.

17 And a thousand rupees is not an inconsiderable sum given that for "two or three hundred rupees a year," Kim can receive "the best schooling a boy can get in India," board included, at St Xavier's (82).

18 A collection of linked short-stories, *Stalky and Co.* (1899) opens with one that establishes the unimpeachable character of his protagonists. "The

Ambush" introduces Stalky and Co. as three spirited boys who find the strict rules of their school somewhat overbearing and accordingly yearn for independence. This desire leads them to trespass on the neighbouring estate of Colonel Dabney where, under the pretence of gathering specimens for the school's Natural Historical Society, they smoke tobacco and idle about. Eventually they are rumbled by King, master of one of the school's rival houses, who, in Stalky's words, "want[s] to catch us *flagrante delicto*" (18: 24). King's antipathy towards Stalky and Co. derives from his conviction that these boys are of a bad sort and, conjuring up the strongest invective one could attribute to the stereotype of a draconian house master, he brands them "self-sufficient little animals!" (18: 19). The ambush of the section's title is the climax of the rivalry between King and the boys. Unlike the young fellowship who "had all Colonel Dabney's estate to play with, and … explored it with the stealth of Red Indians and the accuracy of burglars," King lacks subtlety and is duly captured for trespassing by the groundsman who brings his quarry before Dabney (18: 19). Dabney then berates King and his companions in an elaborate ritual humiliation, while the boys watch on from their secret hiding place with glee. For more on the social reordering that takes place in this story, see Kucich (2007).

19 See Winch's discussion of rules in section 8 of chapter 1 of *The Idea of a Social Science and Its Relation to Philosophy* (1958).

20 J.A. Mangan's *The Games Ethic and Imperialism* (1986) is an excellent history of Richard Wellesley's brother's famous statement about the virtues of the playing fields at Eton. Mangan shows how games like rugby and cricket taught men to complete tasks in dynamic non-linear environments, by autonomously exercising their skills in a cooperative way for the benefit of the collective.

21 The figure of Creighton coincides with the revival of ethnological and anthropological studies in India during the reign of Viceroy Curzon (1899–1905). According to Bernard Groslier, in 1899 Curzon "energized" the Archaeological Survey of India with a speech full of Foucauldian rhetoric: "It is … equally our duty to dig and discover, to classify, reproduce and describe, to copy and decipher, and to cherish and conserve" (qtd. in Groslier 155–7).

22 The inaccessibility of "true" native cultures by "passing" officials reminds me of nothing so much as Heisenberg's principle on quantum mechanics: namely, that the presence of an observer changes the system utterly so that the "true" or real object of scrutiny (whether the "spin" of subatomic particles or the "behaviour" of the natives) inevitably evades detection.

Conclusion: Out of India

1 As John Plotz has argued, it was Anglo-Indians "who provided a series of influential texts … that seem to have circulated as widely in other settler colonies as they did back in England" (47–8).

Works Cited

Ahmed, Siraj. "Orientalism and the Permanent Fix of War." *Postcolonial Enlightenment*. Ed. Daniel Carey and Lynn Festa. Oxford: Oxford University Press, 2009. 167–96.

– "The Theater of the Civilized Self: Edmund Burke and the East India Trials." *Representations* 78.1 (2002): 28–55.

Allardyce, Alexander. *The City of Sunshine*. Edinburgh: William Blackwood, 1877.

Allott, Kenneth. Introduction. *Oakfield; or Fellowship in the East*. New York: Humanities Press, 1973. 7–39.

Anderson, Benedict. *Imagined Communities: Reflections on the Origins and Spread of Nationalism*. 1983. 2nd ed. London: Verso, 1991.

Annan, Noel. "Kipling's Place in the History of Ideas." *Victorian Studies* 3.4 (1960): 323–46.

Arata, Stephen. *Fictions of Loss in the Victorian Fin de Siécle*. Cambridge: Cambridge University Press, 1996.

Arendt, Hannah. *The Human Condition*. Chicago: University of Chicago Press, 1998.

– *The Origins of Totalitarianism*. New York: Harvest, 1968.

Aristotle. *The Nicomachean Ethics*. Trans. David Ross. Oxford: Oxford World's Classics, 2009.

Armstrong, Nancy. *How Novels Think: The Limits of British Individualism from 1719–1900*. New York: Columbia University Press, 2006.

Arnold, Edwin. Preface. *In My Indian Garden*. By Phil Robinson. London: Sampson Low, 1871. i–vi.

Arnold, Matthew. *Culture and Anarchy*. 1869. Ed Samuel Lipman. New Haven: Yale University Press, 1994.

Arnold, William Delafield. *Oakfield; or Fellowship in the East*. 1853. 2nd ed. 1854. New York. Humanities Press, 1973.

Ashcroft, Bill, Gareth Griffiths, and Helen Tiffin. *The Empire Writes Back: Theory and Practice in Colonial Cultures*. London: Routledge, 1989.

Bagchee, Shyamal. "Writing Self/Writing Colony *In Situ*: Expatriate British Poetry in India." *ARIEL: A Review of International English Literature* 23.4 (1992): 7–32.

Bakan, Joel. *The Corporation: The Pathological Pursuit of Profit and Power*. Toronto: Penguin Canada, 2004.

Barlow, George. "Opening Remarks." *Essays by the Students of the College of Fort William in Bengal to Which are Added the Theses Pronounced at the Public Disputations in the Oriental Languages on the 6th February, 1802*. Calcutta: The Honourable Company Press, 1802. i–xv.

Bayly, C.A. *Indian Society and the Making of the British Empire*. Cambridge: Cambridge University Press, 1988.

Beames, John. *Memoirs of a Bengal Civilian*. London: Chatto and Windus, 1961.

Beasley-Murray, Jon. *Posthegemony: Political Theory and Latin America*. Minneapolis: University of Minnesota Press, 2010.

Bell, Duncan. *The Idea of Greater Britain: Empire and the Future of World Order, 1860–1900*. Princeton: Princeton University Press, 2007.

Bellamy, Richard. Introduction. *Victorian Liberalism: Nineteenth Century Political Thought and Practice*. Ed. Bellamy. London: Routledge, 1990. 1–33.

Bhabha, Homi K. *The Location of Culture*. London: Routledge, 1994.

Birdwood, George C.M. *Competition and the India Civil Service: A Paper Read before the East India Association, Tuesday, May 21, 1872*. London: Henry S. King, 1872.

Bivona, Daniel. *British Imperial Literature, 1870–1940: Writing and the Administration of Empire*. Cambridge: Cambridge University Press, 1998.

Bolts, William. *Considerations on Indian Affairs*. 1772. Ed. Patrick Tuck. London: Routledge, 1998.

Bonar, James. *A Catalogue of the Library of Adam Smith*. London: Macmillan, 1932.

Bourdieu, Pierre. "Social Space and Symbolic Power." *Sociological Theory* 7.1 (1989): 14–25.

Bowen, H.V. *The Business of Empire: The East India Company and Imperial Britain*. Cambridge: Cambridge University Press, 2006.

Brantlinger, Patrick. *Rule of Darkness: British Literature and Imperialism, 1830–1914*. Ithaca: Cornell University Press, 1988.

Bremer, L. Paul. *My Year in Iraq: The Struggle to Build a Future of Hope*. New York: Simon and Schuster, 2006.

Breton, Rob. "Ghosts in the Machina: Plotting in Chartist and Working-Class Fiction." *Victorian Studies* 47.4 (2005): 557–75.

– *Gospels and Grit: Work and Labour in Carlyle, Conrad, and Orwell*. Toronto: University of Toronto Press, 2005.

Brontë, Charlotte. *Jane Eyre*. 1848. Oxford: Oxford University Press, 2008.

Brown, Mark. "Crime, Governance and the Company Raj: The Discovery of Thuggee." *British Journal of Criminology* 42.1 (2002): 77–95.

Browne, A. Claude. *The Ordinary Man's India*. London: Cecil Palmer, 1927.

Browne, Stephen A. *Edmund Burke and the Discourse of Virtue*. Tuscaloosa, AL: University of Alabama Press, 1993.

Burke, Edmund. "Articles of Impeachment." *The Writings and Speeches of Edmund Burke*. Ed. P.J. Marshall. Vol. 6. Oxford: Clarendon Press, 1991. 125–57.

– *The Correspondence of Edmund Burke*. Ed. Holden Furber and P.J. Marshall. Vol. 5. Chicago: University of Chicago Press, 1965. 10 vols. 1958–78.

– "Letter to a Noble Lord." *The Writings and Speeches of Edmund Burke*. Ed. R.B. McDowell. Vol. 9. Oxford: Clarendon Press, 1991. 145–87.

– *Letters of Edmund Burke: A Selection Edited with an Introduction*. Ed. Harold J. Laski. Oxford: Oxford University Press, 1922.

– *A Philosophical Inquiry Into the Sublime and the Beautiful*. 1757. London: Penguin, 2004.

– *Reflections on the Revolution in France*. Ed. L.G. Mitchell. *The Writings and Speeches of Edmund Burke*. Vol. 8. Ed. L.G. Mitchell. Oxford: Clarendon Press, 1989. 53–293.

– "Speech on American Taxation." *The Writings and Speeches of Edmund Burke*. Vol. 2. Ed. Paul Langford. Oxford: Clarendon Press, 1981. 406–63.

– "Speech on Fox's India Bill." *The Writings and Speeches of Edmund Burke*. Vol. 5. Ed. P.J. Marshall. Oxford: Clarendon Press, 1981. 378–454.

– "Speech on Opening of Impeachment." *The Writings and Speeches of Edmund Burke*. Vol. 6. Ed. P.J. Marshall. Oxford: Clarendon Press, 1991. 264–471.

Burke, James Henry. *Days in the East: A Poem*. London: Smith, Elder and Co., 1842.

Burney, Frances. *Diary and Letters of Madame d'Arblay (1778–1840) as Edited by Her Niece Charlotte Barrett*. 6 vols. London, Macmillan, 1904–5.

Caldwell, Robert C. *The Chutney Lyrics: A Collection of Comic Pieces in Verse on Indian Subjects*. Madras: Higginbotham, 1871.

The Cambridge History of English and American Literature. Ed. A.W. Ward and A.R. Waller. 18 vols. New York: Putnam, 1907–21.

Campbell, George. *A Scheme for the Government of India*. London: John Murray, 1853.

Cannadine, David. *Ornamentalism: How the British Saw Their Empire*. Oxford: Oxford University Press, 2002.

Canter, H.V. "The Impeachments of Verres and Hastings: Cicero and Burke." *Classical Journal* 9 (1914): 199–211.

Carlos, Ann M., and Stephen Nicholas. "'Giants of an Earlier Capitalism': The Chartered Trading Companies as Modern Multinationals." *Business History Review* 62 (1988): 398–419.

Carnall, Geoffrey. "Burke as a Modern Cicero." *The Impeachment of Warren Hastings*. Ed. Geoffrey Carnall and Colin Nicholson. Edinburgh: Edinburgh University Press, 1989. 76–90.

Chakravarty, Gautam. *The Indian Mutiny in the British Imagination*. Cambridge: Cambridge University Press, 2005.

"Charter Granted by Queen Elizabeth to the East India Company, 31 December 1600." Ed. Panchanandas Mukherji. *Indian Constitutional Documents (1600–1918)*. Vol. 1. Calcutta: Thacker, Spink, 1918. 1–20.

Chatterjee, Partha. *The Lineages of Political Society*. New York: Columbia University Press, 2011.

Cicero. *The Verrine Orations*. Trans. L.H.G. Greenwood. Cambridge, MA: Harvard University Press, 1953.

Clark, Anna. *Scandal: The Sexual Politics of the English Constitution* Princeton: Princeton University Press, 2003.

Cobban, Alfred. *Edmund Burke and the Revolt against the Eighteenth Century*. 1929. London: Allen & Unwin, 1969.

Cohen, Deborah. *Household Gods: The British and Their Possessions*. New Haven, CT: Yale University Press, 2005.

Cohen, Victor. *Jeremy Bentham*. London: Fabian Society, 1927.

Colley, Linda. *Britons: Forging the Nation, 1707–1837*. New Haven: Yale University Press, 1992.

Committee of British Subjects Residing in Bengal. "Letter from the Committee of British Subjects Residing in Bengal, to the Right Honourable Lord North, dated Calcutta, May 25, 1779." *Administration of Justice in Bengal: The Several Petitions of the British Inhabitants of Bengal of the Governor-General and Council and of the Court of Directors of the East-India Company to Parliament*. [London]: [1780?]. 65–72.

Compton, J.M. "Open Competition and the Indian Civil Service, 1854–1876." *English Historical Review* 83.327 (1968): 265–84.

Conrad, Joseph. *Heart of Darkness*. 1899. London: Penguin, 2007.

– *Lord Jim*. 1900. Oxford: Oxford World's Classics, 2008.

Corfield, Penelope J. *Power and the Professions in Britain 1700–1850*. London: Routledge, 1994.

Cotton, Henry. *Indian and Home Memories*. London: T. Fisher Unwin, 1911.

Crane, Ralph J. *Inventing India: A History of India in English-Language Fiction*. New York: St Martin's Press, 1992.
Crockett, Samuel Rutherford. "On Some Tales of Mr Kipling's." *The Bookman* 7 (February 1895): 140.
Cunningham, Henry Stewart. *Chronicles of Dustypore: A Tale of Modern Anglo-Indian Society*. London: Smith, Elder, 1875.
David, Deirdre. *Rule Britannia: Women, Empire, and Victorian Writing*. Ithaca, NY: Cornell University Press, 1995.
Davis, Mike. *Late Victorian Holocausts: El Nino Famines and the Making of the Third-World*. 2000. London: Verso, 2001.
D'Cruz, Glenn. "My Two Left Feet: The Problem of Anglo-Indian Stereotypes in Post-Independence Indo-English Fiction." *Journal of Commonwealth Literature* 38.2 (2003): 105–25.
Dickens, Charles. *Little Dorrit*. 1857. Oxford: Oxford University Press, 1953.
Dirks, Nicholas. *The Scandal of Empire: India and the Creation of Imperial Britain*. Cambridge, MA: Harvard University Press, 2006.
Disraeli, Benjamin. *Tancred; or a New Crusade*. 1847. *Disraeli's Novels and Tales*. Vol. 2. London: Routledge, Warne, and Routledge, 1862.
Douglas, Mary. *Purity and Danger*. London: Routledge, 1966.
Doyle, Arthur Conan. "The Red-Headed League." 1891. *Sherlock Holmes: Selected Stories*. Ed. S.C. Roberts. Oxford: Oxford University Press, 1998. 329–58.
Duncan, Sara Jeannette. "A Mother in India." *The Pool in the Desert*. New York: D. Appleton, 1903. 47–114.
– *Set in Authority*. 1906. Peterborough, ON: Broadview Press, 1996.
Durkheim, Emile. *Professional Ethics and Civic Morals*. Trans. Cornelia Brookfield. London: Routledge, 1992.
Eagleton, Terry. *Literary Theory*. Oxford: Basil Blackwell, 1983.
Earle, Peter. *The Making of the English Middle Class: Business, Society, and Family Life in London, 1660–1730*. Berkeley: University of California Press, 1989.
Edwardes, Michael. *The Nabobs at Home*. London: Constable, 1991.
Eisenhardt, Kathleen M. "Agency Theory: An Assessment and Review." *Academy of Management Review* 14.1 (1989): 57–74.
– "Control: Organizational and Economic Approaches. *Management Science* 31 (1985): 134–49.
Esty, Jed. *Unseasonable Youth: Moderninsm, Colonialism, and the Fiction of Development*. Oxford: Oxford University Press, 2011.
Foote, Samuel. *The Nabob: A Comedy in Three Acts*. London: George Colman, 1778.
Forster, E.M. *A Passage to India*. 1924. London: Penguin, 2000.

– "Some Books: On William Arnold's *Oakfield*." *The Listener* 12 Oct 1944: 410–11.

Foucault, Michel. *Discipline and Punish: The Birth of the Prison*. 1975. Trans. Alan Sheridan. New York: Vintage, 1995.

Furber, Holden. *Rival Empires of Trade in the Orient, 1600–1800*. Minneapolis: University of Minnesota Press, 1976.

Gibson, Mary Elizabeth. *Indian Angles: English Verse in Colonial India from Jones to Tagore*. Athens: Ohio State University Press, 2011.

Gilmour, David. *The Ruling Caste*. London: John Murray, 2005.

Gintis, Herbert, and Tsuneo Ishikawa. "Wages, Work Intensity, and Unemployment." *Journal of the Japanese and International Economy* 1 (1987): 195–228.

Goonetilleke, D.C.R.A. "Forgotten Nineteenth-Century Fiction: William Arnold's *Oakfield* and William Knighton's *Forest Life in Ceylon*." *Journal of Commonwealth Literature* 7.1 (1972): 14–21.

Gramsci, Antonio. *Letters from Prison*. 2 vols. Trans. Ray Rosenthal. Ed. Frank Rosengarten. New York: Columbia University Press, 1994.

Greenberger, Allen J. *The British Image of India: A Study in the Literature of Imperialism 1880–1960*. London: Oxford University Press, 1969.

Griffin, L. "The Indian Civil Service Examinations." *Fortnightly Review* 17 (new series) 1 April 1875: 529.

Griffiths, Ralph. Revue of *Observations on the Present State of the East India Company*. *Monthly Review* 45 (December 1771): 504.

Groslier, Bernard Philippe. *Indochina*. New York: World Publishing, 1966.

Guillory, John. *Cultural Capital: The Problem of Literary Canon Formation*. Chicago: University of Chicago Press, 1993.

Habermas, Jurgen. *The Legitimation Crisis*. Trans. Thomas McCarthy. Boston: Beacon Press, 1975.

– *The Structural Transformation of the Public Sphere: An Inquiry into a Category of Bourgeois Society*. 1962. Trans. Thomas Burger with Frederick Lawrence. Cambridge, MA: MIT Press, 1991.

Hai, Ambreen. "On Truth and Lie in a Colonial Sense: Kipling's Tales of Tale-telling" *ELH* 64.2 (1997): 599–625.

Hastings, Warren. *The History of the Trial of Warren Hastings, Esq*. London: J. Debrett, 1796.

Herbert, Christopher. *War of No Pity: The Indian Mutiny and Victorian Trauma*. Princeton: Princeton University Press, 2009.

Herder, Johann von Gottfreid. *J.G. Herder on Social and Political Culture*. Ed. and trans. F.M. Barnard. Cambridge: Cambridge University Press, 1969.

Hitchens, Christopher. "A Man of Permanent Contradictions." *The Atlantic Monthly* June 2002: 96–103.

Hobbes, Thomas. *Leviathan; or the Matter, Forme, and Power of a Commonwealth Ecclesiasticall and Civil.* 1651. Ed. Michael Oakeshott. Oxford: Basil Blackwell, 1946.

Hobsbawm, Eric. "Introduction: Inventing Traditions." *The Invention of Tradition.* Ed. Eric Hobsbawm and Terrence Ranger. Cambridge: Cambridge University Press, 1983. 1–14.

– *Nations and Nationalism since 1780: Programme, Myth, Reality.* Cambridge: Cambridge University Press, 1990.

Hobson, J.A. *Imperialism: A Study.* London: James Nisbet, 1902.

Hockley, William Browne. *The English in India.* London: Simkin and Marshall, 1828.

– *Pandurang Hari, or Memoirs of a Hinoo.* London: George B Whittaker, 1826.

– *Tales of the Zenana; or A Nawub's Leisure Hours.* London: Saunders and Otley, 1827.

Hogg, James Weir. *Addresses by Sir James Weir Hogg, Bart. M.P. at Haileybury and Addiscombe.* London, 1846.

Hubel, Teresa. "In Search of the British Indian in British India: White Orphans, Kipling's *Kim*, and Class in Colonial India." *Modern Asian Studies* 38 (2004): 227–51.

Hume, David. *Enquiries Concerning the Human Understanding and Concerning the Principles of Morals.* Ed. L.A. Selby-Bigge. 2nd ed. Oxford: Clarendon Press, 1902.

– *Treatise of Human Nature.* Ed. L.A. Selby-Bigge and P.H. Nidditch. 2nd ed. Oxford: Clarendon Press, 1978.

Hutchins, Francis. *The Illusion of Permanence.* Princeton: Princeton University Press, 1967.

Hyam, Ronald. *Britain's Imperial Century 1815–1914: A Study of Empire and Expansion.* London: B.T. Batsford, 1976.

– *Empire and Sexuality: The British Experience.* Manchester: Manchester University Press, 1990.

Jackson, Patrick. "Trevelyan, Sir George Otto, Second Baronet (1838–1928)." *Oxford Dictionary of National Biography.* Oxford: Oxford University Press, 2004.

JanMohamed, Abdul R. "The Economy of Manichean Allegory: The Function of Racial Difference in Colonial Literature." *Critical Inquiry* 12.1 (1985): 59–87.

Jasanoff, Maya. "Secret Signals in Lotus Flowers." Revue of *The Indian Mutiny and the British Imagination* by Guatam Chakravarty. Cambridge: Cambridge University Press, 2005. *London Review of Books* 27.14 (2005): 9–10.

Jensen, Michael. "Organization Theory and Methodology." *Accounting Review* 56 (1983): 319–38.

Jensen, Michael, and William Meckling. "Theory of the Firm: Managerial Behavior, Agency Costs, and Ownership Structure." *Journal of Financial Economics* 3 (1976): 305–60.

Joseph, Betty. *Reading the East India Company, 1720–1840: Colonial Currencies of Gender*. Chicago: University of Chicago Press, 2004.

Kantorowicz, Ernst. *The King's Two Bodies: A Study in Medieval Political Theology*. Princeton: Princeton University Press, 1957.

Kaul, Chandrika. "England and India: The Ilbert Bill, 1883; A Case Study of the Metropolitan Press." *Indian Economic and Social History Review* 30 (1993): 413–36.

– *Reporting the Raj: The British Press and India*. Manchester: Manchester University Press, 2003.

Kaye, J.W. "The English in India." *Calcutta Review* 1.1 (May–August 1844): 1–41.

Keay, John. *The Honourable Company: A History of the English East India Company*. New York, Macmillan, 1994.

Kemp, Sandra, and Lisa Lewis, eds. *Writings on Writing, by Rudyard Kipling*. Cambridge: Cambridge University Press, 1996. 25–6.

Keynes, John Maynard. "Robert Malthus 1766–1835: The First of the Cambridge Economists." *Essays in Biography*. London: Rupert Hart-Davis, 1951. 81–123.

King, Larry. "Interviews with Donald Rumsfeld, Dr. Phil." *CNN Larry King Live*. 3 February 2005. CNN.com. Web. 29 June 2013.

Kinkead-Weekes, Mark. "Vision in Kipling's Novels." *Kipling's Mind and Art*. Ed. Andrew Rutherford. London: Oliver and Boyd, 1964. 197–234.

Kipling, Rudyard. "Anglo-Indian Society." 1887. *Kipling's India: Uncollected Sketches, 1884–1888*. Ed. Thomas Pinney. London: Macmillan, 1986. 184–93.

– *Kim*. 1901. Ed. Zoreh T. Sullivan. New York: W.W. Norton, 2002.

– *Letters of Rudyard Kipling*. 6 vols. Ed. Thomas Pinney. Iowa City: University of Iowa Press, 1990–2004.

– *Life's Handicap: Being Stories of Mine Own People*. London: Macmillan, 1899.

– "Music for the Middle Aged." 1884. *Kipling's India: Uncollected Sketches, 1884–1888*. Ed. Thomas Pinney. London: Macmillan, 1986. 42–5.

– "Prelude." *Departmental Ditties and Other Verses*. Garden City, New York: Doubleday, Page and Co., 1927. 6.

– *Something of Myself*. 1937. *Something of Myself and Other Autobiographical Writings*. Ed. Thomas Pinney. Cambridge: Cambridge University Press, 1990. 3–134.

– *The Writings in Prose and Verse of Rudyard Kipling*. 36 vols. New York: Charles Scribner and Son, 1897–1937.
– "Unpublished Prefaces to Departmental Ditties, 1st English Edition." *Writings on Writing*. Ed. Kemp and Lewis. 25–6.
Kolsky, Elizabeth. *Colonial Justice in British India: White Violence and the Rule of Law*. Cambridge: Cambridge University Press, 2010.
Kreisel, Deanna K. "Wolf Children and Automata: Bestiality and Boredom at Home and Abroad," *Representations* 96 (2006): 21–47.
Kristeva, Julia. "From Symbols to Flesh: The Polymorphous Destiny of Narration." *International Journal of Psycho-Analysis* 81 (2000): 771–87.
Kucich, John. *Imperial Masochism: British Fiction, Fantasy, and Social Class*. Princeton: Princeton University Press, 2007.
Lane, Christopher. *The Ruling Passion: British Colonial Allegory and the Paradox of Homosexual Desire*. Durham, NC: Duke University Press, 1995.
Lang, Arthur. "Mr. Kipling's Stories." *Essays in Little*. London: Longmans, Green, 1899. 198–205.
Lang, John. *The Wetherbys: Father and Son; or Sundry Chapters of Indian Experience*. London: Chapman and Hall, 1853.
Lawson, Philip. *The East India Company: A History*. London: Longman, 1993.
Lawson, Philip, and Jim Phillips. "Our Execrable Banditti: Perceptions of Nabobs in Mid-Eighteenth Century Britain." *Albion* 16.3 (1984): 225–41.
Leask, Nigel. *British Romantic Writers and the East: Anxieties of Empire*. Cambridge: Cambridge University Press, 1992.
Lecky, William Edward Hartpole. *The Empire: Its Value and Its Growth*. London: Longmans, Green, 1893.
Lesjak, Carolyn. *Working Fictions: A Genealogy of the Victorian Novel*. Durham, NC: Duke University Press, 2006.
Lukács, Georg. "Reification and the Consciousness of the Proletariat." 1923. *History and Class Consciousness: Studies in Marxist Dialectics*. Trans. Rodney Livingstone. Cambridge, MA: MIT Press, 1971. 83–222.
Lock, F.P. *Edmund Burke*. 2 vols. Oxford: Oxford University Press, 1998–2006.
Macaulay, Thomas Babington. *The Indian Civil Service: Report to the Rt. Hon. Sir Charles Wood*. London: W. Thacker, 1855.
– "Lord Clive." 1840. *Miscellaneous Works of Lord Macaulay*. Ed. Lady Trevelyan [Hannah More Macaulay]. Vol. 3. New York: Harper and Brothers, 1880. 7–90.
– "Minute on Indian Education." 1835. *Selected Writings*. Ed. John Clive and Thomas Pinney. Chicago: University of Chicago Press, 1972. 235–51.
– "Speech on the Government of India, 1833" *Miscellaneous Works of Lord Macaulay*. Ed. Lady Trevelyan [Hannah More Macaulay]. Vol. 5. New York: Harper and Brothers, 1880. 131–67.

– "Warren Hastings." 1841. *Miscellaneous Works of Lord Macaulay*. Ed. Lady Trevelyan [Hannah More Macaulay]. Vol. 3. New York: Harper and Brothers, 1880. 152–268.

Mackenzie, Helen. *Life in the Mission, the Camp, and the Zenana; or Six Years in India*. 3 vols. London: Richard Bentley, 1853.

Mackenzie, Henry. *The Man of Feeling*. 1771. Ed. Brian Vickers. London: Oxford University Press, 1967.

Malthus, Thomas Robert. *A Letter to the Rt. Hon. Lord Grenville Occasioned by Some Observations of His Lordship on the East India Company's Establishment for the Education of Their Civil Servants*. London: J. Johnson, 1813.

– *Statements Respecting the East-India College with an Appeal to Facts, in Refutation of the Charges Lately Brought against It, in the Court of Proprietors*. London: John Murray, 1817.

Mandeville, Bernard. *The Fable of the Bees*. 1714. Harmondsworth: Penguin, 1970.

Mangan, J.A. *The Games Ethic and Imperialism: Aspects of the Diffusion of an Ideal*. London: Viking, 1986.

Marcuse, Herbert. *One-Dimensional Man*. 1964. London: Routledge, 2002.

Marshall, P.J. "Burke, Hastings, and the Higher Law." *Times Literary Supplement* 7 November 1997. 31.

– *The Impeachment of Warren Hastings*. Oxford: Oxford University Press, 1965.

–, ed. *Problems of Empire: Britain and India, 1757–1813*. London: George Allen and Unwin, 1968.

– "The Whites of British India, 1780–1830: A Failed Colonial Society?" *International History Review* 12.1 (1990): 26–44.

Martin, W.B. "On the Advantages to be Expected from an Academical Institution in India; Considered in a Moral, Literary, and Political Point of View." *Essays by the Students of the College of Fort William in Bengal to Which are Added the Theses Pronounced at the Public Disputations in the Oriental Languages on the 6th February, 1802*. Calcutta: The Honourable Company Press, 1802. 1–15.

Martineau, Harriet. *British Rule in India: A Historical Sketch. Harriet Martineau's Writing on the British Empire*. Vol 5. Ed. Deborah Logan. London: Pickering and Chatto, 2004.

Marx, Karl, and Freidrich Engels. *The German Ideology*. New York: Prometheus Books, 1976.

Mason, Philip [Philip Woodruff]. *The Men Who Ruled India*. 2 vols. New York: St Martin's Press, 1954.

McBratney, John. *Imperial Subjects, Imperial Space: Rudyard Kipling's Fiction of the Native-Born*. Columbus, OH: Ohio State University Press, 2002.

McClintock, Anne. *Imperial Leather: Race, Gender and Sexuality in the Colonial Context*. New York: Routledge, 1995.

McClure, John A. *Kipling and Conrad: The Colonial Fiction*. Cambridge, MA: Harvard University Press, 1981.

Meadows Taylor, Philip. *Confessions of a Thug*. 1839. Oxford: Oxford University Press, 1998.

– *Seeta*. 1873. London: Kegan Paul, Trench, Trubner, 1880.

Mehta, Uday Singh. *Liberalism and Empire: A Study in Nineteenth-Century British Liberal Thought*. Chicago: University of Chicago Press, 1999.

Meštrović, Stjepan. *The Trials of Abu Ghraib: An Expert Witness Account of Shame and Horror*. Boulder, CO: Paradigm, 2007.

Metcalf, Thomas. *Ideologies of the Raj*. Cambridge: Cambridge University Press, 1994.

Mickle, William Julius. *A Candid Examination of the Reasons for Depriving the East-India Company of Its Charter*. London: J. Bew, 1779.

Mill, James. *The History of British India*. 1817. 9 vols. London: James Madden, 1840–6.

Mill, John Stuart. *Considerations on Representative Government. Utilitarianism, Liberty, and Representative Government*. London: J.M. Dent, 1910.

– "The East India Company Charter." *Writings on India. The Collected Works of John Stuart Mill*. Vol. 30. Ed. John M. Robson, Martin Moir, and Zawahir Moir. Toronto: University of Toronto Press. 123–45.

– "To Harriet Mill." 2 February 1854. *Later Letters. The Collected Works of John Stuart Mill*. Vol. 14. Ed. Francis Mineka and Dwight N. Lindley. Toronto: University of Toronto Press. 146–8.

– *Utilitarianism*. 1863. 2nd ed. London: Longman, Green, Longman, Roberts and Green, 1864.

Miller, D.A. *The Novel and the Police*. Berkeley: University of California Press, 1988.

Misra, B.B. *The Central Administration of the East India Company, 1773–1834*. Manchester: Manchester University Press, 1959.

Misra, Udayon. *The Raj in Fiction: A Study of Nineteenth-Century British Attitudes towards India*. Delhi: B.R. Publishing, 1987.

Moore, R.J. "The Abolition of Patronage in the Indian Civil Service and the Closure of Haileybury College." *Historical Journal* 7.2 (1964): 246–57.

Moore-Gilbert, Bart. *Kipling and "Orientalism."* London: Croon Helm, 1986.

Monier-Williams, Monier. "Reminiscences." *Memorials of Old Haileybury College*. Ed. Charles Danvers. Westminster: Archibald Constable, 1894.

Morris, William. "The Socialst Ideal: Art." *The Soul of Man under Socialism: The Socialist Ideal; Art, and the Coming Solidarity*. New York: Humboldt, 1891. 32–8.

Nairn, Tom. *The Break-Up of Britain: Crisis and Neo-Nationalism*. London: New Left Books, 1977.

Napier, Charles. *Defects, Civil and Military, of the Indian Government*. London: C. Westerton, 1853.

Nechtman, Tillman W. *Nabobs: Empire and Identity in Eighteenth-Century Britain*. Cambridge: Cambridge University Press, 2010.

Ngugi wa Thiong'o. *Decolonising the Mind: The Politics of African Literature*. London: James Curry, 1981.

Nora, Pierre. "Between Memory and History: *Les Lieux de Mémoires*." *Representations* 26 (1999): 7–24.

Noreen, Eric. "The Economics of Ethics: A New Perspective on Agency Theory" *Accounting, Organizations and Society* 13.4 (1988): 359–69.

Nye, Joseph. "Corruption and Political Development: A Cost Benefit Analysis." *Political Corruption: A Handbook*. Ed. A.J. Heidenheimer, M. Johnston, and V.T. Levine. New Brunswick, NJ: Transaction Press, 1989.

Oaten, Edward F. *A Sketch of Anglo-Indian Literature*. London: Kegan Paul, Trench, Trübner, 1908.

Osborne, Thomas. "Bureaucracy as a Vocation: Governmentality and Administration in Nineteenth-Century Britain." *Journal of Historical Sociology* 7.3 (1994): 289–313.

Orwell, George. "Rudyard Kipling." 1942. *Kipling and the Critics*. Ed. Elliot L. Gilbert. London: Peter Owen, 1966. 74–88.

– "Shooting an Elephant." 1936. *Shooting an Elephant and Other Essays*. New York: Harcourt, Brace and Company, 1950. 3–12.

Palmer, D.J. *The Rise of English Studies: An Account of the Study of English Language and Literature from Its Origins to the Making of the Oxford English School*. London: Oxford University Press, 1965.

Parry, Benita. *Delusions and Discoveries: Studies on India in the British Imagination, 1880–1930*. Rev. ed. London: Verso, 1998.

Patterson, Stephen. *The Cult of Imperial Honour in British India*. New York: Palgrave Macmillan, 2009.

Paxton, Nancy. *Writing under the Raj: Gender, Race, and Rape in the British Colonial Imagination, 1830–1947*. New Brunswick, NJ: Rutgers University Press, 1999.

Peters, Laura. *Orphan Texts: Victorian Orphans, Culture and Empire*. Manchester: Manchester University Press, 2000.

Philp, Mark. "Defining Political Corruption." *Political Studies* 45 (1997): 436–62.

Philips, C.H. *The East India Company, 1784–1834*. 2nd ed. Oxford: Oxford University Press, 1961.

Pinney, Thomas, ed. *Kipling's India: Uncollected Sketches, 1884–88*. London: Macmillan, 1986.

Plotz, John. *Portable Property: Victorian Culture on the Move*. Princeton: Princeton University Press, 2009.

Pocock, J.G.A. *Virtue, Commerce, and History*. Cambridge: Cambridge University Press, 1985.

Poon, Angela. *Enacting Englishness in the Victorian Period: Colonialism and the Politics of Performance*. Aldershot: Ashgate, 2008.

Poovey, Mary. "For What It's Worth ..." *Critical Inquiry* 30.2 (2004): 429–33.

Prichard, Iltudus Thomas. *The Chronicles of Budgepore, or, Sketches of Life in India*. London: W.H. Allan, 1870.

Rajan, Balachandra. *Under Western Eyes: India from Milton to Macaulay*. Durham, NC: Duke University Press, 1999.

Randall, Don. *Kipling's Imperial Boy: Adolescence and Cultural Hybridity*. New York: Palgrave, 2000.

"Representation from the Court of Directors, 1 July 1803." *India Office Records* H/487 391–430.

Ricoeur, Paul. *Lectures on Ideology and Utopia*. New York: Columbia University Press, 1986.

– "The Model of the Text: Meaningful Action Considered as a Text." *New Literary History* 5.1 (1973): 91–117.

Robinson, Phil. *In My Indian Garden*. London: Sampson Low, 1871.

Ross, Stephen A. "The Economic Theory of Agency: The Principal's Problem." *American Economic Review* 63.2 (1973): 134–9.

Roy, Parama. *Indian Traffic: Identities in Question in Colonial and Postcolonial India*. Berkeley: University of California Press, 1998.

Ruskin, John. "The Roots of Honour." *Selected Writings*. Ed. Dinah Birch. Oxford: Oxford University Press, 2004. 140–53.

Ruth, Jennifer. *Novel Professions: Interested Disinterest and the Making of the Professional in the Victorian Novel*. Columbus: Ohio State University Press, 2006.

Rutherford, Andrew. Introduction. *Plain Tales from the Hills*. Oxford: Oxford University Press, 1987. i–xxxvi.

Ryves, Elizabeth. *The Hastiniad; An Heroic Poem in Three Cantos*. 1785. *The Poetry of British India, 1780–1905*. Ed. Máire ní Fhlathúin. London: Pickering and Chatto, 2011. 11–22.

Said, Edward. *Culture and Imperialism*. New York: Vintage, 1994.

– *Orientalism*. New York: Pantheon, 1978.

– *The World, the Text, and the Critic*. Cambridge, MA: Harvard University Press, 1983.

Seeley, J.R. *The Expansion of England*. 1883. Chicago: University of Chicago Press, 1971.

Sharpe, Jenny. *Allegories of Empire: The Figure of Woman in the Colonial Text*. Minneapolis: University of Minnesota Press, 1993.

Shaw, George Bernard. *The Man of Destiny*. 1896. *Collected Plays with Their Prefaces*. Volume 1. London: Bodley Head, 1970. 605–66.

Singh, Bhupal. *A Survey of Anglo-Indian Fiction*. Oxford: Oxford University Press, 1934.

Sinha, Mrilani. *Colonial Masculinity: The "Manly Englishman" and the "Effeminate Bengali" in the Late-Nineteenth Century*. Manchester: Manchester University Press, 1995.

Smith, Adam. *An Inquiry into the Nature and Causes of the Wealth of Nations*. 1776. 3 vols. London: G. Walker, J. Akerman, E. Edwards et al., 1822.

Sorley, H.T. *The Gazetteer of West Pakistan, the Former Province of Sind*. Karachi: Government of West Pakistan, 1968.

Spivak, Gayatri Chakravorty. "Can the Subaltern Speak?" *Marxism and the Interpretation of Culture*. Ed. Cary Nelson and Lawrence Grossberg. Urbana: University of Illinois Press. 271–313.

Stanhope, Philip Henry. *Life of the Right Honourable William Pitt*. 3 vols. London: John Murray, 1879.

State of the East India Company's Affairs, with a View to the Intended Bill for Regulating the Dividend, December 1767. London, 1768.

Stephen, James Fitzjames. *Liberty, Equality, Fraternity*. New York: Holt and Williams, 1873.

Stephens, H. Morse. "An Account of the East India College at Haileybury, 1806–1857." *Colonial Civil Service: The Selection and Training of Colonial Officials in England, Holland, and France*. London: Macmillan, 1900. 233–346.

Stokes, Eric. *The English Utilitarians and India*. Oxford: Clarendon Press, 1959.

Suleri, Sara. *The Rhetoric of English India*. Chicago: University of Chicago Press, 1992.

Sullivan, Zoreh T. *Narratives of Empire: The Fictions of Rudyard Kipling*. Cambridge: Cambridge University Press, 1993.

Teltscher, Kate. *India Inscribed: European and British Writing on India 1600–1800*. New York: Oxford University Press, 1996.

Tennyson, Alfred. "Ulysses." *The Poems of Tennyson*. Ed. Christopher Ricks. Vol. 1. Harlow: Longman, 1987. 613–20.

Thackeray, William Makepeace. *Vanity Fair: A Novel without a Hero*. 1848. New York: W.W. Norton, 1994.

Thomas, James H. "East India Company Agency Work in the British Isles, 1700–1800." *The Worlds of the East India Company*. Ed. H.V. Bowen,

Margarette Lincoln, and Nigel Rigby. Woodbridge, Suffolk: Boydell Press, 2002. 33–48.

Thompson, E.P. *The Making of the English Working Class*. 1963. New York: Pantheon, 1964.

Thomson, James. "Rule Britannia." 1740. *Eighteenth-Century Poetry and Prose*. Ed. Louis Bredvold, Alan McKillop, and Lois Whitney. 3rd ed. New York: Ronald Press, 1973. 669–70.

Tönnies, Ferdinand. *Gemeinschaft und Gesellschaft* [*Community and Civil Society*]. 1887. Ed. Jose Harris. Trans. Jose Harris and Margaret Hollis. Cambridge: Cambridge University Press, 2001.

Trevelyan, George Macaulay. *Sir George Otto Trevelyan: A Memoir*. New York: Longmans, Green, 1932.

Trevelyan, George Otto. *The Competition Wallah*. 1864. London: Macmillan, 1895.

Trumpener, Katie. *Bardic Nationalism: The Romantic Novel and the British Empire*. Princeton: Princeton University Press, 1997.

Valdes, Mario J., ed. *A Ricouer Reader: Reflection and Imagination*. Toronto: University of Toronto Press, 1991.

van Klaveren, Jacob. "The Concept of Corruption." *Political Corruption: A Handbook*. Ed. A.J. Heidenheimer, M. Johnston, and V.T. Levine. New Brunswick, NJ: Transaction Press, 1970. 38–40.

Varouxakis, Georgios. *Victorian Political Thought on France and the French*. New York: Palgrave, 2002.

Viswanathan, Gauri. *Masks of Conquest: Literary Study and British Rule in India*. New York: Columbia University Press, 1989.

Walter, Henry. *Joseph Separated from His Kindred, and from His Native Land, to Be a Ruler in a Foreign Nation: A Sermon Preached in the Chapel of the Honourable East India Company's College, Haileybury, at the Close of Term*. London: C&J Rivington, 1827.

Watkins, Robert E. "Politics *in medias res*: Burke, Hume, and Deleuze on Empiricism's Secrets for Political Theory." PhD dissertation, University of Pennsylvania, 2004.

Watt, Ian. *The Rise of the Novel: Studies in Defoe, Richardson and Fielding*. 1957. Berkeley: University of California Press, 2001.

Weber, Max. *The Protestant Ethic and the Spirit of Capitalism*. 1930. Trans. Talcott Parsons. London: Routledge, 2001.

Wellesley, Richard. "Notes with Respect to the Foundation of a College at Fort William." *The Wellesley Papers: The Life and Correspondence of Richard Colley Wellesley, Marquess Wellesley, 1760–1842*. Vol. 1. London: H. Jenkins, 1914. 718–55.

Whelan, Fredrick. *Edmund Burke and India: Political Morality and Empire*. Pittsburgh: University of Pittsburgh Press, 1996.

Wilberforce, William. "Speech on Hastings." *The Debates and Proceedings of the House of Commons*. Vol. 9, 1780–1796. Ed. J. Stockdale. 19 vols. London: John Stockdale, 65.

Wilde, Oscar. "Two Extracts." 1899. *Kipling: The Critical Heritage*. Ed. Roger Lancelyn Green. London: Routledge, Kegan and Paul, 1971. 104–5.

Williams, Patrick. "Kim and *Orientalism*." *Kipling Considered*. Ed. Phillip Mallett. New York: St Martin's Press, 1989. 33–55.

Williams, Raymond. "Base and Superstructure in Marxist Cultural Theory." *New Left Review* 82 (1973): 3–16.

– *George Orwell*. New York: Viking Press, 1971.

– *Marxism and Literature*. Oxford: Oxford University Press, 1977.

Wilson, Edmund. "The Kipling That Nobody Read." *The Wound and the Bow*. Cambridge, MA: Riverside Press, 1941. 105–81.

Winch, Peter. *The Idea of a Social Science and Its Relation to Philosophy*. 2nd ed. London: Routledge, 1989.

Wright, Henry Charles. *Songs Sung at Haileybury*. Hertford: S. Austin and Sons, 1889.

Young, Wayland. *Eros Denied*. London: Corgi, 1969.

Žižek, Slavoj. "The Two Totalitarianisms." *London Review of Books* 27.6 (2005): 3–5.

Index

www.ingramcontent.com/pod-product-compliance
Lightning Source LLC
LaVergne TN
LVHW040149080826
844660LV00014B/898/J

* 9 7 8 1 4 4 2 6 4 8 4 6 3 *